W9-DCH-153

"Steeped in sacred mysteries, this novel explores what it is like to be caught between Spirit and Human form, the uncomfortable and uncanny ability to read the energy fields of others, and to feel the agonizing alienation of not-belonging. A love story to the universe, full of deep yet simple teachings, *There's a Whole in the Sky* provocatively challenges you to take another look at the very nature of reality."

Priscilla Cogan,
author of *Winona's Web*; *Compass of the Heart*;
and *Crack at Dusk: Crook of Dawn*

"This book guides us to remember our true selves—that we are spirit in body, light within form, ever connected with the Source and Love. Though fiction, this book speaks truth. This important psycho-spiritual story traces Luna's journey from birth through childhood, into becoming a woman and then claiming her wholeness as spirit grounded in her human body. A must-read book with lessons for us all, it belongs on the shelf with *The Celestine Prophecy*."

Lesley Irene Shore Ph.D.,
Psychologist, founder of Harmony Center,
and author of *Healing the Feminine*

"*There's a Whole in the Sky,* is not your typical novel. It will challenge you. It will stretch your boundaries and make you ask questions about the nature of the universe and your own spiritual possibilities."

C.W. Duncan Sings-Alone,
author of *Sprinting Backwards to God*

May your lessons
be gentle and your spirit
Soar!

Loralee Dubeau
"Spirit Singer"
11-19-12

THERE'S A
Whole
IN THE
Sky

LORALEE
DUBEAU

BALBOA
PRESS

A DIVISION OF HAY HOUSE

Copyright © 2012 Loralee Dubeau

All rights reserved. No part of this book may be used or reproduced by any means, graphic, electronic, or mechanical, including photocopying, recording, taping or by any information storage retrieval system without the written permission of the publisher except in the case of brief quotations embodied in critical articles and reviews.

Balboa Press books may be ordered through booksellers or by contacting:

Balboa Press
A Division of Hay House
1663 Liberty Drive
Bloomington, IN 47403
www.balboapress.com
1-(877) 407-4847

Because of the dynamic nature of the Internet, any web addresses or links contained in this book may have changed since publication and may no longer be valid. The views expressed in this work are solely those of the author and do not necessarily reflect the views of the publisher, and the publisher hereby disclaims any responsibility for them.

The author of this book does not dispense medical advice or prescribe the use of any technique as a form of treatment for physical, emotional, or medical problems without the advice of a physician, either directly or indirectly. The intent of the author is only to offer information of a general nature to help you in your quest for emotional and spiritual well-being. In the event you use any of the information in this book for yourself, which is your constitutional right, the author and the publisher assume no responsibility for your actions.

Certain stock imagery © Thinkstock.
Any people depicted in stock imagery provided by Thinkstock are models, and such images are being used for illustrative purposes only.

ISBN: 978-1-4525-4152-5 (e)
ISBN: 978-1-4525-4151-8 (sc)
ISBN: 978-1-4525-4153-2 (hc)

Library of Congress Control Number: 2011919438

Printed in the United States of America

Balboa Press rev. date: 04/24/2012

For Paul,
The love of my life

Foreword

This is not a novel for the fainthearted. Do not open it unless you're willing to have your basic assumptions challenged.

It is the story of an exceptional woman who, from childhood, has been in touch with the Sky Beings, has had the ability to read the minds of others, can observe the movement of energy within another's body, and communicates with the deceased. Your first reaction might be to marvel at her incredible gifts, but read this book and you will see the awful stress that it has taken upon her life. One can hardly imagine what such gifts would do to a child.

While the story portrays the burden of her gifts, it also shows how she came to harness and value her abilities for the benefit of all her relations.

While written as a novel, it is inspired by many of Loralee's experiences.

Not every story in the book is factual; it is a novel after all. Some aspects of the book may seem unbelievable. But in this age of quantum mechanics, everything she described is within the realm of possibility. The great British physicist, Stephen Hawkins, speaks of the possibility of time travel, other intelligent universes, and the abrogation of nearly every aspect of consensus reality.

I have known Loralee for many years. She came to my lodge community and seemed to be a fine person and very dedicated. One day, a week or so prior to my leaving for the entire summer, my wife and I were hiking with our dogs in the woods when my Spirit Teacher spoke to me, "Sweat Loralee before you leave." I argued that I did not have the time to do that, but He was insistent. So, upon returning home I called Loralee and told her what the Grandfather had said. She was rather surprised but agreed to meet me the following day for sweat lodge ceremony. In the lodge I asked what this was all about and the grandfathers told us that she was to be my Successor and that I was to teach her everything I knew.

And so Loralee became very important to our lodge community and I taught her as best as I could. I have seen her grow and develop and have come to understand that she has had a lifelong relationship with the spirits and has been very familiar with all kinds of paranormal experiences. She was reluctant at first to share the information in this book, but finally agreed to write the book as fiction. I have known of her struggles about sharing her experiences. She has been very private about these parts of her life. No wonder. It was her only way to escape her fear of ridicule and disapproval.

Her spirit guides have told her to open her secrets and write a book. A couple of years ago I urged her to put this information out to the reading public and although I have not had all of these experiences myself, I am so glad because it carries an important teaching and message.

This is not your typical novel. It will challenge you. It will stretch your boundaries to ask questions about the nature of the universe and your own spiritual possibilities, as well as questioning all of your assumptions about reality. And that is why this book is for you.

C. W. Duncan Sings-Alone, Founder and original Principal Chief of the Free Cherokee, author of *Sprinting Backwards to God*

You will remember the story.
It is both the beginning and the return to wholeness.
Remember the love.
Remember the Oneness.
Remember the light.
Remember to balance both form and light.

This was the last conscious memory of the spark before it spiraled through the darkness of the tunnel.

The Entry

It was a tough entry for this little one. Being born into the world while her mother was under anesthesia; feeling alone under the hot white lights. There was no one to greet her except a man in a white mask and sterile gloves. This man turned her upside down, dangled her by her feet, forced a suction cup into her mouth, and slapped her hard on her backside until she screamed. *What kind of greeting is this? What is this physical pain I'm experiencing? What is this sound being released from inside of me?*

No one comforted or coddled her. Actually, she was treated rather roughly, being scrubbed clean and wrapped tightly in a blanket, bound and restricted from flight. Breathing with tightness in her chest, she was now heavy matter. She was trying to expand and flee, but could not. Finally, she was placed in a glass chamber, one of many in the sterile room. And every one of those chambers contained a little one, each making the same unfamiliar high pitched vibrating sound.

She felt separated from the Center. The vibrational energy was different. Everything was different. *So this was Earth? And this was Humanness? This is not what I was promise*d, she thought. *I WANT TO GO BACK!*

The thought that something was wrong ran through her mind. *There must have been a miscalculation. Maybe this wasn't the Earth Star.* The Light of Oneness had groomed her, filling her consciousness with wonderful tales about the Earth Star. It was a place where she would have a physical form called a *body*. The human shell would give her a beautiful experience, with sensations such as touch, taste and smell; and emotions of joy, peace and happiness. *This is certainly not joy or peace!*

Pictures of flowers, trees, animals and other forms of life on this Earth Star were imprinted in her memory. The Center of All-Knowing and Oneness had expressed that all of these new experiences would further her understanding of humanness. It gave her an education that could be kept with her at all times.

She was to remember that her spirit light would always be inside her human physical form. She was to remember they were never separate. Many before her had forgotten this when they entered the human form.

Her mission was to tell the story of origin, the place of being and light, the place where the light is formless, wonderfully expansive and free. It is the place where all life is created and eventually returns to. It is the source of peace and perfection. The place where there is no separation, only divinity and grace. The place where...

As she lay there in the glass chamber, she realized she wanted to return to the Center, and she wanted to return there immediately!

Wait, something is happening. Again, this uncontrollable wail of sound came out of her tiny human body. It vibrated through her being. The loud primal scream caused all the other little ones to make the same sound all at once. Being bound and restricted from movement was frustrating and intolerable. *Why is this human form so restricted? How can this be?* It ached in the pit of her human stomach.

Something inside was burning and making her sick. It started as a small gurgle in her stomach and grew until it escaped from her lips and left a sour taste in her mouth. And then it released. Burp. A liquid mixture spewed from her mouth with full force. The anger and frustration she felt was her first lesson as a human being. The negative mental and emotional vibration could fill her being and affect the physical form, creating an imbalance between the spirit and body.

These loud vibrations caused such a stir that several humans in white masks came into the room to attend to the little ones. She realized that this behavior would attract attention. *I must remember this, it could be useful.*

A female human came into the room to retrieve her, and brought her to another room. While still tightly wrapped, she was placed into the arms of another female. The second human's energy was much softer. A little depleted and nervous, but soothing. This female had smooth tan skin. Her dark shiny hair was shoulder length, and wet with perspiration. Her dark-brown eyes conveyed joy and satisfaction as she spoke.

"Hello, beautiful girl. I am your mommy. You are so precious. What shall we name you? Your grandmother and daddy will be here soon. Grandma will name you. It's a tradition for her. So let's indulge her to keep the peace. I love you so much. You are perfect. Perfect toes, fingers and a cute little button nose." Mommy kissed her gently on the forehead.

Then Mommy's expression changed, and a wet thing started to stream down her face. No sound was coming from her, but the little one could feel warmth radiating from her mother's being. Ah yes, this energy felt very good. It reminded her of Home, the Center of Light and Oneness where she was created from pure love.

She remembered that moment. The Center started to expand, creating an atomic force of energy. It blessed her journey and mission to the Earth Star. It gave her the knowledge that she would have helpers that would come to her aid when needed, teaching her about the stars in the universe. She would have all that she needed to complete her mission.

The Light became more expansive, until an explosion finally erupted. A small spark was released from the Light. It was barely a glimmer in comparison to its size. It floated out and then downward in a counterclockwise spiral, until it embedded itself inside the womb of the female human that was now holding her. Yes, she remembered that moment well. That same free-flowing and unconditional loving energy was now coming from the female that called herself *mommy*.

Maybe it will be a good experience after all. Maybe I will just have to make a few adjustments because of my inexperience with humanness.

Her mission was to remind other fellow humans about the place of creation at the Center and the spirit light within them. She was to tell them the story of their connection to the Sky and stars and to teach them of the expansiveness of the universe. She was to teach them about other life forms in the universe that came from the same Center. And she was to help them understand that the spirit light within them needs to be in balance with their human body.

This might be tougher than I anticipated. Will these humans believe me, or remember themselves? Only time will tell.

The Light had explained to her that when humans are born, they often forget the Center and the spirit light inside them. By the age of seven they are bombarded with experiences and thought patterns that trap the human form. The experiences of touch, taste, smell, sight, and sound become so important to the human personality and mind that all thoughts are consumed by them. Most humans will not allow themselves to be silent or still, to feel and experience the spirit and their connection to the Oneness of Light in all life forms.

The drop of moisture from the Mommy's face fell on her little forehead and startled her, bringing her back to the present.

The door to the room opened and two other humans entered. One was called *Grandma.* She had short salt-and-pepper colored hair, large black glasses shaped like cat's eyes, and bright red lipstick on her mouth. She had a slender form and tan skin, but the lines and creases on her face made her seem much older than the *mommy* who was holding her. The other human called *Daddy,* was a tall thin male with jet-black hair, and a lighter complexion than Grandma and Mommy. His face was handsome and furry. His open shirt revealed curly black hair on his chest. In fact, unlike Mommy and Grandma, all of his skin seemed furry. His hands were strong and secure, and he emitted a calm energy. The little one liked being passed back and forth between both of them. It made her feel light and weightless for awhile. She had experienced this feeling well before she had entered the Earth Star. As they loosened the tight cloth that constricted her, she could feel flappers dangling at the sides of her body, moving around uncontrollably. She worried that these flappers, called *hands and arms,* might fall off. If only she could use them to flap and fly around the room on her own. She wondered when they were going to tighten the cloth wrapping again.

"Well Claire, I have prayed for our new little girl. She was born on the evening of the full Moon. We should call her Luna," Grandma said.

"Luna?" asked Claire while clenching her jaw. "Oh Mother, I don't know. Luna?" she repeated. *What kind of name is Luna,* she thought.

What was I thinking when I agreed to her tradition and let her name the baby? I thought that letting her name the baby would bring us closer.

"Yes, Luna Belliveau," Grandma confirmed.

"Luna? I like it," Tom, Claire's husband and proud new daddy, said.

"The grandmother names the baby," said Anna, the excited new maternal grandmother. "After all, it's my first grandchild."

She folded her arms in front of her, showing no retreat from her decision.

"Okay, okay," Claire conceded, while wondering why it was so important for her mother to name the newborn.

Claire had asked her many times, but each time was told that it was a family tradition. The truth was... Anna could not tell her the truth. Anna had never anticipated having to tell her why, at least not yet.

"Well, if you don't want the name, that's fine," Anna snapped.

Claire dropped the question. "It's fine, Mother. Luna it will be."

Claire silently wondered if the name would have been so strange if it had been a boy. She only hoped the child would not be teased, and grow up hating her name as she got older.

Grandma Anna had a dream that this child was going to be gifted in some way, much like herself. Anna was different—secretive yet powerful. Her own left wrist had a red birthmark in the shape of a star. In her dream she had seen a glowing light of rainbow colors around the child. It felt significant.

She inspected the child carefully for birthmarks on her face, neck, arms and legs. As the infant grabbed her finger tightly with her left fist, Anna inspected her fingers and hands. And there she found her confirmation. The infant had prominently marked lines that formed a star in the center of her left hand, a sign of identification from the spirits.

Grandma Anna knew Luna would have a special gift. She hoped these gifts would not burden Luna the way they had burdened her life. She prayed that a new generation of acceptance from society would come to embrace Luna, so that she would not need to hide. Anna was committed to help and protect her granddaughter.

Anna looked into Luna's deep, dark, almond-shaped eyes. They were wide awake and aware. They were mysterious and mystical. It was as if Luna had come with some great knowledge and wisdom. But there was something almost worrisome about her; the infant had a serious, pouty face and a squinty brow. *What is Luna bringing to this family? What is she bringing to this world? Only time will tell.*

Luna had a full head of dark hair that was soft, shiny and thick. Her skin tone was tanned from the maternal bloodline. She had so much hair that Claire had to put a barrette in it to keep it from falling into her eyes. Claire could see the seriousness on her little face. Luna's eyes were searching, looking intently around the room at everything, as if she were processing and thinking. *No, it's not possible,* Claire thought. *Infants cannot see yet. Can my child already be aware of her surroundings?*

Luna would be the family's first newborn. Claire and Grandma Anna both looked forward to forming a strong bond with her.

The Grounding

In her early years Luna was, as they say, in between the worlds. She had a difficult time being in this human form. She did not want to stay here. It was a struggle. The body she was in was uncomfortable. She could barely move and control these appendages on the sides of her body. They just seemed to flap around uncontrollably. This vehicle she was in was not cooperating. And then there were the liquid and solid wastes that would come out of her bottom and backside. They were smelly, wet and left a leaking mess. But the liquid that she ingested from her mother's breast allowed her to grow in size.

Her tiny body began to reach high temperatures. The convulsive fevers were wearing out her new vehicle. *What had happened? Something must have gone wrong.* Her body was hot and in pain, and shook with uncontrollable tremors. *This must be a mistake.* She wanted to go back Home.

Luna's fevers and convulsions lasted for two days, and seemed to return every month. During these bouts of sickness, Luna drooled from her mouth and her eyes rolled back into her head, leaving only the whites of her eyes visible to others, trying desperately to escape her body.

"Tom, it's happening again!" Claire screamed.

Her parents panicked with each episode. And each time they brought her back to the place of her birth, where Luna felt so sad and alone. *Maybe I can return Home from the same place I entered the Earth Star.* Luna's body was hot, sweaty and in seizure. She was choking on the drool that was spewing from her mouth.

"I'll get the car," Tom said running out the door, nearly missing one of the stairs in his rush.

As they approached the hospital, Claire ran out of the car into the emergency room, screaming.

"Please help my baby. She is convulsing!"

The doctor removed the child from Claire's arms. After inspection, he placed her on an I.V. drip, and put an oxygen tube into her small nostrils.

After parking the car, Tom hurried into the hospital, "Where is she?" he asked.

"They are trying to stabilize her. She is convulsing and barely breathing," Claire replied. "Oh Tom, what if her brain is damaged. Why can't they figure this out? She has been sick for two years. Will she die?" Claire sobbed into her tissues. Tom held her tightly as he lowered his head. They waited in desperation.

It was always the same procedure, cold ice baths and tubes in her arms and nose. Lonely overnight stays with strange masked Earth people. She was held captive in a bedchamber covered with a low-hanging contagion net. They called this a *crib*. Luna couldn't move and she couldn't leave. As if her physical body wasn't enough of a cage. Her body hurt and was twitching uncontrollably. *This life is getting worse by the minute. Why did I agree to come here?* Luna was in and out of the Earth consciousness.

The Center of Oneness had portrayed Earth as a wonderful and exciting place. The experiences of smell, touch, sight, sound and taste were nothing that she liked. It seemed she had been misinformed, misled and wanted desperately to be released from this body. She wasn't grounding the human vehicle, and she didn't want to accept it. As she angered, her body temperature shot up to 105 degrees. The nurses worried that she would slip into a coma and experience brain damage.

The Guide

Cyrus was his unspoken name, and from afar, he watched this little one struggle for her human life on this star called Earth. He felt responsible for her. He was the one assigned to guide her through the young years of her journey. His presence hovered around her. Although he was invisible to most adult humans, the infant's eyes followed him everywhere as he floated around the room.

She saw his spirit light. It was much easier for her to see him than the other humans. His ghost-like appearance was more transparent and familiar to her. The little one could see him around her all the time. Sometimes Luna would smile and giggle for no reason at all, or so people thought. The reality was that he would light up the room and dance around her. He would brush her cheek and softly stroke the top of her tiny head, especially when she cried to leave her body and this world.

Cyrus' mission was not his first one. He had guided new beings to this place before. But he had failed each time. By the time each child was seven years old, the youngster would usually forget all about Cyrus and the mission.

This Earth was full of fear, ego and unawareness. The two-legged beings walked around wanting to control one another, and every other form of being. This race was going to be destroyed because of their ignorance. They needed to connect to the spirit of Oneness within themselves.

Cyrus would never give up on his mission to bring enlightenment to these human beings. He would guide this one with persistence. Somehow, Cyrus knew it would be different this time. This little one had entered the world and still had all of her memory from the Center. *This is a good sign,* he thought, *since most little ones lose over half of their memory upon entry.*

Although she struggled within her body and despite her thoughts telling him that she wanted to go back, Cyrus still had much hope due to the family she had chosen to be born into. Their secret lineage understood the stars and the balance of the spirit. This culture would help her make her way through the human form and connect to the Earth and all of its beings.

Cyrus was determined to work really hard with this one. He would teach her with more diligence than he had done with the others before her. He had to succeed this time, or this race of humans would get further away from the light and then eventually cease to be.

He believed her essence would understand, remember, and eventually agree to stay here. Now if he could just get her to stop struggling in her human body.

The choice was difficult for many little ones. The human vehicle was so heavy and the life process seemed so hard that many chose to leave by using their own free will to create illness. Others would forget their mission and struggle throughout their whole earth life, adding more destruction to their race and the Earth.

Cyrus was with her at the birthing place when she entered this world. She was brought back there again and again, during the first two-and-a-half years of her life when her convulsions and fevers were at their worst. But she was a warrior, full of strength. *Good,* he thought. *These qualities will serve her well here.*

There had been two reasons why Cyrus had failed on his previous missions. The first reason was that many of the little ones lost all of their memory at the birthing place. Second, the human parents would unintentionally reprogram the memories and thoughts of the little ones before they were seven years old. Their memories became long lost and forgotten. He could no longer help them on their missions if they had no memory.

On one of Luna's return trips to the birthing place they called a *hospital,* she was weak and her body was shaking. Her body was placed in a tub of ice. She felt her body become very light. Looking down she could see her body in the tub below, but she could not feel the pain. Her spirit had lifted out of its tiny shell, feeling free and happy.

I've escaped, she thought. *I'm going Home.* She began floating and dancing around the room, above her body. Moving towards Cyrus she thought, *I'm free. I'm free,* only to be disappointed by being pulled back into her body with a thump and experiencing the excruciatingly cold temperature of the ice.

"I think she is coming around," the nurse said. "Her eyes are open. Let's get her out of the tub, dress her, put her into the crib and start the I.V."

Oh no, Luna thought. She despised the bars on this thing they called a crib, and she hated the net over it. It trapped her, like a caged wild animal.

She was poked and prodded with pointed objects by women who had no mouths. They wore masks as they conducted their tests. Luna saw them extract a red liquid from her tiny arms. It hurt, and it made her feel dizzy. Luna kicked and screamed so much that they had to strap her down in the crib. The tests gave her arms a black and blue sore.

Luna had a hard time adjusting. The only power or control she had was with her eyes and mind. Her eyes darted around the room staring at the form of Cyrus that floated around her. At least he kept her entertained. He soothed and calmed her. His thin outlined veil of a human form emulated a teenage boy in a shimmering rainbow-colored robe. Only his face and hands had form. He had an angelic face with soft, iridescent blue, transparent eyes. He was beautiful. The brilliant lights surrounded him like an egg as he floated and glowed.

"Look at her eyes. What is she looking at?" the first nurse asked.

"She looks so far away when she stares, and yet she moves her eyes as if she is following something very distinct and solid," the second nurse added.

"She has convulsed so many times since she was born, maybe her little brain is not right."

"The poor child, hopefully the tests will tell us what is wrong with her," the second nurse replied.

Despair engulfed Luna. This body and life had been her misery for the last two-and-a-half years. She struggled to get out of her little body.

She wanted to escape this sterile place that caused her excruciating pain and confinement, and to go back to the world she remembered.

On what she hoped would be the last of her hospital visits, the doctors placed an oxygen mask over Luna's nose and mouth as her body convulsed. Once again she escaped her body. As her light danced around the room like a butterfly, Cyrus approached her.

"Luna, dearest, you must retreat and merge back to your human form," he guided.

"No. My form hurts and it's too much work. I don't want to stay there," she protested.

Luna's spirit light dashed around the ceiling. Cyrus continued to persuade her as he chased her.

"Remember your mission agreement. The Earth Star needs you. You must help mankind remember their connection to Oneness, the place where they have all come from and their connection to the stars. You cannot go back Home yet. I will help you here."

"It is too hard. My vehicle is heavy and moves too slow. This is not what I was promised. I don't want to be human. It has too many restrictions. Please help me go back," she pleaded in desperation.

"Dearest, you must learn to live among them and have this experience in order to become complete. It is the process by which the spirit evolves. You have chosen with free will to accept the human form and all of its experiences. You have not even allowed yourself all the wonders available to your humanness. You can help many human beings remember and learn to truly merge the love and light within. You're angry, and you feel separated from everything. This is what each human experiences. But, you still remember your spirit light and where you came from. Almost all of these beings have forgotten. Your anger and fear will rebel against your human form. Anger and fear will cause your body to break down. You must learn to use and accept the human form while balancing your light within. You must remember that it is inside of you and every being."

Luna expanded her free-flowing spirit. She wanted to reach back to the Center. Remembering that there is no separation between her body and her spirit, she retreated and fell back into her human body once again with a hard thud.

Claire

Luna's mother Claire came from a small blue-collar town in Massachusetts, known for shoe and textile manufacturing. In later years, it would expand to the field of medical filter manufacturing. It was a small country town with a landscape consisting mostly of oak and elm trees sprouted between the small cottages and old farm houses. Most of the old houses, many of which were built in the 1700s, were being converted to apartments. There were no major highways and there was hardly any traffic.

Claire was an only child, and there weren't many children in the neighborhood her own age to play or talk with. Aunts, uncles, paternal grandparents, and her parents were her companions. She was not allowed to have friends over after school. Claire was a lonely and isolated child. Claire really didn't remember having a childhood. Her activities were limited; she spent a lot of time alone reading or with her father in his basement wood shop. Helping her mother with daily chores allowed Claire to learn domestic ways. Except for tending the small vegetable and herb garden in the backyard, she could barely remember a time when she played or even went outdoors. And whenever she did go outside, she was fearful of even the smallest spider, bee, or bird.

Her parents had relatives over for Sunday visits. Claire helped prepare the food for the summer barbecues and birthday dinners. She learned how to be quiet, listen, and speak only when spoken to. She withheld her emotions and buried her loneliness deep inside. Claire became skilled at serving people, a cold drink for this aunt or a napkin for that uncle. Serving others was always expected. Claire tried hard to please her mother and get her attention. The relatives would rave about her, complimenting on how obedient and helpful she was to the elders.

What a prize daughter. Yet Claire never felt prized, she felt alone and distant from her mother. Anna spent a lot of time in silence and in her special room.

Growing up, Claire was obedient. But when she got to be a teenager, Claire realized she had never experienced a child's playful, imaginative life. Because of her mother's special room, Claire's school playmates were not allowed to visit. Claire had become the babysitter for the younger cousins at the family gatherings. She never had fun, although her father could be quite funny after a cocktail or two. Her serious face camouflaged her fear and frustration.

There was only one place in her home that she was not permitted to enter, her mother's mysterious room, which was a dim candle-lit place that smelled of sweet smoke and flowers.

Claire got a glimpse of the secret room only once. She was five years old when she made her one and only unauthorized entry. She opened the door to the dark room and saw four white-pillared candles arranged in a cross-like manner on a small table. On the table, was a glass bottle of aromatic oil, soft dried gray leaves rolled into small round balls, a long braid of sweet smelling grass, many different sized colored stones and a skinned pouch. On a nearby shelf were small jars of dried herbs and dark bottles of liquids and pastes. She quickly took in as much as she could observe. Claire noticed a wing of a bird that looked like a fan. The room was much cooler than the rest of the house. She inspected each thing with her eyes and wondered how her mother might use it. The inspection ended abruptly once Anna noticed the room's door was ajar. Anna caught Claire with a tight grip and swiftly ushered her out of the room.

"Claire, I told you to never to go into that room," Anna yelled.

"But I just wanted to see where you go. What is all that stuff for? Why is it cold in there?" she asked.

"Never you mind about that," Anna reprimanded. "That is my room and you are to keep out. You must never speak about it to anyone. Just forget about it. Do you understand?"

"Yes, but...," Claire stammered.

"No buts," Anna snapped.

Claire reluctantly agreed, not fully understanding what she had seen. She was left with many unanswered questions in her young mind. Claire felt the pain from her mother's grip. All she wanted was to be with her mother and to understand why she went to that room. Claire's face grew angry and cold. She would carry that day's memory in her heart from that day forward, as she began to distance herself from her mother. Anna's fear and anxiety was revealed in that moment. She hoped that Claire would obey her and forget what she had seen.

From time to time in the late evening, after she went to bed, Claire would hear people come to the house. She never knew who they were. Anna would greet them and bring them into the secret room. Claire would hear singing and low whispering, but she could never make out the words. After a long time, they would leave the room, hug, and the unknown person would be on their way.

Before Claire entered primary grade school, she was tormented by her dreams. Something would touch and awaken her, pulling her out of bed and trying to lead her somewhere. She could feel it but could not see it. Then she would hear a loud screeching noise in her ears. It scared her to death and made for some sleepless nights. Claire would fight it and resist it while cowering under the covers. She called for her mother to help, but only once did Anna come to Claire's aid.

Claire shared her nightmare with her mother. Anna explained that there are guides who watch over each person and communicate with them. Anna told Claire that she did not have to be afraid and that she had guides of her own as well.

"Mommy, what do you do in your secret room?" Claire asked.

Anna was reluctant to answer. But she realized maybe that if she answered some of her questions, Claire might forget about it once and for all.

"I help people who are sick and troubled," Anna replied. "That's all you need to know. Don't ask me anything else about that room."

Claire did not want anything to do with unseen guides and their teachings, help, or protection. Claire needed her mother. She was fearful, unlike her mother, and would hide under the bed covers until she drifted off to sleep. By the time she was seven, the nightmares had become but a distant memory. They made no formal contact again. Claire's resistance had won.

Anna's absence from Claire was because of her gift. Those she helped called her a healer. She was someone who could intervene on the behalf of sick and ailing people. Anna would ask for a healing to come. Praying that the energy and power would flow into her and show her where she should transfer it into the troubled person.

Did it work every time? No, but most of the time it did. It was always dependent upon the individual's free will to accept the healing or not. Her guides told her which people she could help.

Anna never used the word healer. She referred to herself as a helper. She was able to feel, hear and know things that most humans could not. Protecting her secret, at times, was burdensome. Healing was not widely accepted by her small town. It was viewed as black magic, and it created fear and what was feared was destroyed. She was concerned about her family's safety and security, which was why she was so secretive about her room.

Claire's mother had many late night friends who seemed to be grateful and loving. Claire, even as a young girl, dreamed of escaping from her mother's bizarre room of secrets, and then getting married and having children of her own. Children that she would love and spend time with and have no secrets.

When Claire met Tom at the tender age of eighteen, she felt all her dreams had come true. She could at last begin to make a life of her own. The dream of a wonderful home with lots of children and laughter was her hope.

At present, Claire was twenty-two years old, with dark short hair that she curled daily. She treasured her husband's affection and wanted to look good for him.

Sitting at the kitchen table, she was waiting for her homemade chocolate cake to cook. She was four-and-a-half years into her marriage and where was her dream? What had happened? Her only child Luna was not well. The toddler with shoulder length jet-black hair and deep, dark-brown almond eyes was in and out of the hospital. Claire was exhausted from the back and forth trips to the hospital and trying to maintain her household at the same time. For some unknown reason, she had been unable to get pregnant again and she was terribly worried about the thought of losing her only child.

Claire was desperately searching for an understanding of her situation and the tears silently made their way down her cheeks with anguish and fear. She wondered if she had been selfish and should have had her mother try to help. She could vaguely remember the secret room. Anna had not used it for a couple of years. Claire remembered the conversation.

"Claire, would you like me to take Luna to my room and try to help her? I can help my grandchild."

"No, Mother. That room is scary. I won't subject her to that."

"Claire, please let me try. I love that child. I believe I can help her," Anna pleaded.

"No," Claire said firmly. "Where were you, for me, Mother? You wanted your secret room over me."

Claire was still struggling with resentful feelings of abandonment. The old anger resurfaced, reflecting her inner child desiring her mother's attention. Claire pushed it down deeper. *I am a good mother. I will be there for my child,* she reassured herself in her private thoughts.

She refused Anna and it was never offered again.

My mother was not there for me. She helped strangers, but not me. When I needed her as a child, she was depleted and had to rest. My father was my only protector and source of affection thought Claire, as the wound opened again.

Anna loved Claire and tried to reach out to her many times. But it was too late. Claire's anger had built a wall between them.

A child should have her mother, Claire thought. *One that was there for them at all times.*

But for Claire, being there for her own child Luna was running her ragged and filling her with anxiety and stress. She was in the midst of drowning in her own thoughts when a sound suddenly alarmed her.

Beep! Beep! Beep! The alarm signaled the cake was cooked and should be removed from the oven. It awakened her from her distant thoughts. It was now time to set the table for dinner. Her pot of stew and warm homemade bread were ready to be served. She awaited the arrival of her beloved Tom. Together they would make the ritualistic trip to see their only child in the hospital, hoping for some answers this time.

Tom had dark clean-cut hair, dark eyes, thin lips, and a perfectly white smile. He was really good looking. He had stopped Claire's heart when they first met. But his best quality was his tender heart. He was a kind and thoughtful man. He was full of laughter and fun, a very affectionate man who was loved by everyone who met him. He was a hard worker, taking on two jobs to pay for Luna's medical bills.

Tom was the oldest of six children and understood the importance of family and a loving home. His parents were born and raised in Canada, and they both had died before Luna was born. His mother passed ten months after his father. Some say she died from a broken heart and that she did not want to live without him. Tom had wanted the same loving marriage that his parents had. He was happy and grateful to have found that with Claire.

At seventeen, Tom enlisted in the Air Force for four years to provide income to his parents and younger siblings. He enjoyed the traveling and being stationed at many places across the country. He had a sense of adventure and a personality to match it.

When Tom met Claire after the Air Force, it was love at first sight. The attraction was like fire. They instantly knew they were meant to be together.

After six months of dating they were happily married. Tom did not come from riches or wealth, but his heart and passion for life won Claire's heart. Like Claire, he wanted a family with lots of children. For Claire, he was responsible, loving, and the man of her dreams.

"Honey, I'm home," he called.

"Dinner's on the table," she said, as she greeted him with a kiss.

"Sit down and start eating before it gets cold. Visiting hours end at eight o'clock. We can get a quick visit in before your part-time job. My mother and I saw her this morning. Her fever is down and she seems to be stable again. She may come home tomorrow."

"It feels so empty when she isn't here. I wish the doctors could stop this from happening."

"Oh, Tom," Claire sat down next to him at the table and broke down in tears. "What's wrong with her? I'm so afraid that we'll lose her if she convulses one more time. It can't be good for her little body. I'm also worried that I can't have any more children. We have tried for months. What kind of woman am I that I can't get pregnant again?" Claire lamented.

"Come on, Claire," Tom replied. "The doctor said it may just be stress on your body, and right now we need to focus on getting our little girl well." He soothed her by rubbing her back.

"Yes, you're right, honey. We need to see that our little girl gets well. At least it hasn't impaired her walking or speech. Finish eating and I'll do the dishes when we get back," Claire continued. "I need to see her before she falls asleep. She needs to see her mommy before she falls asleep."

The little one was standing up in the crib and waiting for them. The nurse had removed the overhead netting, giving Luna the freedom to walk around in the crib. She was really getting to be too tall for the crib. She stood at attention looking at the door and hallway beyond, watching the nurses and doctors walk back and forth past the room. Mommy and Daddy would always come to see her in this lonely place.

She was in her nightgown and stood on her little sock-covered feet and rocked from side to side in the crib. She waited in anticipation for them and the new stuffed furry present they would bring to cheer her up. She had a room full of them from each of her previous incarcerations. But the only thing she truly wanted was to go Home. Not the house where her mommy and daddy lived, but her real Home. The place she still remembered clearly. The place of beautiful lights where the air was perfect and her essence could float easily and free. Luna smiled and relaxed as she thought of it.

Just then, the door flew open and she fell out of her little memory.

"Luna, baby! Mommy and Daddy are here, sweetheart," Claire announced.

And with that, Tom plopped a large stuffed monkey into Luna's crib. The monkey's right plastic thumb was in its mouth and its left hand was holding a fake banana.

"Do you like your monkey?" asked Tom. "He's almost as big as you are."

Luna jumped up and seemed excited to see them. Her arms were extended and she said "Mommy" as she reached for Claire. But her daddy picked her up first and bounced her around and kissed her cheeks. He handed her to Claire, who smothered her with kisses.

It was good to be reunited with them even if she wasn't really going Home.

The nurse came in during the reunion and announced:

"The doctor said he will release her tomorrow. The fever is gone and everything is back to normal. He'll talk to you more in the morning. Call him around ten o'clock to confirm her release time."

Claire and Tom visited for a little while. They rocked Luna to sleep, placing her back into the crib and tiptoed out of the room before making their way back home.

"I hope the doctor has found what's been causing these episodes," Tom stated.

"Well honey, in a way I almost hope he hasn't, because then there wouldn't be anything terribly wrong with her, like a deadly disease," she said. "You know my friend Joan said that children can start with epilepsy at a very young age."

"Maybe the bloodwork will tell us this time," he responded.

The next morning, Claire found herself in the same position as in the past. The doctor had not found anything in the child's bloodwork.

"Well, I guess we'll wait and see if there is a next time," the doctor shrugged. "That's all we can do."

Claire took her little girl home once again, and resumed her daily life of worry.

The next episode came a month later. Once again Luna was brought to the hospital. Once again, everyone in the sterile place wore a mask and gloves. Their cold robotic voices sounded muffled and routine. They pulled and tugged at her, and once again poked a sharp object into her arm. She was dehydrated from the fever. They hooked her up to long tubes that had a clear fluid flowing into her. It was supposed to make her feel better.

The needles made her little arms black and blue like a human pincushion. Bruised from uncaring beings, it would take at least a month for the bruises to heal. Still, no one could figure out her sickness. Luna knew she didn't want to stay *here*.

Take me back Home, to the Center. This place is hard. I am not happy. It's much darker here than back Home. I can't move freely. This vehicle I'm in doesn't work properly. Everything is slow and takes too much effort, she thought. Her impatience with this place was growing stronger by the minute.

Up until now, no one had ever noticed that Luna had a raspy voice. However, on the next trip to the hospital, a young new doctor named Dr. Wright found that many small sores in her throat had caused an infection. He said that these sores had been making it difficult for her to speak clearly.

Luna didn't need to speak in her former world. She used telepathy for communication. It required less energy and was much easier.

No, thought Luna, *I don't want to communicate this way. I want to communicate like we did back Home, no words, only pictures and thoughts.*

The doctor decided that he would remove something called *tonsils* from her throat. He told her parents that surgically removing her tonsils would end the recurring infections, high fevers and emergency visits. The date and time were scheduled. Claire and Tom took her to the hospital for the surgery.

Luna cried in terror.

"No, Mommy! No, Mommy!" she protested.

"It's okay, sweetheart. The doctor is going to fix you this time and make you all better."

It was so hard for Claire to leave her child again. Each time, it broke a little piece of her heart. Luna looked so helpless and frightened. Claire filled up with tears when she was separated from her terrified child. Her daughter was wheeled away and admitted to the same place she had been for much of her short life. Luna was prepared for surgery and rolled down a long hallway into an extremely bright room.

As Luna lay on the cold hard table, they placed a mask on her face. Air and gas came through the mask and made her very sleepy. Two women wearing gloves, green caps, suits and masks told her to repeat counting to *three*. Luna only got to *two* before drifting off into a deep sleep. Her spirit lifted out of her body easily. She floated and danced around the room once again.

"I'm flying. Hey, look at me up here," she said.

But no one below could hear or see her. The ladies and man in the green suits were talking excitedly to each other.

"She is bleeding too much. Her blood pressure is dropping. Hurry up before we lose her!" the doctor yelled.

She did not understand, nor did she care because she was flying around and happy. Then she saw a sphere of bluish-green light on the ceiling in the corner of the room. It was getting larger and brighter. The young being emerged out of the sphere. Luna had seen him many times before, floating around her, watching her. His essence was older than hers. He was what the Oneness called an old soul, one that had been around for a long time.

"Hello, little one. Remember me? I'm your friend. I have come to take you Home. You have resisted so much that your spirit is more out of your body than in it. Once again, I guess I have failed. Your human form has died and the spirit has left to go Home."

The people below desperately tried to revive the young child.

Yippee! I'm going Home. I'm going Home, Luna thought with relief. He took her spirit light and led her into the sphere of bluish-green colors. They traveled into the blue Sky, far past the clouds, until it became a dark tunnel. At the end of the tunnel many lights appeared.

Oh yes, she remembered, the place in the Sky beyond the stars and the doorway into all knowing, awareness, peace, love and tranquility. It was the place of creation and spirit light of being, the Center, the true Home.

They appeared among many beings of light. These beings did not have faces. Just an elongated shaped light with gold flecks floating in the formless essence.

Luna heard them speak. The voices were chattering away in her head, the old way of communication through transference of pictures and thoughts.

"It's not her time. Why did you bring her here?" they asked.

"I was told to take care of her. She was having trouble staying in her earth body. Her vehicle died, so I brought her here to the Portal of the Center," he said. "Maybe you can give her another form to be reborn into?"

"No, that will take too long. We need to send her back before she forgets. She has much to do back there. This child must live the life and tell the story. She needs to help the humans on the Earth Star to understand. She has not learned all of the teachings of the universe," the light beings of the Portal spoke firmly.

Luna was confused. She wanted to merge with the light.

Go back? Live the life? Tell the story?

Luna thought, *I remember I agreed to go to the Earth Star and help the beings remember their spirit light within and their connection to the Oneness at the Center, and to remember the connection to all beings from the stars and the true essence of all life. But, I have not met the beings from the stars yet...*

Luna realized that being on the Earth Star for three years was erasing a small amount of her memory. And then, as soon as she thought about Earth, she felt herself being tugged away from the light through the darkness, down into the blue Sky, through the clouds, through the ceiling, and falling back into the hospital surgery room. As she looked at the being that *claimed* to be her friend she was afraid. Luna was falling fast and far away from Home through the wormhole.

What is happening?

"Don't be afraid, little one. My name is Cyrus and I am your guide. I will teach you and show you many things. I will come back to see you soon and, in time, you will learn. Your body has been revived. Don't reject it again."

With that, she crashed hard into the body that the doctor and nurses had stabilized in a deep sleep of recovery.

She awoke hours later in a room with her parents and grandparents.

Oh no, she thought, as she cried. *I'm back!*

Her throat was burning and was in great pain. She tried to speak but her mother Claire, just hushed her.

"Luna, don't talk. I know it hurts baby, but it will feel better soon. Don't cry."

They were presenting her with gifts and candy. They hugged and kissed her. She tried again to speak, but couldn't. She wanted to tell them about what she saw and where she had been, but her throat felt like it was on fire.

For the first few moments she just sobbed large tears as she looked around. She was back *here* again.

Please let me go back! My head, neck and throat hurt! Luna screamed inside. Her body became tense and tight.

Claire soothed, "It's okay, sweetheart. Your throat will hurt for a little bit but it'll get better. And you can have lots of ice cream."

And with that, she took a spoonful of chocolate ice cream and spooned it into her daughter's mouth. The taste was unbelievably good. It was cold and soothing on her throat. It was creamy and sweet, and rolled around so smoothly in her mouth. A smile emerged from her lips. At last a taste that she liked. It was one of the sweetest and satisfying tastes that had been promised by the Center of Oneness.

Maybe, this place isn't so bad after all. This ice cream is pretty good. Maybe I will stay here for a little while, at least to have some more of this ice cream.

Cyrus

Once her throat had healed and she was able to talk, Luna told her mommy and daddy about her flying, Cyrus, the Center, and coming back to tell the story.

Sure, okay, so you had a dream, they thought. They amused her by letting her go on about it, at first. But after a couple of weeks, it became troublesome to them.

"Okay, dear. Now let's forget about this dream and talk about something else," Claire said.

"But it wasn't a dream," Luna responded. "It was real."

She couldn't think about anything else. It was all she thought about. The feeling of being free from her body, flying through the Sky and seeing the beautiful light. It was simply unforgettable. And she promised herself that she would never forget it, no matter how much time passed.

Luna, now able to communicate using her voice after surgery, began to ask incessant questions. Pointing and asking, "Why? What's this? How does that work?"

Luna realized she needed to understand this world if she was going to stay here.

The one thing she did enjoy was eating. She loved the taste and texture of many foods: cream, cheese, candy, cookies and cake. She also loved butternut squash and pumpkin. Eating was her favorite experience in her earth vehicle. It would become her comfort in times of great stress.

She awoke one night, and noticed the brightness of the Sky outside her bedroom window. She climbed out of her big girl bed, and looked outside. There she was, the Moon, full and bright. Luna could see a woman's face in it that seemed to be looking back at her and smiling. This made her happy, for the moment. And then suddenly a wave of despair came over her. Looking at the stars only reminded her of Home, beyond the darkness of the Sky. She sighed, wandering back from the window with tears in her eyes and crawled into bed. A clouded mist came in from the window. A bluish-green sphere emerged from which Cyrus made his entrance.

"Oh yes," Luna said. "I'm going Home. You have come to get me. My wish has come true."

"Hello, little one. No, dearest. Sorry to say that I'm not taking you Home. Your life will be here on the Earth Star for a long time. I have come to bring you teachings from other places and beings," he said.

"Cyrus? Why do you visit at night?"

"Luna, it is morning here, even though the Sky is dark over your Earth and the clock reads 2:00 a.m. I come in the dark because it is much easier for you to see me, and for you to travel without being missed by your parents. The time of the full Moon is a powerful one in the stars. It is easier to see the celestial realm and travel through it. The time before sunrise is when the veil between the Earth and stars is the thinnest, and dimensional passage is easiest."

"For tonight, we will just practice going through the dimension of your bedroom wall," he continued. "Follow my breathing and watch me. Practice with me, Luna."

Luna watched him take several short quick shallow breaths. She repeated his example. It made her feel light-headed and dizzy, the same as when she would run around in circles.

"No, dearest," Cyrus coached. "Try breathing with your mouth open."

Luna tried again, breathing with her nose and mouth open slightly, sounding close to hyperventilation. The breath transformed her body into thin transparency, becoming airy and light. The bluish-green sphere enveloped her, changing the molecular structure of her form into a mist of energy.

Luna reached for his hand. The hand was just an image filled with a pocket of air. His shrouded human-like form was designed to make the child feel safe and comfortable and enabled him to easily befriend her and appeal to her senses.

"Okay, Cyrus," Luna replied.

They breathed together in unison. Luna felt her body and head get lighter. She had started to float.

"That is very good, Luna. Now close your eyes, and in your mind, see yourself floating right through your bedroom wall to the outside," he said, as the sphere started to move forward.

Luna silently focused and concentrated on her shallow quick breathing, and before very long, she and Cyrus were outside in the backyard above the swing set, floating several feet above the ground.

Luna was excited. "Can we go higher off the ground?" she asked.

"Yes, but let us practice this for tonight. We have many days ahead of us to journey together," he replied.

He played with Luna as she floated above and around the swing set. They had fun the rest of the night, effortlessly shifting between indoors and outdoors.

Morning came, as Luna awoke and jumped out of bed, still feeling light on her feet.

"Mommy, Mommy! I was flying last night with Cyrus. We went outside through the bedroom wall and my feet didn't touch the ground!" exclaimed Luna.

Claire had just woken up and was having her first cup of coffee.

"Luna, it was just a dream," remarked Claire.

"No Mommy, I was really outside floating up in the air. My feet were off the ground. I was flying above the swing!"

Claire knew that her daughter loved the swing set. Luna desperately pumped her feet to get higher and higher, but she could never get high enough for her liking. "I want to go up there," Luna would say as she pointed to the Sky.

"Luna, you just dreamed you were flying," Claire replied firmly. "Sit down and I'll fix your breakfast."

"No, I don't want to eat. I'm not hungry," she stammered as she stomped to her bedroom, crying. Mommy did not believe her.

Claire could not believe this tantrum. "All right, don't eat," Claire snapped back.

Luna had been excited to share this with her mother. But thanks to the response she got, her excitement did not last very long.

Luna now saw that communication was harder here on the Earth Star. *Maybe if I could just show Mommy the pictures in my mind, she would understand,* Luna thought with her arms tightly folded over her chest. Luna closed her eyes and tried to telepathically send a visual message to her mother. But it was as if Claire's mind had a door that was closed and sealed. The pictures could not get through. Luna tried several times, to no avail. Finally, she gave up.

Maybe Cyrus can teach me how to show Mommy and help her see, she thought. Luna could not wait for Cyrus' next visit. She was overwhelmed with excitement just thinking about it.

It was around this time that Luna fell in love with music. She danced and mimicked the words to the songs when her parents played the radio. Singing and dancing made her happy and helped her get accustomed to her body. She enjoyed the movement of dance; the sensations of sound pulsating through her body and the vibrations of her voice reflecting the energy of her singing gave her joy. Her body felt lighter when she sang and danced. The music moved both the energy and emotion inside of her.

Claire and Tom also loved music, and the radio would often be on. Luna swayed her hips and rocked back and forth whenever music was on in the house. She would take her hairbrush and pretend it was a microphone, just like the ones used by the singers on the television. Luna loved how her ponytail, which was tied in a colorful ribbon, swung back and forth on her neck and shoulders as she moved with the music.

Sometimes she'd change the words of the song's lyrics, and make up her own.

Claire would often say, "Luna, you are singing the wrong words to the song."

Luna would just reply, "I know Mommy, but I like these words better."

Luna would take her improvised lyrics, set them to her own melody and perform for Mommy, Daddy, Grandma Anna and Grandpa Joe.

Her performances would lighten the mood of her family, with everyone smiling and laughing. And making other people happy made Luna feel good. She sang to the trees, the frogs, and even the swing set. Singing was a natural sensation for her to create in her physical vehicle.

Several months later, Luna was outside in her backyard while her mother was chatting with a neighbor. Luna saw a beautiful black and yellow snake slithering in the grass. She followed it and started to sing to it.

"Come here pretty snake. Come here, little dear. Come here pretty snake. Just let me come near."

The snake slithered toward her, and just as she was reaching down to pick it up, Claire screamed and threw a rock on the snake's head, killing it. Luna gasped for air. The breath was knocked out of her as she felt a crushing blow to her skull. The snake's physical pain had become her own pain. Luna grabbed her head and screamed as the pain passed through her body. She didn't understand what had just happened and why her mother had killed the snake.

"Why, Mommy? Why did you kill the snake?" Luna shrieked.

"Luna, calm down," Claire said. "That snake could have hurt you. You cannot play with those kinds of things. Leave them alone."

"You were killing me, too. He was my friend. I am him and he is me," she cried. "He wouldn't have hurt me. I called him to me."

"Luna, you did not call him to you. It's just a snake and it doesn't think like you and I do. You are not a snake and I am not killing you."

"Yes, he understood. I could feel it. I was connected to him," she rebutted.

"Luna, do not argue with me. Leave the ants, snakes, spiders, frogs and everything else on the ground alone. Do you hear me? They have diseases and can bite you and make you sick."

"They won't hurt me if I talk to them," she argued.

"Luna, you cannot talk to them. It's impossible. They don't understand."

"No, you don't understand!" Luna screamed at a deafening pitch, tears streaming down her reddened cheeks.

Luna shook her head in disbelief. She was trembling and felt nauseous. She vomited, discharging her energy and emotion.

She wondered if she should have left the snake alone, and not called it to her. She glanced at the snake and said she was sorry, hoping it would forgive her for calling him over and indirectly causing his death.

Why couldn't her mother understand? Why did she do such a terrible thing?

Claire took Luna's hand and brought her into the house to calm her down.

Luna was sensitive to all living beings, including the ants. She would watch them for hours as they built their mounds in the dirt and carried food into their holes. Luna marveled at how strong they were and how well they worked together as a family. On one occasion, while Luna was watching the ants, Stevie, the boy next door, came over and asked, "What are you looking at?"

"I'm looking at the ants on the ground. Look at how strong they are," Luna replied.

Stevie promptly stomped on the mound, crushing the ant hill and several ants.

"They don't look so strong now," he said laughing.

Luna screamed, falling to the ground in pain. Her eyes and mouth opened in horror. "Why did you do that? They weren't hurting you."

She curled into the fetal position and rolled back and forth on the ground until the pain passed.

"How would you like it if a giant came and stepped on your house and killed you and your family?"

Stevie thought about it for a few seconds, and said, "I guess I wouldn't like it. But Luna, they're just ants."

"They're just ants?" she screamed again.

She narrowed her eyes and glared at him; she wanted to hit him and knock him down. Instead, she shook her head and cried, trying to displace the anger she was feeling.

"What is wrong with human beings? I don't understand how they can be so mean and hurtful. No connection to other living beings!" she said as she released her fury.

Luna's mind, emotions, and vocabulary were much more advanced than that of a typical four-year-old child. More sensitive than anyone else she knew, she felt the physical sensation of pain in other living beings that she connected to. These sensations would only intensify as she got older. Her only solace came from her hope that her friend Cyrus would visit soon. He was the only one who could help her understand.

Merope

It was two o'clock in the morning, her favorite time. As she waited by the window for Cyrus, she remembered how the Moon outside always shone bright when he came for her.

This was her playtime. She loved the Moon. She watched it in the night Sky from her bedroom window, feeling a kinship to it. As she gazed at it again, she could still see a woman's face in it.

It was also why Grandma named her Luna, because it was a full Moon on the eve of her birth.

Tonight she was excited and full of anticipation for Cyrus' visit. He had come for her often since her operation, and they had become fast friends. Luna had fun waiting for him, knowing he was coming to play. She always knew when he was coming ahead of time, because she would get faint and light-headed, and hear a low-pitched buzzing sound. Cyrus said it was the way he would prepare her for ethereal movement. He would help her body adjust.

Cyrus was so much fun to be with. It already seemed like he had been her playmate forever. Her heart raced as she lay awake in bed, waiting for him. She wondered where they would play tonight. On his last visit, he said that the next visit would be to someplace special. Her celestial friend sneaked past everyone who was asleep and came into Luna's room. Thanks to his quick, quiet, shallow breaths he walked with an invisible appearance. Luna was now ready to travel further.

"Hello, little one," he spoke.

"Hello, Cyrus. Where will we play tonight? You said it would be special."

what most cannot see or know. It will not harm you; it will only make your life force stronger."

As soon as he lifted his hand, Luna felt full. She had been filled with something, and it felt good. It was uneasy at first, as she tried to adjust to this energy. Luna noticed she was slightly dizzy, and her head was aching. Though there were many new beings around her, she wasn't afraid of them.

The second-tallest being came forth. "I am Matar." He took her hands and again transferred a cold tingling, numbing sensation into her hands. This time wasn't so bad. It actually felt good; cool, tingly and refreshing. Lighter than the first time.

"Just relax and breathe slow and deep. This will help you with your work on the Earth Star when you need to offer assistance. It will help you feel, move, and transfer energy within other creatures and beings."

And last, the third of the taller beings stepped forward. "I am Alcor."

"Are you going to touch me too?" she asked.

"Yes, but I will fill your earthly heart. It will help you to understand the energy of every living thing. This will feel like a hardship at times, but it will help you to become compassionate and sensitive for the future."

Alcor placed his metallic-form hands on her heart, and for a moment, she felt her heart stop, frozen in time. There was a sharp pain at first, like a stabbing in her chest. For an instant, she couldn't breathe. She wanted to scream but she couldn't move her lips. Then a wave of emotions filled her heart. She felt sorrow, joy, overwhelming love and finally, a rush of peaceful bliss. As she came to the end of this energy transfer, a large tear fell from the corner of her eye. She would remember this feeling and experience forever. It was embedded in her every cell.

Luna's eyes caught a glimpse of a beautiful waterfall in the distance. It was a rush of cascading water that glistened like a rainbow sparkling in the light. She wandered away from the group toward the water, as it seemed to beckon her. It sounded almost like it was whispering to her at first, but as she got closer and focused her attention; she could actually hear it speak.

Luna noticed that all of these things seemed to glow more here than back on Earth. There was a light around each and every one of them.

"Welcome," the waterfall crooned. "You will notice that everything here can communicate, the plants, trees, animals, birds, fish, stones, wind, fire, water, and even the ground on which you stand. All have voices that can be heard. We vibrate energy, and we can communicate visual thoughts to your mind, so that you may understand us. Here on Merope, our life force appears brighter and clearer than on Earth. Learn to be silent and focus your attention. Become what it is you see by stepping inside of it with your heart and mind. You will hear them speak from the little light inside of them."

"Wow, this is a magical place!"

"No, little one. It is a place for you to train, and learn the techniques that you'll need to use when you go back to your Earth Star," the waterfall replied.

"You can do all of this there as well. We will teach you to hear, feel, see and understand."

The waterfall opened up and she saw herself inside the crystal blue ocean. She felt the roar of the waves and the coolness of the water inside her body and on her skin, as if she *was* the ocean. The large white foam crowning the waves was flowing around and inside of her. It felt like the bubble bath her mother would wash and scrub her clean in.

"This is not a bubble bath," said the ocean. "The element of water can soothe and clean all things within and without. It can refresh and renew the being. It can wash away great sadness and cleanse and balance the body."

"Clean within and without what?" she asked.

"Clean and clear within your heart, mind, and body. Just close your eyes and hear the sound of the waves singing, and the vibration of the waves flowing in and out, rocking you. Let the sound relax and calm you, feel your body tingle. When you are full of the energy of water, you are able to heal many things."

"Oooh, this feels nice," she sighed.

This was the first teaching about the element of water. She would learn and experience more on future visits. At last she opened her eyes. The ocean and the waterfall had disappeared. Cyrus was calling to her, for it was time to return.

Her little face pouted and cried. "I don't want to go. I want to stay here. I am so happy here."

She tried her little human tantrum, but it did not work. He soon came to her side and they started the quick and shallow breathing. Soon the misted sphere surrounded and merged them through the tunnel. Cyrus placed Luna back into her bed.

"Cyrus?" Luna asked.

"Yes, dear one?"

"Why do the people on Earth want to kill snakes, and hurt ants and other things?"

"Luna, human beings are afraid of every thing that is different. They want power and control over the things they fear and don't understand. I know it's hard for you here, because you see and think differently. But that is precisely why you are on Earth, to help them understand the idea of Oneness. Even if you can only enlighten a few people, it could raise the consciousness," he replied.

Luna did not completely understand the meaning of the words *enlighten* or *consciousness,* but was confident she would understand one day.

"Cyrus, please don't go. Stay with me!" Luna cried.

"No, child. You must have time to live here and be one with your humanness. You need to adapt and bond with the other humans in your life," he replied.

Luna loved to see Cyrus, but hated feeling so lonely after he left. Luna remembered the shiny floor in the dome house. Mommy would sure love to have a shiny floor like that. She had seen Claire scrub the floor on her hands and knees many times. She decided to go into the kitchen and do just that. Mommy would sure be surprised.

Luna took out the sponge from under the sink and looked in the lower cupboard. There she found the bottle of clear liquid that she would use to scrub the floor.

"Yes. This is it. If I wash Mommy's floor, it will be just as shiny as the one on Merope," she said.

Luna started her project and worked until the Sun came up. She sat on a kitchen chair with a smile on her face, and waited for the praise that Mommy was sure to give her.

Claire woke up and proceeded to the kitchen. She took one step and went sliding across the floor and fell on her backside.

"What the he...?"

"Hi, Mommy. I cleaned the floor. Do you like it? It's real shiny." Luna was smiling, and waiting for her praise.

Claire looked around silently. She was almost in tears. The entire floor was covered with some kind of grease.

"Luna, what did you use to clean the floor?" she asked, holding her breath.

Luna reached behind her and pulled out the bottle of vegetable cooking oil.

"I poured it on the floor and washed it just like you do, Mommy."

Oh my God, Claire thought. *This will take forever to clean off the floor. Well at least it wasn't a harsh chemical. She could have gotten burned or sick.*

Claire tried not to appear angry, but the tears started to flow. She was tired and it would take her hours to clean this completely.

"What's the matter, Mommy? Why are you crying?" she asked.

"Luna, this was not the right thing to use. Please do not get up in the night and do any cleaning. Leave that to Mommy. Okay? If you get up and can't sleep, wake Mommy up. Okay?"

"Okay, Mommy. But I saw the floor last night when I went with Cyrus and met the Sky Beings on Merope. It was real shiny and I thought you'd like it. So I tried to make our floor just like it. I guess it didn't work." Luna hung her head from disapproval.

"Luna, you had another dream," she said, as she began to raise her voice.

Luna proceeded to tell more of her adventure. "Mommy, I went to the shiny domed house and I talked to a waterfall and I became the ocean."

"Honey, you had a dream while you were sleeping," she said, clenching her jaw.

"No. It was real. I was really there. I went into a bluish-green cloud. The cloud took us to the round house. It was all shiny and it glowed like Christmas lights. And I saw some people with no faces!"

She was talking so fast and with such excitement, that it almost sounded garbled.

"Luna, you *did* have a dream. There is no such place. Please don't talk crazy today. Mommy is tired and has a lot of housework to do, especially after all of this."

She seemed discouraged and overwhelmed as she looked at the greasy floor.

"But, Mommy..."

"No buts, little girl. Go to your room."

Luna ran and slammed her bedroom door and threw herself on her bed. She felt like a balloon that had just been popped. All the excitement was gone. *I wish she would believe me,* she thought. *I wish I could show her.* Luna punched her pillow over and over until she finally embedded her face into it and sobbed.

Cyrus had explained many times that adults did not understand these things, because they had long forgotten their memories of Oneness, as well as the stars, they had when they were children themselves. Some people became fearful with age and had forgotten all of their teachings as they were growing up. Others forgot because they became more concerned with money, possessions, and ego. They learned to manipulate each other's energy through drama.

Cyrus was putting his trust in Luna, hoping that this child would be the one to remember, and help many others on the Earth. Humans needed to remember and reconnect to the Spirit of Oneness within themselves.

Merope was all she could think about for the longest time. Claire and Tom thought it was a product of her vivid and imaginative dreams. But after a while, they became concerned and irritated. Little did they know that these *dreams* were not going to go away.

"I don't know whether to punish her or not," Claire said to Tom.

"She is four years old," Tom replied. "She has been talking about these crazy dreams ever since she had the operation."

"The strange places and this boy named Cyrus; I just don't know what to do."

"Well, honey, she is still little. All children have imaginary friends," he said. "I wouldn't worry too much about it. Once she goes to school, she'll have too many friends to remember Cyrus."

"Do you think she has brain damage or psychological problems from the convulsions and the fevers?" she asked.

"No, I don't think so. Stop worrying. You worry too much," Tom chuckled.

But deep inside, the hidden truth was that he was just as concerned as his wife. *How do you cope with a child that is as insistent as Luna?*

"Well, I hope you're right. But let's not encourage her to talk about him, okay?" she suggested.

"Okay," he replied.

The months passed and there were many other secret visits from Cyrus and trips to Merope. She remembered the many things she was shown. She would tell Mommy and Daddy about each visit the next morning, and they would quickly change the subject every time, leaving Luna feeling deflated, frustrated, and alone.

Spirit Light

After having been on the Earth Star for six years, it was time for Luna to experience her first day of school. She found the school day to be long and boring. She knew the answers before the teacher even asked the questions.

Her head busily processed information. Cyrus' teachings helped Luna to read the thoughts of other beings. He also told her not to misuse that ability and, for her own safety, not to invade someone else's mind. She was permitted only into another's mind when she was asked to help, and that wasn't likely to happen until she was quite a bit older. But sometimes people's thoughts were so loud to her, that she could not help but hear them. She often wished that people would stop thinking so much.

Silence was so much better, as she learned from Alcor. The Sky Beings of Merope spent most of their time relaxing in tranquil peace. The mind was open when quiet, able to connect with the plants and everything else in nature. Luna could see that nature gave energy back to humans by raising their vibration to help them evolve. Energy was exchanged from humans to nature and from nature to humans. This energy was composed of the spirit light of the Divine Oneness.

Luna learned through silent observation. The days after her nocturnal visits with Cyrus became the hardest time for her. She had been so quiet on the visits that she felt the need to chatter away the next day. Bottling up all of her thoughts and not sharing what she had experienced the night before was hard for her.

There were many times on the first day of school that she raised her hand before the teacher asked a question. When the teacher called upon her and asked, do you have a question, she would reply, "No, but I have the answer."

Then the teacher would reply, "But I haven't asked the question yet."

Of course, the children in class giggled and laughed at her. But Luna had heard the question clearly in her mind.

She had learned to hear the thoughts of others by really focusing her attention. Luna had learned this on Merope. She remembered it so clearly. On his last visit, Cyrus had said, "We will go to Merope again, and the Sky Beings will show you how to communicate without words."

That night, they went into the night Sky and beyond in their usual way. When they arrived on Merope, the circle of the humanoid metallic beings came forth. As in the past, Chara, Matar, and Alcor, the taller familiar beings, were there.

The first of the three Sky Beings, Matar, came toward her.

"Dearest, tonight we will teach you how to hear and see with your mind. Everything has a spirit or life force. It is a tiny star inside each creature and being. If you look deeply into the eyes or heart of the being, you can see the light."

Matar continued, "Here, look at what I'm holding."

"It looks like a frog. Mommy doesn't let me play with frogs," she giggled.

"Yes, it is. It is the same as the ones on Earth."

Oh how Luna loved frogs. She would pick them up and hold them and talk to them, especially when she felt there was no one who would listen to her. Her mother would find her and scold her for handling something that could give her germs, but Luna was not afraid of germs.

Matar gave her the frog to hold and spoke.

"Now look deep into its eyes and focus, until you can see right inside him. See beneath the physical matter that is made from the vibration of tiny atoms. Take your time. Look until you see the light and become one with it. Once you see it, listen with your heart and mind. It will express its thoughts and sensations."

She looked deeply into the frog's eyes. Its large bulging eyes were dark like marbles. Luna finally found herself inside the body of the frog.

There it was, between the heart and the belly: the light looked like a little star. When she recognized it, she opened her heart and mind to feel and listen. She lingered for what seemed like a long time, feeling what a wonderful creature this was.

"It is warm inside me," she offered out loud.

"Yes, you are feeling the energy of love and contentment, little one. Each being has pure unconditional love inside it. That is what the spirit life force of light contains. The frog means no harm to you or anyone. Yet most humans are either afraid of it or repulsed by it."

"But can it really feel love?"

"Every living thing has a spirit light and a reason for being. Everything is equal, no matter how big or small it is. Everything is just as important as you, for everything is a part of you," Matar continued. "The spirit is the same size, no matter how large the body may be. When the body dies, the spirit light lives on until it is reborn into another form or becomes one with the Light of Oneness at the Center again."

"I think I want to go back to the Center and not be reborn again," she spoke decisively.

Luna wanted to see another being's spirit, a different one. She asked if she could work with ants next. She liked to play with the ants and watch them build their underground homes.

Alcor was the next to come forward, and he brought an ant for her to hold. As she looked down at its head it slowly crawled up her arm and then back down into her hand. Although she could not see its eyes, she focused her attention closely on its head. Suddenly she was inside and she again saw the spirit light. It was the same size as the frog. Amazing! Then she lost her focus and attention, and was outside again watching the ant sitting in her hand.

Luna decided to ask once more, "What about a dog? I would like to see inside a dog."

She loved dogs and wanted one as at pet on Earth, but Claire said there was no room for one in the home. She guessed Mommy did not like animals.

"What about me? Look inside me," Cyrus said.

"You mean I can do it with you, too? But you are not really a solid form like the others," she questioned.

"Then I should be easier to see," he laughed. "Why don't you try? And this time, if you focus real well, you will understand my thoughts."

Luna looked into his eyes and she saw the light right away. But there was something different that she didn't quite understand. It was easier to see into him. Even though his spirit light was the same size as the frog's and the ant, there seemed to be more of a glow beaming from him. She did not have to go inside him to see it. His eyes shimmered so brightly that it startled her.

Luna had never seen him like this before. She had always seen the ghost-like form. Then she focused and tried to hear with her heart. She had seen his energy enveloping her, protecting her like a loving blanket. It made her well up with tears. The separation she occasionally felt was washed away. The sadness of her mommy and daddy not listening or believing her stories didn't matter at this moment. She heard him speak, though his lips never moved.

"Little one, your time on the Earth may seem hard because you won't always be understood. You will see things that are possible, but many will not believe or understand. But it is real. You will know and remember these things. And in time, you will help many people. Do not give up and do not come Home until we come for you. Choose to live on the Earth Star with your humanness. You must agree with your own free will. I will leave you one day when I have given you all that you need to know. You are love. I am love. You are me and I am you. There is no separation. Please, always remember this."

Luna could hear all of his thoughts. They were coming to her so quickly that she could barely keep up with them. *Help many people? Don't come Home? You will come for me? My free will?*

It was too much for her mind to follow. Little did she know that he would speak of this often. She would not be able to forget and, in time, would come to fully understand.

She understood that she had seen the spirit light star within Cyrus, the frog and the ant. And she heard Cyrus talk when his lips weren't moving. The energy of the spirit light was love.

After this visit, she began to see, hear, and know things clearly. Her awareness and sensitivity expanded and it was becoming difficult for her to disguise it.

The Center

First grade recess was disappointing. A few of the boys decided to call her *Luna Lunatic*. This went on for several days. Luna disliked the boys tormenting her. She finally told Cyrus one night and asked him for guidance.

"Cyrus, the boys in school make fun of me. They call me Luna Lunatic. I don't know why. I am nice to them. They laugh and make fun of me," Luna said sadly. "I feel bad inside."

"Luna," he said. "The boys will continue until you stop the drama. Identify the emotion within them. Then tell them what they are feeling. You see Luna, the boys suck your energy and power away. They manipulate your energy by making you angry, fearful or feel weak. They take your joy, a good energy, away and replace it with their own negative energy like sadness, anger and jealousy. They are trying to steal away your happiness and peace. They do this all unconsciously. It is a pattern they learn from their interactions with their parents. Do not allow the negative energy that they send out to affect you. They eventually will try to engage with someone else."

"But why do they want to take my energy?" she asked.

"It is because they feel no good energy of their own. They are fearful, sad and angry, but they are too young to realize it. They want to make themselves feel good, but it will be only temporary. The environment where they live with their parents must not be a happy place. That is where they learned this behavior. Do not be upset with them. You have a choice. Do not allow yourself to receive the negative energy. Stay calm and peaceful in your own good energy. Tell them what they are feeling and send them loving energy to lift their vibration.

Please don't let them take away your smile, for you have such a lovely one," he answered.

Luna went to school the next day and decided to experiment with Cyrus' teachings. She was having fun playing jump rope with the other girls during recess.

"Uh oh," Jean warned. "The boys are coming, Luna."

"Luna, Lunatic! Luna, Lunatic!" the boys taunted.

Luna jumped into the swinging jump rope, keeping her energy high and laughing.

The girls giggled with her. The boys continued to taunt. Luna stopped jumping and confronted them.

"I think that you are nice boys. I know that you are sad and angry and that's why you pick on others. Why do you feel this way?" she asked as she sent loving thoughts.

The boys just stared at her. They paused for a moment and then one of them spoke.

"My daddy works all the time. He promises to take me places, but he always works instead and breaks his promises."

Another boy spoke.

"My mommy and daddy don't live together anymore and my mommy says bad things about my daddy. She's always mad at him and me." The other two boys chimed in with similar stories.

"I am sure that makes you feel bad. But trying to hurt others by calling them names will not really make you feel better. It will just be for a moment. The pain will still stay inside your heart. Let's be friends, and you can tell me when you are feeling bad and I will listen. Then we can play together at recess and have fun," she suggested, hugging each of them.

"Okay. Okay. Okay. Okay," they all agreed. And with that, as children often do, they all became fast friends.

Cyrus was right, she thought. In the years to come, she would learn how to deal with and help these earth people.

After recess, while Luna was returning to class, she overheard Mr. Marks, her gym teacher, talking to another teacher named Mrs. Morand.

"Bea, during gym class, Luna Belliveau seemed to be talking to thin air. Her lips were moving and she was looking into the empty bleachers.

I have caught her several times. Does she have mental problems?" he laughed.

"She is a strange child. Her first grade teacher commented that Luna often raises her hand before a question is asked. Luna would say she had the answer even before the question was asked. Pretty odd I'd say," Mrs. Morand replied.

"I also heard that she was sick as an infant. Maybe she has brain damage? Or maybe, she is just a child who acts strange, because she's starved for attention," she added.

"Well, I wish she wasn't in my class. I have to reprimand her everyday to focus her attention on our exercise activities. It's very disruptive to the class," he complained.

"At least the grade teachers only have to deal with her for a year. But Bob, you must endure her until junior high," Mrs. Morand chuckled.

Luna could not believe her ears. Her eyes started to mist over. She wiped her eyes with the back of her hand and made her way back to the classroom. Her stomach felt queasy, and her eyes hurt from holding back tears the rest of the day.

So this was the talk of the teachers behind my back. I hate it here on the Earth Star. How am I supposed to fit in? Am I supposed to be like everyone else? But everyone I've met has forgotten. I hate being different. I'm not talking to thin air! There was a dead spirit there that needed help. Someone that Mr. Marks could not see. Why can't I just go Home?

The private school Luna attended enforced strict discipline. The teachers were not amused by her otherworldly ability to see, hear, and know things that were not apparently there.

Luna could see spirit beings that no longer inhabited their human bodies. On one of Cyrus' night-time visits he said, "Tonight we will go to the place where the spirits of all beings are waiting to be reborn. The Portal to the Center is where each spirit light returns to upon completing their earth life. It is a place consisting of all knowledge and wisdom. It is a place where you can ask any question and find the answer. It is the place where one's life is reviewed and decided if it will be reborn or return to the Center of the Light of Oneness."

"What question shall I ask," she pondered, as she remembered the Center of light from which she came, and the Portal to its entrance.

"No questions. Just watch, listen, and pay attention," he suggested.

He loved Luna, but sometimes she was a handful. She was a source of endless questions. And every time he answered them, she got into more trouble on the Earth. Whenever Luna passed this information on to her classmates, teachers, and parents, she was always greeted with disbelief, fear, and concern.

"Okay, let us go now child. Remember your breathing," he said.

The misty sphere came and spiraled around them quickly, but this time it was different. The beam around them was clearer, like a bubble. She could see well into the night Sky. They were approaching a dark spinning hole that seemed like it was going to suck them both in. Luna started to get frightened.

"Don't worry, Luna. It's okay. This is the way Home, remember? It is where you began and where you will come back to. Do you remember when your vehicle was failing in the hospital, and we left the Earth Star to come here? Well tonight, it's time for us to go there again. But you won't stay there. We're only going to visit the Portal for a teaching."

Luna wasn't sure if she wanted to just visit. It might make her sad again upon leaving.

"Merope has taught you many things. It is now time for a new teaching at the Portal. The Portal is the place where the spirit being stays before the final merge Home," Cyrus said.

They were there within seconds. It was full of white light. It was so bright that she could barely see.

"Yes, it's bright here and hard to see with your human eyes. Remember, if you look out of the corners of your eyes, you'll be able to see the light beings."

Sure enough, it took her a little time to adjust, but she could see them. Small specks of light that grew brighter as they spoke to her mind. They vibrated, even without mouths or lips. She could hear them all.

"Welcome. Welcome, dear one," they said.

"Remember, she is only here for a lesson on how to communicate," Cyrus cautioned. "Luna, do not reach out to touch them." Cyrus knew if a being from the Portal touches a human it will merge the spirits together, causing the end of that lifetime for the human.

Luna listened to the light beings reveal their own experiences on Earth. She heard how some of them had gained enough knowledge from their Earth mission, and that they were finally going to be allowed to merge to the Center forever. Others would be reborn until they reached the perfection of knowledge needed from the human experience. All of them told her how difficult it was to keep going back to Earth to perfect their missions. They were much happier here at the Portal. The Portal allowed each being to review their life and decide if more experience was needed. If so, they were reborn. If not, they merged with the Center of Oneness.

One point was always emphasized: No one on Earth should try to call a spirit who was at the Center or Portal back to Earth. Everyone was insistent on this when they spoke about this.

They explained, "You see child, once we have completed and are here, we must be allowed to merge back with the Oneness, or review our past life and choose what lessons and experiences we have yet to learn."

"Sometimes, we may choose to wait to merge, until we guide our loved ones on the Earth Star Home to us, once they have completed their life missions. We may choose to go to them in times of their earthly woes, or if we have unfinished business we need to take care of. The Portal is a place that allows us to relive every memory of our humanness. If we have not completed our mission, we will return and be reborn. Many spirit lights stay in the Portal and move back and forth to the Earth until they choose to merge back into the Center."

"Every being has to completely master similar strengths and abilities during their lifetime, but each person is given a special reason to be there. We are all eternal beings. The spirit light never dies it merely releases the physical form. When we move into the human body, the eternal light emanating from the Light of Oneness gives it the energy necessary for movement. Physical matter is the vehicle for each being's journey. Each journey or lifetime allows the being to evolve, experience and finally become whole upon returning to the Center forever. That is each being's ultimate mission."

"That is the reason I have to stay on the Earth Star?" she asked.

"Enough questions, Luna," said Cyrus.

"No, let us tell her again, before she is too old to remember. You know, the older they get, the more their mind becomes clogged with trivial thoughts."

"Your mission is a large one, dearest. This will be your last time on Earth if you can complete your mission. You have almost completely evolved. You will remember the Center's teaching and the stars, and use your gifts to help the beings on the Earth. You will see more than you want to see, hear more than you wish to hear, and know more than most beings will believe. But first you must learn what it is to be human and balance your spirit light within it. You have embraced the light, but not the human form. When you are finally able to do this, you will be able to help the others remember their origins, as well. The Sky Beings will teach you. You will use our teachings to help people remember their connection to Oneness and then pass these teachings on to those who will listen. Only after achieving this will you complete your earth life and your mission. You must tell the story of the Center and the Sky Beings you have met. Remind them all of their wholeness, and help them realize that their spirit within is their connection to everything and that every being is made from the same spirit energy and life force. Then maybe they will stop destroying all life, the Earth, and each other."

The information overwhelmed her. But her heart knew its truth. In time, her mind would fully embrace this knowledge and understand.

The light beings explained that when they come as guides to help, they usually appear in the form of a small star light. Sometimes they can appear as a face. Other times, they appear as an entire body, almost looking human, but in a thin transparent form. They then transformed into each of these forms so that Luna would know what to look for.

"Our truest form is a twinkling light, like a star. The blue light beings are recognized as former incarnates of the Earth who travel back and forth to the Portal as helpers. The white or gold light beings are from the Center itself and have never incarnated as humans. Once the human completely evolves, the spirit light melds back into the Center forever."

Luna was amazed, already looking forward to returning Home for good. This place was magnificent. The vibration was calm. The brilliance of the light in the Portal made it hard to leave once again. To think she was in the place that was one step away from the Center. She was so close.

"Now Luna, you must not get too attached here. It will take a long time on the Earth Star to complete your mission. Then you'll be ready to come Home," Cyrus confirmed.

Yeah yeah, I know. The mission, she thought.

The teachings always ended with a reminder of her mission. And as usual, Luna awoke from her nightly journey filled with heightened energy.

School Daze

Daytime had become difficult for her since visiting the Portal. The spirit world door was now truly open to her. Dead spirits would appear to Luna to communicate for them. They had their own agenda and chose to appear whenever they pleased. It made it difficult to concentrate in class. Especially on one day, when Luna was in the third grade.

Luna knew that her teachers were more fearful than the children, and that they had more negative thoughts and conversations. Luna was sitting in the classroom and eating her lunch, as was her teacher Mrs. Morand. As Luna looked up, a light appeared out of the blackboard, behind her teacher, and produced an older woman's face, shrouded with a luminous veil.

Luna could hear the old woman's voice racing in her mind, speaking too quickly to understand. So she listened closely.

"Your teacher is my granddaughter, Bebe. I'm happy to see so many children around her since she could not have any of her own. This is good. Bebe has had a good life."

She understood the message, and Luna decided to tell her teacher the good news.

"Mrs. Morand, did your grandma call you Bebe?" she asked.

"What did you say?" Mrs. Morand questioned.

"Did your grandma call you Bebe?"

The teacher turned white as a ghost and asked, "Why are you asking this?"

"Well," she paused. "*She* told me. Your grandmother Estelle, she's sorry that you couldn't have children because your body could not make a baby. But she's glad that you became a teacher and that you're

"Mrs. Morand told the principal that you claimed to talk to her dead grandmother."

"But I did. She told me that Mrs. Morand could not have any children, and that she was glad Mrs. Morand was a teacher and could have many children around her and in her life, and that she had come back to her."

Luna's face turned to excitement as she now understood.

"That's it, Mommy!" Luna's mind understood now. "She came to be with her when she had a heart attack. She really didn't die, Mommy. She came to take her Home to the Portal of the Center."

"Stop this! You do not see or hear voices from people that are not here! They are dead! Put in the ground. No more bodies or voices. Please stop this game. This talk is crazy. Do you hear me?" Claire banged her fist on the able. Her face became red with fury.

"But it's not a game! It's real," Luna yelled back.

"There is no Cyrus and there is no Merope! It is imaginary. You are pretending. When people die, they die. They do not come back. We never see them again!" she yelled.

"You are wrong! Why don't you believe me, Mommy? I'm not a liar! Cyrus told me that grown-ups don't understand. Why can't you believe me? Please," she choked as she screamed.

"Not another word about it, Luna. Not another word," she huffed.

Luna ran to her bedroom and slammed the door. Tears flowed as she punched her pillow over and over.

"She thinks I am crazy," Luna sobbed exhaustedly. She threw herself on the bed and smothered her tears in the pillow.

Claire's heart was aching. Luna would be ostracized, first in school and then in the small town in which they lived. She didn't want that for her child. Only now did she begin to understand her own mother's fear and her need to keep the special room a secret. Anna was trying to keep Claire safe and protect her from the societal ridicule that Anna's room could cause. Claire was now dealing with something similar with Luna. But Luna wasn't as quiet and mild-mannered as Claire had been. Luna was engaging with a curious energy. She was both resilient and stubborn.

Claire remembered her own fear and worry that others might find out about her mother's secret room. It was difficult to maintain the secrecy as she grew up without fully understanding her mother's gifts and burdens. Claire did not want to cause trouble or make things worse. So she obeyed and kept quiet, for fear of losing her mother's love. She wanted her mother's attention. Anna would give many others the time they needed, but not Claire. This caused years of pain for Claire.

Claire loved Luna and wanted her to feel that love, but Luna frustrated Claire. Luna was not outgrowing this difficult imaginary friend. How could she help her? Did she really want her daughter to experience the same emotional pain of feeling unloved as she did with her mother? She did not want to fight with her daughter. Claire wanted to protect Luna and her sanity. In her heart, Claire knew that Luna truly believed that she experienced these episodes and was not acting out just to get attention. But she couldn't really believe her daughter. Her own fear was too great. Claire reached for the phone and dialed her mother's number. She was at her wits end. Maybe Anna could help make her *normal*.

"Hello… Hello?" Anna answered the phone.

Claire closed her misty eyes and muffled her tears into her forearm, and gently hung up the receiver. It was all too much. She could not ask her mother for anything. The pain from her childhood was too great.

Lyra

Although the day ended with sadness, Luna knew the Moon was going to be full and bright on this evening. She knew Cyrus was coming. Luna could not wait to close the door to her bedroom and await Cyrus' visit. As she looked out the window, the clouds in the Moon-lit Sky started to flash like a lightning storm. Except this time, the light came from inside the cloud. The cloud came closer and closer to the Earth, and when it arrived at her window, she backed away. The light hovered silently in the air outside her window. Then she heard his voice.

"Luna, come here. It's your friend, Cyrus. Don't be afraid."

She approached the window. "What is that light out there? Where did it come from?" she asked.

"It's from the world of Lyra. It is far away from here. We're going there tonight. You'll meet a different race of Sky Being. This is how they travel. Come, let's go."

The cloud thinned out and revealed a silver, oval, cylinder-shaped craft, lights lining the underside and inside. The door opened and they both floated on a beam of light until they reached the inside. It made no sound. It did not feel like it was moving, but it was. Through a large window, she could see the darkness of the Sky and the bright stars that twinkled and danced in the distance. It only took what seemed like minutes for them to arrive at their destination. The door rose and they both floated outside onto the light beam.

"This is the world of Lyra. We are on its main star Vega," Cyrus announced.

This was a dark and gloomy place. The Sky was gray and the ground was full of pinkish dry mounds. It looked deserted. No buildings. Not much vegetation, just some dry weeded plants. No water. It was very cold and hard to breathe in the thin air.

"Breathe gently here. Take short breaths. Your body will get used to the cold."

"I don't like it here. It's scary and cold and my head hurts," she cried.

Luna heard a deafening humming noise and felt movement under the ground below her feet. The ground was buzzing. Luna could barely keep from falling down. In the distance, something was rising from underneath the pink mound. A large hole erupted, ejecting the dirt into air, thumping to the ground in a pile. The ground shook and vibrated violently. A large creature emerged. It looked like an insect and was a few feet larger than an adult human. It had two antennae and a hard shell covered its body. Its large black bulging eyes took up most of its head.

Luna wanted to scream, but was afraid the creature would hear her. Suddenly, creature after creature emerged from the hole, in formation like an army.

"Don't be afraid, dear. They're not aggressive. They can survive here when others cannot," Cyrus explained.

One of the creatures came forward and started to produce a humming vibration. Luna could understand what it was saying. It wanted her to climb on its back as it walked on all six legs. It was going to take her somewhere.

Luna and Cyrus climbed on its back and began to journey down the hole in the mound and further underground. The ground below was filled with tunnels and cave-like openings. Some of the openings contained food stored from the sparse vegetation. It was warmer below the ground than above. The creatures survived by receiving energy from the minerals below the ground.

Luna observed many creatures at work, building tunnels and moving soil and large clear stones. The digging was precise. The stones were carved and arranged to form specific patterns and designs. The tunnels were mostly dark, but there was a slight light within them. She recognized that the light was actually the reflection of little pools of water that had dripped from the ceiling above. The long, clear icicles were embedded in the ceiling. They were crystals, like the ones on Merope.

The creature came to a stop and allowed Luna and Cyrus to climb off. It began to hum again, and many others creatures followed suit. The vibration began to shake the tunnel and one of the long clear crystals fell to the ground. The creature picked it up and loaded it on its back.

"What is it used for?' she asked.

With that question, the largest of these creatures came forward. *It must be the leader*, she thought.

It began a low humming vibration that intermittently sounded like a voice forming words.

"The crystals are formed from ancient water that has been hardened by the freezing temperatures of this star. You have many on your Earth Star under the ground as well. They are conductors of information and energy. The energy can be used to vibrate and move things. Crystals also store knowledge of the stars and the land on which they live. They can amplify and transmit magnetic energy, light and sound waves."

The creature demonstrated by allowing her to hold onto the large crystal, which was twice her size. Luna felt its fluid motion as she held onto it. She also felt a slight hum within her being, as if a light switch had been turned on inside her.

"Smaller pieces of these crystals can be placed around or on top of things to charge or discharge energy. They can bring energy to your body or they can remove energy and static when the vibration is too high."

They placed the crystal pieces on her in seven places and began to hum. The humming made the crystal pieces disappear and enter her body. They lodged in the top of her head, forehead, throat, heart, stomach, lower belly and tailbone.

"These implanted crystal points will allow you to charge and discharge energy from beings, helping them when their energy is not equally balanced. The Earth Star has many beings that will need your help."

Next, they had her place her hands on some larger stones within the tunnel. "The stones will teach you. Touch them and listen."

As the creature spoke, the large stone began to fill her head with the stories of Vega and its beginnings. She could have sat there forever, listening. It taught her many things to remember for future use. When she held them, she could see both the future and past.

"The place in which you live also has these great ancient rocks. Learn to listen to them for information. They will guide you. They can tell you of many things to come if you use them above the ground. They each have a different vibration for charging and discharging. They will teach you about polarity. They respond to negative and positive waves of energy. Both are needed to have balance in the universe. Molecules and ions have positive and negative vibrations, and are the make-up of all things with form as well as in the space around us."

They allowed her to feel the different types of crystal formations and the difference between a charge vibration and a discharge vibration. The discharge vibration seemed to have more of a thrusting impact more hum or movement. The charge vibration was slow, melodic and very soothing. It increased gradually to the right level of attunement. Luna was fascinated. In the process of taking this all in, she forgot how scary looking this creature was just a short while ago. Now like a friend, she realized it would never harm her. She looked deep to see the spirit light within its hard shell.

Luna would return again to use the crystals and perfect her internal hum. But for now, it was time for her to leave. Again they climbed onto the creature's back until she was out of the tunnels and above the ground. The flying craft brought them back to Earth once again. The Sun awakened Luna for another day of school.

I wonder what will happen today with the new teacher.

Luna had hoped it would be a quiet day. She had much to think about from the night before. Luna decided not to tell her mother about her journey. It was best to start the day without upsetting her. In the days ahead Luna began to withdraw, sharing less of her journeys for fear of disappointing Claire.

For the next year, she visited Lyra's star Vega with Cyrus to learn more about the vibration of the crystals and the humming sound the insect-like creatures made. They taught her how to use her own voice to recreate that sound. They also taught her how to charge and discharge vibrations through sound, and how to use the crystal rocks to move energy with her hands. The insect race had become her friends just as Cyrus, the light beings, and the metallic race had become.

Full of the vibration, she practiced humming quietly as she walked to school. Luna started to get dizzy and had to stop for a moment.

I guess I must not hum unless I'm moving the energy, she thought. *It has nowhere to go. The creature told me to use it with care. I must remember this.*

Luna remembered a group of the insects demonstrating a high pitched humming underground. They broke a large crystal formation into pieces. It was remarkably dangerous if used incorrectly, they had warned her.

As the years passed, she was nearly ten years of age and was sitting at her desk in class when the boy behind her began to think *very* loudly. She heard his thoughts over and over, to the point where it began to hurt her head. Charlie was going to kiss her in the schoolyard at lunchtime and tell her he loved her.

He was obsessing about this in his mind. Luna turned around to look him in the eye and gave him a glare that said *no boy is going to kiss me!* Being sensitive to other people's energy, she felt every emotion near her. The metallic Sky Being, Matar, taught her to how to protect herself by not letting anyone except family come within arms-length, placing a grid-laced sphere around her when she wanted protection. This protective grid, as she learned when she got older, could interfere with electronic, magnetic, and sonic waves. It caused clothing stores and car alarms to go off. Radio receivers would have static and electrical appliances would not work if the vibratory charge of the protective field was too high. She would have to learn how to master the grid energy and lower the vibration enough so as to not interfere with other mechanical devices.

As recess began, Charlie was so dreamy eyed, he hadn't noticed Luna's glare. Luna was not a violent girl and always got along with other children. But the thought of this boy touching her and giving her what the other girls called *cooties* was too much. He needed to stay away from her.

Luna tried to stay far away from him in the schoolyard at lunchtime by playing jump rope with the other girls. But as soon as she jumped out of the circle of the rope, he grabbed her shoulder, turned her around and planted a kiss right on her mouth. All the girls giggled and started to tease Luna. As Charlie tried to speak of his undying love for her, she pushed him so hard that he fell back onto the cement, scraped his hands and began to cry.

"Charlie, you had better never try that again. Stay out of my space. And that goes for the rest of you," she yelled as she pointed to the other boys.

Cyrus had taught Luna about *her space*. He had said that energy can build in the spaces within and around beings. It was important to keep both the spirit light (the space within) and the aura (the space around the body) clear. When beings attached themselves through this energy to other beings, they could cause confusion and imbalance if the energy was not properly aligned and accepted. Luna figured she would just not let any energy that she was not willing to accept to come too close. And Charlie was definitely not wanted. None of the boys were ever going to bother her or laugh at her again. She claimed her own space and scared every boy in the schoolyard that day.

Hearing other people's thoughts got her into trouble. Luna needed to learn if and when to act on them.

An informant ran into the school to report what had happened on the playground.

You can always count on there being a tattle-tale, Luna thought as she and Charlie were brought in to explain their stories.

The principal decided to send a note home with each of them.

No, please. Not the note. Not this again. Luna silently complained.

She didn't want any more reports going home about how strange or difficult she was. Luna wanted today to be a good day. She walked home, dreading her parents' reaction.

She decided to get it over with. Luna handed the note to her mother and waited for the yelling to begin. Claire yelled when she was nervous. The note from school was always a reminder of her daughter's bizarre behavior that she was powerless to stop.

"Luna, you know that hurting someone is wrong," her mother said.

"But he kissed me. Daddy said not to ever let any boy touch me," she shot back in disgust.

"Well, yes he did. But you should have told the teacher, not pushed him to the ground. You could have hurt him. I'm sure your father will figure out a punishment for you."

But Claire knew Tom. He was mush when it came to Luna. He did not want to be the bad guy. He wanted his daughter to love and adore him.

Why must I always be the hard one? Claire thought to herself.

Tom possessed a laid back personality. He didn't worry as much as Claire, who demanded that Tom dole out the punishment.

"Tom, she can't go around pushing and lashing out at people. No one will like her. She won't have any friends and other children will be afraid of her."

"Honey, she is a likable, sweet child. It's okay for her to protect herself. She didn't understand that it was an innocent mistake. She is a good girl and has never had tirades or outbursts of violence. I think you're over-reacting to a normal misunderstanding between two children."

Still, Claire insisted on some kind of reprimand. Luna's punishment was no television at night for a week, an apology to the boy, and of course, a lecture about hurting people. Luna apologized to Charlie the next day, but made a point to remind him that he had better not ever try it again. The punishment came and went with no real effect on her. Instead of television, Luna read her beloved books. Personal space was important to Luna and she wasn't going to let anyone in it.

Most classes didn't challenge Luna. But she enjoyed spelling class. Luna could see the words in her mind clearly before the teacher called upon her.

Mrs. Martin, the fifth grade teacher, would call three children up to the blackboard to write the word she gave each of them to spell. Each child would be given a different word from the dictionary.

"Joseph, Luna, and Maria, take you place at the blackboard," Mrs. Martin commanded.

"Maria, your word is *bright*."

"Joseph, your word is *brim*."

"And Luna," Mrs. Martin stopped speaking in shock. Luna had already written the word *brilliant* on the blackboard before Mrs. Martin had told her which word to spell.

"Luna, I haven't told you which word to spell."

"Oh yes you did. You said *brilliant*," replied Luna.

The children giggled. Mrs. Martin was confused. Yes, that was the word she was looking at in the dictionary, but she had not spoken the word out loud.

Mrs. Martin let the episode go the first time, without making a big deal of it. Little did she know that this would happen every time she called Luna to the blackboard. She wondered if Luna read and memorized the dictionary, but she quickly discounted that as being highly unlikely. Like other teachers in the past, Mrs. Martin sent a note home with Luna, asking Claire to come in and have a chat. Claire was irritated that she was summoned to school once again.

"Mrs. Belliveau, Luna is a smart child. She is perfect on her spelling assignments and homework. Does she memorize the dictionary?"

Claire was confused. Mrs. Martin was telling her something good for a change.

Claire replied, "Luna likes to read. But I don't believe she uses the dictionary. I don't believe we even have one at home. Should we get her one?"

Mrs. Martin decided not to press further. She had heard many comments from Luna's teachers about her weird behavior. Still, she saw Luna as a very intelligent child. But Mrs. Martin was still concerned. Luna spelled the word she assigned before speaking it out loud, even when she did not assign the words in alphabetical order. Laughter would follow and the children would get distracted. Mrs. Martin could also sense the awkward pain it caused Luna. Mrs. Martin decided to question Luna.

"Could you come and see me after school for a couple of minutes?" Mrs. Martin asked.

"Okay," Luna replied. "Am I in trouble?"

"No, dear. Just see me after school please."

Luna had that knot in her stomach again. She knew it meant trouble. As she approached Mrs. Martin after school, the knot became tighter.

"Luna, how do you know which word to write on the blackboard before I say it?" she asked.

"Um," she paused.

The truth was she would see the word in her mind, through telepathic transference. She was taught how to receive the thoughts by Alcor.

"Luna, do you memorize the dictionary? That's called having a photographic memory," Mrs. Martin explained.

Against her better judgment Luna replied, "Yes, I do."

Luna continued to feel sick all the way home, because she had lied. The guilt of not telling the truth felt terrible. But the truth gets you into trouble. She hated not being able to just tell people the truth. It was possible for everyone to tap into the connection if they just focused.

The gossip from other teachers had already alerted Mrs. Martin that Luna was different, and the idea of exploring that uniqueness made her uneasy. Mrs. Martin eventually decided to stop using the blackboard for spelling exercises. Luna's performance had become too much of a sideshow for the other children to take spelling seriously.

During recess, Luna would hear the thoughts of the other children. The flow of thoughts would not let up until she passed this information on to them. It was the only way she knew to clear her head and release it. As she got older, the thoughts became louder and clearer in her head.

Vinny was the chosen one on this given day. Against her better judgment, she decided to share her information.

"Vinny, I sure am going to miss you when you move away this summer and go to another school next year," she said.

"I'm not moving away," Vinny replied.

"Oh yes, you are. But it'll be okay. You'll like it there," she said confidently.

Vinny argued with her and then finally, scared and in tears, ran to tell his teacher. Once again, a note went home with her. It happened so often that it seemed like the note had become an extension of her hand.

Claire once again read the note, paused, and looked at her daughter with a stern face.

"Okay, listen to me. You have to stop this right now. You're scaring me and other people. You cannot make up stories like this. That little boy is upset because you told him he was going to move away," she said firmly.

"But he *is* going to move away," Luna replied.

"You don't know that. You don't know the future!" she yelled.

"But I saw that he was going to move away, and the pictures are always right," she said stubbornly.

"What pictures?" she asked, treading carefully.

"They are the pictures that I see in my head as I go inside the person's energy field," Luna explained.

"What on Earth?" Claire muttered with exasperation.

"Well, it wasn't on Earth, it was on Merope. The star in the Pleiades that Cyrus and I visited. It was the time when I had energy put into me," she said sheepishly.

"Stop! Just stop!" Claire screamed. "Cyrus is imaginary. He is not real. You have to stop this!"

Claire went on, "Look, if you don't stop this, they'll take you away from us and put you in a hospital with other crazy people that hear voices. Do you want to never see Mommy and Daddy again?" Claire was so frantic, she was now screaming at a deafening pitch.

"No. I don't want to go to the hospital," Luna replied in defeat. "I don't like the hospital and I never want to go back there."

"Then let's forget about all of this. I don't want you to pretend or talk about this Cyrus again. Look, if I give you ten dollars and we go shopping for a nice toy or something for you, will you promise never to talk about this again?"

Ten dollars! This must be real important to her, Luna thought.

Her allowance was only two dollars a week for helping with chores. Luna wanted to cry but she did not want to upset Claire anymore. It turned her stomach inside out to take the money and make the promise, but promise she did, and that seemed to make her mother happy for the moment. Luna told herself that the promise only said she would not talk about it. She did not promise to stop listening or believing.

Luna went to school the next day and apologized to Vinny. As usual, this episode triggered a lot of discussion among the teachers.

"Did you that hear Luna told Vinny that he was going to move away this summer?" Mrs. Martin asked.

"How does she come up with these things? Does she daydream?" Mr. Marks, the gym teacher, joked.

"I heard that she sees pictures in her head. At least that's what she told one of the children," Mrs. Parks added.

"The poor child must need to make up things to get attention. Well, we won't let her disturb our classes. All of you keep a close eye on her next year. She'll be in sixth grade, and then hopefully out of our hair after that," said the principal, Mr. Arnold.

The school year was finally ending and the teachers wondered what kind of summer Luna would have and what stories she would come back to school with and tell the other children.

The Secret

Summer was a happy time for Luna. She observed the ants, frogs, spiders, and snakes. She watched the clouds pass while sitting under the trees. She loved to be outside; nature was her teacher.

The Earth felt like a pillow as she laid her body down on it. The grass smelled wonderful and sweet. The dandelions grew all around her. Gazing up at the Sky, she followed the clouds as the wind shape-shifted them into many different pictures. Sometimes they looked like a castle or an animal. Today was different though. The clouds formed faces, similar to those of the Native Americans Indians from one of her history books, the faces of both men and women. Luna could not believe her eyes. They were ancient and beautiful. The faces looked both serious and sad. Four faces in particular formed over and over again. Luna remembered those faces throughout the summer, but hadn't yet realized that they would become a part of her life forever.

"Luna," Stevie, the boy that lived next door, called. He was a year older than Luna and went to a public school. Stevie and a few of the other children came running into the backyard toward her. Luna's eyes broke away from the clouds and she stood up to greet them.

"Hi, Stevie," she replied.

The neighborhood children had decided to play *Astronauts Walking on the Moon*, a game which involved going into space on rocket ships. The boys were busy making rocket ships from cardboard boxes they had found in their cellars.

"You don't have to have a rocket ship. You can just breathe real fast and put yourself in a sphere of energy. Then you can go into the Sky," Luna offered.

The boys all laughed.

"That's crazy, Luna. Who told you that?"

Now she was in trouble. She had promised her mother not to talk about this, but she had opened her mouth once again.

"Well," she proceeded slowly as she watched their faces. "There in the Sky, are beings that live among the stars. Just like you and I live here."

Luna had been talking as if she were from another place, filled with great imagination and wisdom.

"That is where *they* come from. We all come from one place called the Center... up there," as she pointed to the Sky. "Most of us can't remember it. We are all made up of the light energy that is called the spirit. It is a light that shines within each living being. Someday, I will go back Home to the Center. We all will," she said with a dreamy smile on her face.

Luna had all of the other children's attention. They loved listening to her stories that filled their heads with imagination. But this was the first time they heard her speak of the Sky. Most of them thought she might be recounting a dream. Luna's face looked mesmerized as she spoke of it, recounting the landscape of Merope and the light of the Center in her mind. In fact, she could tell that some of them were trying hard to remember for themselves. But the truth was, no one would openly agree with her for fear of being ridiculed.

Cyrus had told her that most children would forget all about the star teachings by the age of seven. Parents would program their own personal fears and concerns of acceptance into their children's minds. The child would then adopt the adult's way of thinking.

Luna continued to speak intently.

"One night, when I was four, my friend came and helped me float through my bedroom wall. He opened a beautiful small sphere with bluish-green lights and made it big enough to climb into. He took me to this star and then..."

"Luna!" Claire came and grabbed her arm and pulled her away from the group of children. "I told you not to talk about that anymore," she said angrily. "People will think you're crazy and strange. Why must you do this to yourself? Why must you draw attention to yourself? Why are you doing this to me?" she cried.

"I have to tell them, Mom. It is my mission. They need to remember. Everyone needs to remember. They need to stop hurting and destroying the Earth and its creatures. They need to stop hurting each other!" Luna screamed as she sobbed.

Luna was embarrassed by being grabbed away by her mother in front of the other children. She wanted to make herself small enough to crawl into an ant hole and live with them.

My mother actually thinks I am crazy. How can I complete my mission if my own mother doesn't believe me?

Claire dragged her into the house and continued to yell so frantically that Luna was sure everyone in the whole neighborhood could hear her. Claire was pulling Luna by one arm as she sat her down and tightened her grip.

"That's it, Luna. You have disobeyed me. I have told you not to talk about these dreams of yours."

"But they aren't dreams, Mom. They're real."

"You are old enough to know the difference and old enough to obey me when I say don't talk about these things. Maybe a good spanking will help you remember. You're not too old for that!" she yelled.

Claire bent Luna over a chair, and with the palm of her hand, whacked her butt several times until Luna cried out. At ten years old, the spanking hurt her more emotionally than physically. Luna was embarrassed and angered at the same time.

"I'm sorry, Mom," she said as she bit her lip. "Please stop. I won't do it again."

Claire stopped the spanking and wiped away the tears that were flowing down her own face as well.

I don't know what else to do with her. She can't keep making up stories like this, Claire thought.

Claire was worried and afraid that Luna still had not outgrown and forgotten these dreams. She had never spanked Luna before, and couldn't believe she had gone to this extreme. Claire felt awful and regretted her actions. The threat of spanking had always been a tactic to just scare and intimidate. Feeling ashamed and out of control, she sat there weeping.

"It's okay, Mom. I won't do it again. I'm sorry," Luna said as she hung her head.

The truth was that she would probably do it again. She needed to accomplish her mission and would have to talk about it someday. But how could she talk without upsetting Mom and the others?

"For your punishment, you are not allowed to go out to play with your friends for two days," she said firmly.

Not being able to go outside would have been the most severe punishment for Luna, because she loved the outdoors. However, when she thought about how embarrassed she felt with her mother dragging her into the house in front of the other children, she realized it might be okay not to see them for a couple of days.

Claire finally decided to get advice and went to talk with her mother. After all, Claire had obeyed Anna and kept her secret. Luna loved her grandma and there was a natural bond between them. Maybe Anna could talk some sense into Luna. Claire went to visit her when Tom came home from work.

"Mom," Claire began.

"Yes, Claire," Anna answered.

"Mom, I'm having trouble with Luna. She's still telling stories about her invisible friend Cyrus. I thought she would forget this nonsense once she went to school. I have begged her and forbidden her from talking about this crazy stuff. I even bribed her with ten dollars. But yesterday I spanked her. I put her over a chair and gave her a few whacks with my hand. My hand still hurts from doing it. I feel terrible about it, but I didn't know what else to do."

"Claire Ursa! How could you hit your child over a story? I never spanked you. You bribed her with ten dollars? Did she take it? Well, of course she must have taken it. It was ten dollars for heaven's sake. What that child must feel inside. Claire, I believe Luna is a gifted child. I admit I don't understand all of it, but I believe it." Anna's voice now softened. "My gift, and I haven't used it in some time, is that energy from outside of me somehow passes through me and into my hands. We have never discussed this before. I tried to keep it away from you. I am sorry. I thought it was best."

Claire winced. She knew her mother was disappointed in her if she called her by her first and middle name. Claire hated her middle name, *Ursa*. It was such a strange name. It brought back some embarrassment from her childhood. While discussing middle names with her friends, Claire was asked what her middle name was.

Claire would reply, "I don't have one."

She would have rather died than been laughed at.

"Let's not get into this, Mother. The only thing you kept me away from was you and that awful room! You never gave me an explanation about your gift. You only told me to stay out of your secret room and to keep quiet about it. If you didn't want a child around why did you have me?" she lashed.

"Claire, I am sorry. I most certainly wanted you. I was not trying to keep you away from me. I also didn't know how to handle it. I was afraid of people harming you or the family if you knew too much. What I did was real Claire, but not accepted. I helped many people in those years. I needed to help them. What good was my gift if I didn't use it? Why should people have to suffer if I could help alleviate their pain?" she asked.

"What about *my* pain, Mother? Maybe you were gifted. But you spent more time with strangers than with me! You loved helping others, but did you love me? You were always too tired for me. *I* needed you!" Claire shouted. For the first time in her life, Claire released and spoke the truth of her childhood fear and resentment of her mother's secret gift. Claire wept into her hands, covering her face.

Anna was shocked. She had thought that Claire was an independent child who didn't need her. Claire was her own person, strong and distant at times. Claire loved being with her father, or so she assumed. Anna had not intentionally pushed her child away. Yes, she was tired at times and needed to rest, but she would have always given Claire the time if she thought Claire needed it. Anna was saddened at Claire's anger. Now she understood the reason for her distance and anger from all those years.

"Claire, I am so sorry. I do love you. I have always adored you. I thought you didn't need me. It seemed that you had always wanted to be with your father. You were always so strong and independent. You grew up so fast. I realized now you turned away and inward. I'm sorry if you felt unloved. Parents make mistakes because they want to protect their children and don't always know the best way to do it. They do the best they can, just like you're doing with Luna. You love her and want to protect her."

"Claire, Luna has told me the story of her friend Cyrus before. You know you used to have a visitor when you were young, if I remember correctly?" she added.

Claire could barely remember her visitor, but she knew that it was scary and not fun. She didn't want to go anywhere with it and hid under the covers until it left. Although she was unable to see it, she could feel the pressure on her bed and the tug on her hand, trying to lead her. Unbeknownst to her, that fear blocked any chance of seeing it and unlocking her own memories. That is until her daughter started with her *own* stories.

Claire wondered if that's what made her so angry with Luna. That Luna *did* go with him? Why couldn't he just leave her alone? Was this payback because she didn't go with her guide when she was a child? Claire tormented herself with these questions and continued to agonize over her private fears. Were they punishing Claire and making Luna crazy? Did they cause the child's early sickness? How could she get them to leave Luna alone? If she believed all of this, then maybe Claire too was losing her mind. Nevertheless, Claire was determined to put an end to her daughter's crazy talk. She would make sure of it.

"Claire, how do you know if they are dreams or made-up stories? What if she has a gift like I have, only different?" Anna asked.

"Gift? More like a burden. Your gift was to keep a secret in a dark room with a lighted candle. What did your gift ever do for you besides making you tired and having to sleep for a long time after using it? She has an active mind, not a gift. Please discourage her from talking about it, Mother. Promise me. Maybe you can work on her in your room to make her normal?" Claire begged. "Otherwise she will be an outcast, a weirdo, ridiculed all of her life. I don't want her to carry the sadness of not having friends, like I did. Keeping your secret, Mother, cost me friends. I could not bring friends home after school because you were resting or making your herb tinctures. I did not want to explain why that room was closed off. Life was not easy for me, Mother," she sobbed.

"Claire," Anna grasped Claire's hand. "Don't you see, you are making the same mistake I made with you. Luna cannot share or talk with you. Luna has to keep secrets. You are not allowing her to be herself, but are instead trying to make her into what you expect her to be."

"I want her to be normal, Mother. I can't handle this," Claire cried.

"If you don't allow her to be herself, you will drive her away and she will be distant. It hurts a mother's heart more, believe me I know this. All these years, I have missed you. I had no idea how you felt. I am just finding out now why you resent me. Claire, she *is* normal. This is who she is. Please don't make the mistake that I made with you. I did not mean to push you away and make you feel unloved, yet I did unknowingly. Don't make her resent you. Luna needs you to believe in her and love her. I will not discourage her if she chooses to share. The poor child needs someone to talk to, someone who can understand her and help her. I cannot take her into that room to change who she is. Please forgive me, Claire."

Anna felt weak and dizzy and had to sit down. Small tears fell from the sides of her glasses.

"Mother, I do forgive you. I was too stubborn to talk to you about it for so long. I know you did your best. I wish it would have been different though," Claire spoke softly. "Mother, I love Luna with all of my heart but I am too scared to believe. Oh…" Claire sobbed openly as Anna wrapped her arms around her shoulders.

"Claire, you must love her unconditionally and that means total acceptance. That, my dear, I know all too well is very hard for anyone to do."

Anna was glad she had this conversation with her daughter. Perhaps it was the beginning of mending the relationship.

After a while, with a softening in her heart, Claire wiped her eyes, blew her nose and left. Her mother admitted she loved her after all. Anna was sincere. As Claire replayed the conversation with her mother in her mind, she began to understand. Her eyes filled with tears again.

She had wanted her mother's love and attention, just like any child. Claire wondered if she was indeed making a mistake with Luna. Was she pushing Luna away? Did Luna know that she was loved?

Claire wanted her relationship with Luna to be better than the one she had with her mother when she was young, but she didn't understand her daughter any better than she had understood her mother when she was a child.

Realizing this, she desperately wanted to help Luna. Claire wasn't going to give up hope, holding onto her belief that Luna's *dreams* needed to stop, that she needed to be normal. She loved Luna, but she wanted this nonsense to stop.

Ancestors

The two days of punishment went by quickly and Luna soon returned to the backyard underneath her favorite apple tree. The beloved tree was rooted partially in her backyard and partially in the neighbor's yard. Her neighbor, Mr. Grady, never minded her trespass. Luna would water it with her beach pail and talk to it. He actually got a chuckle out of seeing how much she loved the tree. And when the tree would release its little crab apples, Luna would gather them in a blanket, drag them to his front door and ask if he wanted them or if she could have one or two to eat. Sometimes Luna would eat more than one or two and end up with a severe bellyache, but would never reveal to her parents what caused the problem.

Sitting under the apple tree, she could see the clouds through its branches. Every year, after the tree's flowering season, its flora fell to the ground and would surround Luna, making her feel as if large snowflakes were falling all around her. During its growing season the tree gave her shade, its branches full of apples.

Luna enjoyed resting her back against the trunk of the tree. When she sat there silently, she could feel the tree pulse like a heartbeat. She watched the flowers and leaves on the branches dance with the wind. When she leaned against the tree, she could feel the rhythm of being rocked back and forth like when she was a baby. Luna loved trees, especially this one. Often the tree would talk to her. Not in a voice, but rather as a thought.

Luna would conjure up all kinds of questions in her head and the tree would answer. She would ask how long trees could survive. The tree would show her pictures in her mind of ancient times and how the trees would last as long as man and nature would permit. In the pictures she would see trees being cut down for houses and furniture, and many trees dying from floods, fire and high winds.

These pictures upset Luna and she hoped to find a way to help the trees survive. She lay beneath the tree once again, gazing at the Sky.

On this day there was one cloud in the Sky.

A voice rumbled down from the Sky, seemingly coming from the cloud. It said, "See your Ancestors."

Luna jumped up off the ground. She looked up at the Sky and the cloud stood still as the wind quieted down. Again she heard the booming voice.

"Clouds are a part of the Sky, just like the stars, Sun and Moon. They carry the life-giving waters that feed the Earth and her oceans, lakes, rivers, and ponds. Clouds convey messages and can express when the snow is coming and when the rain will fall. When necessary, lightning and thunder can accompany them, using their tremendous power to clean the air and purify the Earth."

Luna was mesmerized. The cloud appeared as if it would rain, then as it would before a storm was coming, and then as it would before a heavy snowfall. When the cloud finished transmogrifying, four more clouds blew in and formed four old, familiar Native American Indian faces. Faces she had seen in the Sky before.

"These are the faces of your ancestors," it said.

"But the faces look like Native American Indians?" she said with a little confusion in her mind.

"Yes, and so are you. These ancestors will guide you in this life. Remember their faces, for you will see them again and again and be guided by them throughout this life. They will not always appear as clouds."

Luna sat there all afternoon memorizing all she had seen that day. The cloud was teaching her how to read the Sky and the weather; the wind, rain, and snow. What about the faces she had seen and the fact that she had Indian ancestors? Luna didn't know if that was something she should talk about. Maybe she would mention it to Grandma.

The next day was Sunday. Luna looked forward to Sundays because that was the day of her weekly visit with Grandma and Grandpa. She loved

Grandma's hugs. No one could hug like Grandma. It was the way Grandma wrapped her arms around Luna, kissed her on the forehead and gently rubbed small circles on her back. It would make Luna tingle all over.

Claire brought Luna to Grandma Anna's front porch and then left to run some errands. Luna flew through the open door to run into Grandma's arms, but Grandma wasn't in the room waiting for her. She ran through the house until she came to the room that was always closed when Luna came to visit.

This time though, the door was ajar just enough for Luna to observe. Grandma was in the dark with the shades drawn. Four white pillar candles were flickering just enough to dimly light the room. Smoke filled the room from a burning shell. It smelled pungent yet sweet. Grandma was singing in a language Luna did not understand. Her hands were on the top of a young boy's head. Tears were running down her face as she sang and rubbed the top and side of his head with a winged fan. Grandma put down the bird's wing and used her hands, gliding them gently over the boy's head, shoulders, and heart.

Luna saw a white light flowing down through Grandma's arms and into her hands. It was the same as the metallic Sky Beings on Merope, when they had put energy into her head, heart, and hands. All of a sudden, Grandma stopped and the white light discontinued its flow. Grandma fanned the sweet smelling smoke over the boy with a bird wing again and then sparingly sprinkled some kind of water on his head from a brown glass container.

Luna backed away from the door and ran into the living room. Grandma came out of the room wiping her eyes with a tissue, and sent the boy off to his home down the street with a big hug. It had been years since she used her gift. It was also unusual for her to use her gift during the day.

"Grandma, what were you doing?" Luna asked.

"Oh Luna, you're here. Is it that time already? I was trying to help the neighbor's son. His hair has been falling out and the doctors can't figure out why. His mother asked if I could try to help."

Anna had not used her gift in a few years but had decided to help her friend in need. Anna was now ready to reveal her secret that had been hidden from her granddaughter.

"But why did she ask you? And what were you doing to him?" Luna prodded.

"I was offering up a healing for him, praying for his well-being. Luna, I send loving thoughts and pray for his highest good to help him heal."

"I know. It's like you send him energy to raise his vibration in his energy field. Grandma, I could see light going from your hands into his head."

"You could see light?" Grandma seemed surprised.

"Uh-huh. Grandma, can I tell you something? Promise you won't laugh at me?" she asked.

"I promise," she replied.

Luna proceeded to tell her about the star Merope, the metallic Sky Beings and the energy they had filled her with. After she finished her story she waited for her grandma's response.

"Well dear, that is very interesting."

"Do you believe me, Grandma?" Luna's eyes looked desperate and her voice cried out for acceptance.

"Well of course dear, I believe you."

Anna did know that Luna had never lied to her before. It seemed that Luna had understood Anna's experiences even more than she did herself. She wondered if this child would be burdened or blessed.

"Grandma, what were you burning in the shell?" she asked.

"It is a mixture of sage and cedar," she replied.

"What was the liquid you put on his head?" she pressed.

"It is sacred water from the rain of the thunder spirit used for a blessing and healing," she explained.

"Grandma, will you teach me how to do your healing?"

"No dear, it takes a lot of time and sacrifice. I have just come to realize that when you're of service to people, there are things that you have to give up and sometimes it affects the people you love the most. People will need your help at the most inconvenient times. You must take care to prepare yourself ahead of time and rest for a while afterwards. And you must live by the code of nature's law. You spend a lot of time alone to focus on prayer so that the energy may pass through you, allowing the ability to heal. I don't expect you to understand all of this."

"I understand spirit light energy. Cyrus told me about it, and Alcor, Chara and Matar passed the energy to me."

Anna held Luna's hands and looked down at them.

"Luna, I believe you have your own gifts, hidden in your hands, heart and mind. You will find your own way. Honor your gifts and use them with love and integrity."

Luna never forgot those words. The belief that her grandma had in her was so positive and affirming. This type of conversation was the first of many they would have over the next two years. Luna was happy to finally be able to share her stories and journeys with someone. Keeping all of this bottled up had been tough and frustrating.

Luna and Grandma had another conversation a week later. Luna spoke of her experience with the clouds.

"Grandma, I was talking to a cloud, and the cloud told me about my ancestors. It said that I was very close to the Earth and Sky and that I was that way because of my ancestors. It showed me the faces of my ancestors. They were very old and wrinkly. And guess what, Grandma? Their faces looked like Native American Indians!" she said excitedly.

Grandma Anna nearly fell off her chair. She paused and thought for a moment, deciding if she should reveal the secret of her past.

I suppose the timing is right, and I cannot lie to the child, Anna thought. *Maybe this is my prompt to release the story,* she pondered.

"Grandma, did you hear what I just said?" Luna asked.

Grandma Anna tried to remain calm so that she could find the right words to reveal her secret to Luna.

"Luna, Grandma is going to tell you a story. It's a true story that has been kept secret out of fear. I guess the time has now come for it to be told," she confessed.

"There was a young Indian woman who was the daughter of a Plains tribe holy man, a healer. Years ago, the government forced the Indians to live on reservations, land that was set apart from where they used to hunt the buffalo. It separated them from European settlers who had come to America. European farmers eventually arrived at the reservation, along with the military and the missionaries, to teach the Indians how to farm. They gave them equipment to use. But some of the land was not made for farming and many of the Indians starved and perished from sickness. The daughter of this holy Indian man fell in love with one of the European men and became his wife."

"She gave up her home on the reservation and moved to the province of Quebec in Canada to be with him, and lived a life away from the Indians. She missed her family, but she loved this man. The couple had a child, and although she lived away from the reservation, she could not live apart from her culture and her childhood teachings."

"Her culture lives on in our own family, Luna. She was my mother. You see, the Indians were thought to be savage animals. Most Europeans did not understand the Indians and feared them. Many Indians were killed and treated poorly. It wasn't safe for anyone to know you had Indian blood. So our family kept the lineage hidden for our safety. Luna, I am told there are reservations in the southern plains of Montana and in Canada, but I have never been there."

"Wow, Grandma. So we really have Native American Indian heritage?" Luna asked.

"Yes, it's in our ancestral bloodline. Luna, you have a rare gift of communication. You must learn when to share your insights and when to hold them back. It could be a great burden for you until you figure that out. You must only help when you are asked or given permission. You will learn this as you get older. I have some memory of my mother's teachings. I guess this means I need to tell your mother," Anna paused. "My mother had recipes from her people for doctoring with plants. She related to the animals and trees just like you. I bet one of the faces you have seen was hers."

"Grandma, do you have any pictures of her?" she asked.

"No, dear. Sad to say she didn't like her picture to be taken. She believed the picture would steal her spirit and that her spirit would be captured and trapped in the photograph."

"You mean like the spirit light I see inside of things?" Luna questioned.

"Yes, I suppose that might be what she was talking about," she replied.

Luna was jumping up and down with excitement.

"Let's go tell Mom now!"

Claire was sitting outside in the car, sneaking a smoke as she waited to pick up Luna from her visit. She tried not to smoke in front of Luna, but the stress got to her every once in awhile.

"Claire?" Anna called.

Claire quickly put out her cigarette and fanned away the smoke.

"Yes, Mother?"

"Claire, are you still sneaking those cigarettes?"

"Sometimes the stress gets to me. I don't smoke much and never around Luna," Claire admitted.

Luna came outside and caught the end of the conversation with a puzzled look on her face.

"Mom, you smoke?" Luna asked.

"Only sometimes Luna, but don't worry. Mom will stop."

"Claire, I have something to talk to you about. I have just discussed it with Luna. It's time for me to tell you something about our family. Come inside."

Anna began the story and Claire followed the entire story in disbelief.

"Mother, what are you telling me? My grandmother, whom I've never met, was a Native American Indian? And was a healer's daughter? Are you kidding me?"

"Claire, it's true. It was hard in those days. There was so much fear and prejudice, that I still carry that worry to this day."

"But why now? What made you tell us now?" Claire asked.

"Claire, whether you want to believe it or not, you and I both know that Luna is gifted. I think she takes after your grandmother. Your grandmother was intuitive and talked to the spirits, like her father. She had knowledge of doctoring and working with plants that most people didn't understand. She taught me only a small amount of what she knew before I married and moved to New England. The rest passed with her. I would like to teach Luna, while I am still able."

Claire was silent and Luna grinned, beaming from ear to ear. Her chest puffed out, proud as a peacock. Luna would now be able to learn the stories of her great grandmother Marie from Grandma Anna. The secret was out.

"Claire, do you remember all the corn recipes? That was from your grandmother's people," said Anna. "The herb patch that I made for the cyst over your eye when you were small was also your grandmother's recipe. The oil I would put in your ear when you had an earache was from a root recipe from my mother."

Claire was surprised. She remembered those memories fondly.

"And your middle name *Ursa* that you've always hated. When a child was born, they were given a name that represented an animal or something special that defined the characteristics of that child. A name was given to the child so that they could grow into it."

"We couldn't name you in the Indian language for fear of other people finding out, so we used the Latin equivalent from the Christian Bible, the religion that most people followed. My mother came from Canada to New England to visit only once, and that was to name you. *Ursa* is the Latin word for bear. When you were born, you were always ravenously hungry, like a bear after hibernation. Your grandmother gave you that name the year before she died. My father died right after I married. I believe my mother missed him so much that she willed herself to the other side. I'm sorry you never really got to know her. I met your father Joe, on a weekend camping trip to New England. He was camping with his family. We wrote to each other after that summer, and we eventually married two years later. I moved here with him and his relatives," Anna smiled. "The old custom was that the men would move to be with the woman's family, but my mother and I broke the tradition and went to be with our men," she laughed.

Claire was too young to remember her grandmother. She had never met either side of Anna's family who lived in Canada. Although a bear was not necessarily how she wanted to be personified, it was sweet of her grandmother to continue her traditions through the secret naming.

"And what is your Indian name, Mother?" Claire asked.

"My middle name is *Felis*, which represents a cat in Latin. While my mother was giving birth to me in her home, two cats came on the windowsill to watch her. They meowed and sang the entire time to welcome me into the world. So she thought the cat was the name that represented me the best: strong, feminine, and independent. My mother called me *Little Felis*. She did not have her mother around to name me, so she sent a letter to the reservation about the cats singing at my birth. My grandmother sent word that cat should be part of my name. *Cats Call to Her,* was my actual name but my mother decided to just use the Latin word *Felis* for cat to honor the tradition and yet keep it hidden."

"Well, what about Luna? Luna does not have a special middle name."

"Traditionally, it was a longer name. At puberty, my mother's name was changed to *Bridges the World.* My grandmother knew that the times were changing for the Indian people and her daughter would have to live in both worlds, that of the white Europeans and the Indian world on the reservation."

"My mother started using an Indian middle name to keep our heritage hidden amongst the Christian culture. With Luna, I named her using a first name, but still used the Latin word. Times are changing, dear. So Luna means *Moon* in Latin. She was born on a full Moon. The full Moon was a very powerful force that was honored by Native American Indians, especially within the women's circles," Anna explained. "It is a connection to the Sky and a reflection of the Sun to the Earth. It has strong feminine energy."

"So you really did name her Luna because of the Moon? I thought it was just an odd name you liked," said Claire.

"Mother, I'm just not ready to tell anyone yet. Luna, you let Mommy tell Daddy about this when Mommy is ready. So, let's not talk about this just yet. Okay?" Claire said.

After getting so excited over the news, Luna once again felt deflated, unable to share something that was important, something that made her happy. Luna nodded in agreement with Claire, feeling defeated once again.

Two weeks later, Claire approached the conversation with Tom.

"Honey, my mother laid a bombshell on me a couple of weeks ago and I am trying to wrap my mind around it," she said.

"What is it?" Tom asked.

"My mother's family has Native American Indian heritage. Her mother was a full-blood from the reservation on the western plains," Claire explained.

"Really, what made her reveal this to you now?" he asked.

"Luna had a dream of some sort, that told her she was Indian and then my mother decided it was time to let the secret out. Mother said it was kept a secret because the Indians were discriminated against and treated poorly," she answered.

"Claire, do you think this is the cause of Luna's eccentricity?" he surmised.

"Tom, being Indian does not make one strange or eccentric. But my mother has asked to spend more time with Luna to teach her the old ways, the stories and herbal remedies, the ones she still remembers," Claire added.

"I think that is a great idea. We can have her spend Sundays with her. It will give Luna something to do and maybe bring a smile to her face. At times she seems so sad and distance, maybe this will perk her up and give her something to look forward to," he agreed.

Luna began her sessions with Grandma Anna the following week. They spent the entirety of every Sunday together. Grandpa would either visit neighbors or work on wood projects in the cellar. He was a good carpenter who could make beautiful shelves and tables. It kept him occupied for the day so Luna could have Grandma all to herself.

Grandma told Luna stories about the old ways, how to grow and identify plants in her garden and what their herbal medicine properties were. She explained how she prayed to each plant to begin a relationship so the medicine would work and the plant would agree to give its life.

Grandma began their sessions the same way each time. She would light a small ball of sage in an open shell and fan the smoke over and around herself and Luna.

"Luna, this is called *smudging* or cleansing. We cleanse ourselves with the smoke to prepare our focus and intention in a sacred way to work with the Grandmother Earth and her plants. It will help you hear the plants voices better. They can tell you when they are ready for harvest," she winked at Luna.

"Then we offer a little tobacco with a prayer. We ask for the plants to grow strong with medicine out of the Earth, so that they may help us when we need them. We offer our gratitude for their healing and balancing powers," said Grandma. "Do you understand?"

Luna nodded. Luna observed and listened to all of Grandma's teachings intently, writing down the various names of the plants and what parts she should use.

"Mint leaves are used as a tea, Luna. It helps stimulate digestion and eases stomach aches. You may also place the leaves in a warm compress over the forehead for headaches."

Luna helped to weed the garden, which kept the plants strong. Then she would gather the plants' flowers and leaves in the morning during late spring and summer. The roots of plants were gathered in the evening in autumn.

"Gather the leaves of the dandelion, Luna. We will put them in a salad, and the root we will gather later to make a tea and tincture to flush the kidneys and organs. It is what we call a *diuretic* for the body."

Luna did not like dandelion salad leaves. They were too bitter for her liking. But she did enjoy the teas that Grandma made for her, especially the mint. Luna learned how to prepare the salves, tinctures, and oils, as well as the teas. She wrote down all of the details in her notebook.

Luna loved having her hands in the soil. It helped her to become grounded in her body and connect more to the Earth. Grandma hoped it would give her a sense of belonging here.

"Today, Luna, we are going to make licorice oil. We will boil the root, press it to remove the juice, and add the mixture to a small amount of pure olive oil," said Grandma. "Then it will be ready when we need it for an earache. Mullein flowers can also be used for earaches."

Each week Luna learned about new plants and their preparation. Red clover, coltsfoot, sumac berries, and lavender were just a few.

Grandma often sung to her plants in the mornings and evenings. She explained to Luna that it was her way of blessing them for growth and offering gratitude for their life's purpose.

"It is a way of connecting to them, Luna. My mother always told me to stay connected to nature, especially to the plants, for they will help you when you need them."

"I understand, Grandma. The metallic Sky Beings have shown me that all life is connected. It is a tiny light inside each and every living thing. We all are created from the same light. It is our life force or spirit energy. When the body dies, it goes back to the Center, the main source of light," she added.

"Yes, I believe that is what my mother was trying to explain. So the Sky Beings taught you this?" Grandma asked.

"Yes, I could see the light clearly. It is the same size in everything. It looks like a tiny star."

"Luna, Grandma feels those things, the energy or the life force. But unlike you, I cannot see it. I know it is there. It is special that you can see it clearly."

"I can see *and* feel it, Grandma. I even hear people when they are thinking. I don't try to, it just happens," she said.

"Luna, I believe that you have been given these gifts for a reason and someday you will understand how and when to use them. But please dear, don't worry about this. Okay?" she said as hugged Luna.

"Okay, Grandma."

Grandpa Joe had a vegetable garden. Luna help him plant, weed, and harvest the cucumbers, tomatoes, summer squash, zucchini, and green beans. She was happy working with the Earth, and enjoyed eating the harvest as well.

Besides working with the sage, Grandma taught Luna about the use of sweet grass and cedar in their culture. She explained how they were used for purification, in clearing energy, and in opening up the channels of communication between herself and her guides. Grandma brought out a braid of sweet grass, lit the end of it with a match, and fanned the smoke over and around Luna.

"The spirit guides love this sweet smelling smoke. It makes them happy and pleases them. We burn cedar to ask for help."

Grandma placed the small ball of sage in the shell, placed a sprig of cedar leaf on top of it, and relit the sage. The cedar crackled as it burned, and its smoke was fragrant. Grandma offered a prayer, asking that her teachings be planted in Luna's memory for use when she needed them. Luna's sessions with her Grandma became the highlight of her week on the Earth Star.

Draco

It was 2:00 a.m. when a large metallic sphere hovered outside Luna's bedroom window, emitting a light of glowing energy. The craft was encased inside a triangular-shaped frame. Luna awoke from the magnetic force pulling her out of her bed towards the windowsill. Cyrus appeared through the bedroom wall from the ethers, exposing Luna to a different type of flying craft.

"Tonight we will take this craft to the world of Draco, and its brightest star Etamin. It is the most distant star in your night Sky that you will visit," he said.

Luna was excited. *A new place,* she thought excitedly. She boarded the glowing sphere craft. The door had no visible seal or outline. Upon telepathic command from Cyrus, the door became illuminated for them to walk through to begin their journey. The large pod craft traveled quickly through time and space and landed on Etamin. The atmosphere was dark-skied and gloomy, but very warm. Many small fires in the landscaped craters lit up the ground. They looked liked fiery pits of lava, and resulted in an atmosphere much hotter than the other stars Luna had visited. The portions of the ground that were not on fire were made rock-hard from the large molten mounds of ash.

A creature in the distance was running toward them. It appeared to be a lizard, but it stood upright. It was huge and scary, and had long razor-sharp teeth. It reminded her of a dragon or dinosaur.

"These are the reptilian Sky Beings. They are forceful, and the beings from other stars fear them," Cyrus stated.

"Why?" Luna asked.

"They have an aggressive and intimidating energy. They have more of a predatory nature than the insect race on Lyra, the metallic humanoids on Merope, and the highly evolved beings of light from deep within the Center's Portal."

"They are possessive and can cord their energies," Cyrus continued. "They are known as *Maters*. They see with the pineal glands located in the back of their forehead. They are visionary creatures. They like to connect with other life forms by merging their energy source to a receptive being. They are great protectors and guides. However, they are very territorial. Those to whom they connect with can become captives of a sort. The reptilians have connected with humans on the Earth for many years and provide them with great protection, insight, and knowledge. Many of the humans have withdrawn from intimate bonding within the human race once they have merged with the reptilians. They will find no need to engage in a human relationship again; the illusion of complete fulfillment with the mater is too strong."

Luna did not fully understand. As the reptilian creature stepped closer to peer at them, Luna felt an energy of excitement emanating from it. While it looked intimidating, it had the intensity and nurturing nature of a roaring fire. Luna was attracted to the acceptance it emitted. Or was it protection? In any event, it was drawing her in.

The creature towered over them. It was taller than some two-story buildings on Earth. More creatures came forth to completely encircle Luna and Cyrus. They communicated with high-pitched screeches that hurt her eardrums. But as always, Luna concentrated to see the spirit light inside of them.

The creature named Rastaban wanted to take Luna and Cyrus to one of the large craters in the distance that was fully aflame. It was there that he would show her something. The creature floated quickly over the ground. His body was made for this star. Luna floated to the crater with his help.

The crater was ablaze with beautiful red and blue flames. She dared not stand too close to the edge for fear of being burned to a crisp. There, a large group of reptilians stood in silence. The fire seemed to hypnotize them. As she inched closer, she focused her attention on the flames in the crater. The flames appeared to open up, and she could see pictures inside the flames. The pictures were of people and animals. The last one appeared as her house on Earth. The fire was speaking to her through these pictures. The flames foretold of a new baby sister coming to her house, and that her mother and father would be very happy.

Although Luna wasn't sure that she herself would be happy, it seemed like it was going to be a good thing for the family. She also saw Grandma Anna leaving the Earth and the death of her physical body. Her heart would stop, her body would go back into the ground, and her spirit light would be free. In that moment, Luna felt sad knowing she would miss her grandma.

Luna wondered if the fire was foretelling the near or distant future. Luna was confused.

Rastaban approached her with a screech. As Luna listened to the vibration, she could understand the screeching in word form. His energy was masculine, dominant, and self-assured.

"This star foretells prophecies through fire. Stillness within the body and mind will give you access to the sacred fire within all living things, no matter where you are. The fire is within you, as you know. We long to help the humans and other star races. Our energy is very expansive. I would like to protect you and be your friend," he spoke.

Luna knew the truth of what Rastaban had communicated. Accepting him within her being and mind, Rastaban lifted her, and soon the two separate energy forms of light had merged together. He placed his forehead to her face. He wrapped his large webbed appendages around her in a loving embrace. He gently pressed them together. Light and heat started to emerge from his forehead. Her smaller body had melded with the reptilian. Luna enjoyed the completeness of this merge and felt secure in the protection he offered. It allowed Rastaban to be corded to Luna energetically, while the protection formed a force field around her. Rastaban would now know when that force field was being tampered with, or if Luna was allowing her heart to become too close to other beings. Rastaban promised to visit and help her whenever she needed comfort. Luna was not aware of how this connection would later complicate her life by lowering her desire for male relationships.

During the melding, Luna experienced a euphoric vibration within herself. It was expansive and made her shudder and shiver. A million stars were exploding inside and around her. It was a wonderful experience. This feeling would return whenever Rastaban came to visit her on Earth. He would supply her with the energy of security and comfort, a feeling that she would continually mistake for love.

Cyrus was wary of Luna melding with Rastaban, but it was Luna's free will to choose. Cyrus knew that soon he would have to leave Luna, and that Rastaban could help protect her while she was a teenager. Luna was unaware that Cyrus knew from prior experience that melding with the reptilians could become a problem. Once melded with a mater, a human found it difficult to have a happy, stable, intimate relationship with a human partner. It eliminated the human's desire for intimacy and procreation.

Cyrus would later take Luna back to Vega and have the insect race teach her the process of disconnecting from the mater energy.

Luna experienced prophecies from the fire and hoped she would remember all of them the next day.

"The reptilian race holds valuable information. They use the fire to retrieve information from other stars and beings in the universe, like a crystal ball. It is a sacred thing for them. Fire is aggressive, and it can harm and destroy. But it also has the power to promote insight," Cyrus explained. "Our time here is done. We must leave and return to the craft."

They floated quickly to the waiting craft. Luna bade farewell to Rastaban. They boarded and quickly returned to her dark bedroom. Luna sadly parted with Cyrus once again.

They visited Draco's star Etamin, once more during that year. For Luna, now eleven years old, it was becoming more difficult to be on the Earth Star and away from Rastaban and the Center. She was not as excited to see Cyrus and go on journeys with him, as she was when she was younger. For she knew, she would have to return to Earth. Being away was wonderful. Coming back was disheartening.

The more she learned and grew to know, inevitably the more secrets she had to keep. She shared most of her insights and experiences with her grandma, but withheld the Rastaban stories, feeling that the relationship with Rastaban was too private to share. Rastaban had told Luna that her grandma would not understand their melded relationship and in the process, Luna felt increasingly disconnected from other humans. The star world was her reality and she wanted that to be her only life.

The loneliness that Luna felt on Earth grew exponentially after her visit to Etamin. She knew that no one on Earth could understand her fully. Cyrus wasn't with her for every moment of her existence on Earth. Human emotions were getting more difficult for Luna to manage. The more secrets she had to keep, the more her feelings of anger and sadness would surface.

Luna put her arm over her eyes at night, pretending not to see Cyrus when he came. He would shake her, and beckon her to accompany him. Luna would become increasingly angry with Cyrus' insistence that she return to Earth at the end of their journeys. Existence was easier for Luna, much happier and more peaceful, away from the Earth Star. Earth was still not home to her.

When she was younger, Luna would look out her window, gaze at the night Sky, and cry to her mother.

"I want to go Home," she said.

"You are home. This is where you live." Claire would reply.

Saddened, Luna would then look up in the Sky and point her finger upwards, and say, "I want to go back Home...there."

Claire would shake her head dismissively at these episodes. *I cannot, for the life of me, understand this child. What is wrong with her?*

Eventually, Luna stopped displaying any emotional longing and bottled it up inside her.

In the month after their journey to Etamin, Cyrus' attempts to coax her to go with him were feeble. But this night he insisted.

"Luna, Luna, we must go back to Vega this evening," he said.

Luna covered her eyes and pretended to not see him.

"Luna, *please* come with me," he begged.

"Why? I will just have to return here, and then you'll leave again," Luna whined.

"Luna, the insect race will teach you how to disconnect your melded energies. It is very important."

"I've learned that already."

"No, this is different. Come, let's go."

Luna half-heartedly arose, stepped into the craft with him, and off they went.

When they arrived, the pink mounds and insects greeted them with their familiar humming sound. They again led her through their system of underground tunnels. But this time, they arrived at an open and pristine area at the end of one of the tunnels: a cave awash in shimmering light. Eight large crystals were embedded in the ground in a circular formation, their points facing upward, with one large crystal in the center. The crystals flickered like candles and lit the circle like a ring of fire.

The insect Sky Beings explained that this circular formation represented a grid of protection. "Here, let us enter the circle," their leader, Antic, guided. Luna followed.

They stood in the center of the circle. The other insects hummed a certain melodic chant that created a vibration. Soon she saw a very thin, crystallized grid of energy in the form of a dome constructed of pinpointed lights above the circle. The lights connected like a web and were attached to the crystals below.

"This protective shield of energy will keep you safe. Remember this formation and our humming chant," Antic said firmly.

Luna practiced the hum until it became a part of her very being.

Antic explained, "You will need to use this when you disconnect the melding energies from yourself."

"What kind of energies?" Luna asked.

"Powerful integrated energies, those that are melded or corded in nature," he replied.

"Those of the reptilians?" she questioned.

"Yes. The energy of the mater can be overwhelming, possessive, and interruptive. As protective as it can be, it can also hold you back from your humanness, forcing you somewhere else outside of the human form. This could prevent you from being completely grounded in your physical body, making human mating rituals difficult for you. One can get caught up obsessively trying to capture the same vibration of their energetic melding back on Earth, which is a futile exercise, as this vibration cannot be replicated on Earth. Humans need to be fully integrated in their physical bodies in order to fulfill their missions and experiences," he explained.

Luna wanted to maintain her connection to Rastaban, and still did not understand why it would ever be necessary to disconnect from him. It would be many years later until she would understand.

"Now we will show you how to disconnect," Antic directed.

The rhythm of Antic's chant changed. The high pitched hum he exuded dimmed the overhead grid formation, darkening the circle. Luna memorized the chant until it became part of her. The energy within the circle was vibrating frantically, calling forth a reptilian to the circle above. Luna watched as Antic demonstrated how to sever the cord between the reptilian and the insect that it had melded with. The reptilian was thrashing, trying to force its way through the protective grid. Luna became afraid.

"Do not fear. The reptilian's energy feeds on fear. Continue the humming, which calls him forth and hypnotizes him. Then, sever the cord," Antic demanded.

The reptilian gradually became less aggressive until it calmly floated as if in a trance. Antic then severed the cord in a sacred manner, and the reptilian's life force disconnected, sending him whirling back to Draco.

"Remember this circle formation, and how to sever the energy with the vibrational chant. You will use this ritual one day on your Earth Star," Antic asserted.

Luna nodded. She was exhausted, as if she had run a marathon or fought for her life. It was an intensive and depleting vibration to hold. Luna vowed to remember, hoping she would never have to use it.

This would be her last visit to Lyra's star Vega. They were soon brought above ground and returned to the Earth in the craft. Once again, with tears in her eyes, she parted from her beloved Cyrus.

The Prophecy

The new school year was beginning and the teachers were all huddled together and whispering amongst themselves.

"Luna is here. I wonder how she'll react to the news?" they gossiped.

Luna was entering the sixth grade, her final year in this school. She had the same classmates every year. That is, every year except this one. All were accounted for, except for Vinny.

"Where is Vinny?" one of the children asked.

Yes, where is Vinny? Luna thought. The look on her face conveyed a bit of smugness.

"Well, Vinny has moved to Puerto Rico to be with his mother's family. He will be going to a new school there," Mrs. Johnson, her new teacher, answered.

The teacher watched Luna carefully and waited for her to speak. She was well aware of Luna's predictions through the previous teacher's report. But Luna just smiled and didn't say a word about it. She felt she had gained some respect and credibility that day, at least from most of her classmates. The teachers were not so enthused, however.

"It was a lucky guess," Mr. Marks said.

"Just a mere coincidence," Mrs. Martin added.

Hopefully this will be the last time, thought Mr. Arnold, the school's principal.

The wooden school desks were old. The children had to bend over to slide their books into and out of the open desk shelf. Luna was bending down to retrieve a book from her desk, when Shaun bumped into her. Her temple slammed forward into the desk and knocked her unconscious, sending her to the floor. Luna was in blackness. She recognized Cyrus coming toward her. He brought a rainbow of colors in the formation of a tall column. From the bottom, the column had bands of red, orange, yellow, green, blue, purple, violet, and white.

"What is this?" she asked.

"This is the prism of light. Each color has its own energy and vibration. Put your hands inside the column and feel each of the colors."

"Cyrus, you're right. Each color does feel different."

"These colors can be used to create and move energy. They can clear different parts of the body, energize them, and make them stronger," he stated.

He proceeded to show Luna the colored bands within her body and where they were located. It was as if she was looking down and into her body, clearly seeing the banded energy deep inside her. The energy moved around in a circular motion. As soon as she became aware of her body, with her eyes still closed, she could hear the children's voices around her.

"I think she's dead," John said.

"No, I think she is sleeping," Mary added.

"Aw, she's just faking and pretending," Charlie argued.

"No... she's dead. I know. I saw my grandpa when he died. She looks just like him," John cried.

And with that, she opened her eyes and bolted upright into a seated position on the floor. Cyrus was gone, but the colors were still present in her mind. Her classmates circled around her. Mrs. Johnson pushed them aside.

"Luna, are you alright? What happened?" Mrs. Johnson asked.

"I don't know," she replied rubbing her head.

Luna couldn't remember how she fell to the floor until the informant's voice replied.

"Shaun bumped into her and she hit her head on the desk," John tattled.

"It was an accident!" Shaun cried. "I didn't do it on purpose. Luna was bending over and reaching into the desk and I tried to go around her but I bumped into her."

Mrs. Johnson took Luna by the hand.

"Luna, come with me to the school nurse. We'll have her check the bump on your temple and make sure that you're okay."

Mrs. Johnson was frightened as Luna's temple began to swell with a large red bump.

"Gee, Luna, we thought you were dead," John joked.

"There is no such thing as dead. Our spirit light lives on. Our body just returns to the Earth. Sometimes we will come back in a different body if we need to complete our learning," Luna explained.

"Are you cuckoo? You must have hit your head really hard," John laughed.

Now all the children were laughing.

"Argh!" Luna screamed. *Stupid people* she thought.

Mrs. Johnson was well aware of Luna's strange ideas through conversations with her former teachers. She was the gossip of the school. She hurried Luna out of the classroom to the nurse's office.

Luna felt dizzy and wanted to sleep. When she looked at her classmates, she could now see the banded colors inside and around every person. She wanted to go back with Cyrus because she hated being ridiculed. The nurse called Grandpa Joe to take her home for the rest of the day.

"Hit your head, huh?" Grandpa Joe asked.

"Yes," Luna replied.

"Does it hurt?"

"Yes, it hurts a little. You know, Grandpa, I saw a whole bunch of colors."

"Yeah, and I bet you even saw some stars, too," he chuckled.

Luna just froze and looked at him very seriously. *Does he know about the stars?* She quickly realized he was joking and didn't know that she had really been to the stars. She started to giggle and then let out a roar of laughter. She could hardly speak.

"You wouldn't believe the stars I've seen, Grandpa," she replied.

Grandpa Joe was a good man, and very quiet. He was tall, gray haired, and had a bald spot on the top of his head. He usually wore a soft brown fedora and had a cigar in his mouth. He had large black-rimmed, thick-lensed glasses, and a hearty loud laugh. He loved puttering in his vegetable garden. He also kept busy with the woodworking he did in the cellar. One Christmas, he made Luna a beautiful bookshelf. He liked making tables and shelves, and sold them at the local flea market and craft stores. He would go to bed when his wife was working in her secret room. It was an acceptable balance that he and Anna had both agreed upon, and the reason why their thirty-two years of marriage worked.

Grandpa Joe brought Luna to his house and Grandma Anna took care of her until Claire came home from work.

"The nurse said to watch for a concussion. Keep her awake for a while," Anna told Claire.

"Okay, thanks I will," Claire agreed.

Luna sat on the couch and watched television for the rest of the evening. Luna's favorite shows were science-fiction. She became frustrated with some of the unrealistic scenes and the ridiculous looking creatures that were called *aliens*. She knew they did not like to be called aliens. *Sky Beings* best described them. Nevertheless, Luna still enjoyed the show and the fictional family's adventures, fully knowing it was unlike her own experiences.

Claire was busy preparing dinner for the family. Tom would be coming home from work soon and she had some good news to tell him. Luna wondered what it could be, and looked within her mother's mind and spirit in an attempt to find out.

Oh my, Luna thought. *There are two lights in her. One light is in the usual place. The other one is just below her belly.*

As she concentrated more, she could see a little girl's face, just like the one that had appeared in the flames on Draco's star Etamin. They were going to have another baby, and it was going to be a little girl. Luna wasn't sure she was as excited as her mother, but if it made her mother happy, that was a good thing. *At least she won't be worrying about me,* she thought.

Tom arrived home, and they sat down to eat. Supper was delicious, as usual. Claire was a great cook. She prided herself on making most things from scratch. She had baked a chocolate cake for dessert and it was still warm when she served it, with whipped sweet cream on top. *Yum,* Luna thought, *having a new baby sister sure is good news for my tummy.*

"Tom, I have a surprise, honey. It looks like we'll be having a new addition to the family."

He smiled and took Claire into his arms and kissed her. It had been eleven years since they brought Luna home. Now there would be another child. How wonderful, Claire was finally pregnant again.

"What do you think about that, Luna?" her father questioned.

"I guess it's okay to have a baby sister."

"You know, Luna, it could be a little brother," her mother replied.

"Nope, it's a girl. I saw it."

"Now how did you see it?" she asked.

"I saw it inside you, below your belly. It's a girl."

"What, you saw it in my belly?" she asked. "I don't even have a bump showing yet."

"How do you know it's a girl?" her father quizzed.

Luna looked up from her cake, with whipped cream dripping from the corner of her mouth, only to see both parents glaring at her. She knew she was in trouble and had to come up with something quick.

"I guess...I'm just wishing for a sister," she replied quickly.

"Well, that's okay. But don't forget, it might be a boy," her mother hoped.

Whew. I almost got myself in trouble again. When will I learn to not blurt out everything I see in my mind, she scolded herself.

It was hard to not blurt things out as a matter of fact. Keeping secrets about what she could see and know made living here very hard. *When will I be able to just be myself?*

Sunday came and Luna went to visit her grandma. Claire and Tom stayed for a short while in the morning, and let Luna stay without them for the rest of the day.

"Grandma?" Luna asked.

"Yes."

"Did you know that when a mother carries a baby inside her, there is a little spirit light inside the baby, too?" she asked.

"Well, I guess that makes sense. If you say you have seen that everything has a spirit light inside, then I guess a baby should have one too. I wish I could see like you, dear. I have more of a knowing," Anna replied.

"Cyrus said that as soon as a human is sparked into life, it begins its journey. But he said most people never remember. You know Grandma, Mom is going to have a baby girl in six more months."

"No, Luna. It will be seven more months. A baby takes nine full months to grow."

"Well Grandma, then this one will be early. I have seen it," she confirmed.

"Have you been having your visions again? How often do you get them, dear?"

"Yes, Grandma. I always have them, even when I'm trying not to have them. It's like my head fills up with things I don't want to know," she replied.

"Luna, I know you've been given a gift, though it may seem to be a burden. Hopefully you'll figure out how to use it at the right time, and how to turn it off when you don't need it. I only turn my gift on when I open myself up to help others."

"How do you do that?" Luna asked.

"Well, I quiet myself and breathe in very slowly, relaxing my body and centering my mind. I say a prayer, and then I am open to receive. When I want to shut it down, I say a prayer of gratitude, release the energy, and see myself back in the room where I am," Anna explained.

"Cool, Grandma."

Maybe that will be my next chat with Cyrus, Luna thought to herself. She needed to learn how to turn *it* off.

This was her last year in this private school before moving on to the public junior high school. This year Luna felt older. Her body was changing and would soon become a big sister.

Eventually, her mother did have a baby girl. Just as Luna had seen, the baby had come early, six months later, only eight months after conception. The infant was weak and she had trouble breathing on her own. She struggled for her life.

She was born with a wild full head of hair that stuck straight up all over her head. Her constant crying sounded like a low roar. Her little fists made punching movements while her eyes were closed. She was a fighter.

Grandma Anna told Claire she should name her *Leana*, derived from the Latin word *Lea* for lioness. Her hair and her low pitched roaring cries made her look and sound like a lion. The lion would give her power and courage, and serve her well. Claire and Tom agreed it would be a good name for her. They weren't entirely accepting of the Native American Indian belief in animal medicine, but they approved and liked the name *Leana*. Claire was not as resistant as she had been before with Luna's name.

Luna was old enough to visit the baby in the hospital. The baby didn't gain weight the first week. She vomited her mother's breast milk after each nursing. Projectile vomiting, they called it. The baby was in a glass chamber they called an *incubator*. Leana was tiny and much smaller than most of the dolls Luna used to play with as a child.

Luna had to wear sterile gloves in order to touch her inside the incubator. Cyrus told her that she could help baby Leana. He asked her to look inside her to see what was wrong, and to use the color light energy to help.

So that is exactly what she decided to do. Luna touched her tiny head with one hand and her belly with the other, and looked inside of her. The rainbow colors were not right inside. The yellow band and green band were twisted together. Luna stirred up the energy from inside and outside of her, and projected it out of her hands and into the little one, allowing it to flow freely. The baby cooed and started to breathe easier. Luna began to see the bands inside slowly untwist. She removed her hands. The nurses thought it was cute to see Luna lovingly touching her baby sister. They had no clue about the energy transfer that had just taken place.

Luna repeated the same procedure for four days, until the bands were mended. Cyrus told her it would be time to stop when the bands were restored. By the end of the week, little Leana had stopped vomiting and was holding down food. She had gained ounces of weight and was breathing much better. Leana came home from the hospital two weeks after Luna helped mend her bands. Leana was so small that she fit into a shoe box.

All was well in the household. Luna was very attentive to her baby sister and helped her mother tend to her. Luna loved to rock and feed her.

Cyrus came to visit sporadically. He had told Luna that he would visit less as he had less to teach her. But the truth was that his time with her was almost complete.

Moon Time

The full Moon always brought Luna joy. Her memories of her Home in the stars were still vivid. Oh how she wished she could be on the Moon. The old woman's face that seemed to appear in the Moon smiled brightly. It was the time of year when the Moon was moving closer to the Earth, and Luna could see the face most clearly. As she gazed at the Moon and wandered in her thoughts, she heard a voice.

"Luna…Luna."

She looked around to see where the voice was coming from.

"Luna, it is I, the Moon, your Grandmother."

Luna could not believe her ears, although she had seen and heard many things.

"You're my grandmother?" Luna asked.

"Yes, the Earth's Grandmother. I keep the cycles of the seasons, the ocean's tide, and a woman's body in balance. I am the reflection of the great Sun in the celestial Sky. I hold the light and reflect it through the darkness in the night Sky to the Earth. I am the keeper of dreams and visions, the processor of emotions and mental awareness."

"Dearest, your body is slowly becoming that of a young woman and is therefore forming a great connection to me and to the cycles of birth and death. The blood within you will flow and release every month. It is a time for you to honor your body, mind, and spirit. Pay attention to your dreams, dear, for they are very powerful. Dreamtime is when you will reconnect to the source of light and regenerate. I will give you dreams for you to reflect upon and balance yourself, and release the emotional thought patterns you may have."

"But I'm not even twelve years old," Luna confessed.

"Yes, but you see how you now have hair in places where it once did not grow? You see how your chest and hips have become larger and more developed?"

"Yes," Luna said.

"Well, you are reaching an age when a woman's blood fills the parts of the body that can give life and when there is no life, then the blood flows out of you. It is called your Moon time, because it flows with the natural cycle of the Moon, just like the tides that flow in and out of the great oceans. It is nothing to be ashamed of. It is a powerful time for you and other women. It releases and cleanses the insides of your body where a new life can grow and where your body can renew itself with vital creativity. It's a time of dreams, creativity, and rest. It will help you become grounded in your body and connect to the Earth Star."

"Like when my mom grew a baby inside of her?" Luna asked.

"Yes," the Moon replied.

"Luna, you will have your Moon for many years, but your body will never grow a baby. Your mission here will not give you children of your own."

Luna did not really care. She was not thinking of having any babies yet. She was not even interested in boys. So what did it matter. But years later, when her cycle changed in her fifties, she would mourn the children she never had.

The Moon gave her a vision of a ritual to perform when she began her first cycle, a ritual to respectfully honor herself and connect to the Earth in a blessed way. Luna would remember and perform this ritual every month, for the years she would have her menses.

"What is it like on the Moon? Is it cold? Can I travel there like I do with Cyrus?"

As she looked out of her window, many tiny lights began to gather and flicker in the bushes. She looked up into the Sky and noticed that the stars were twinkling. It was so bright that it looked like it was snowing. It reminded her of her Christmas snow globes. The tiny flecks magically circled and surrounded her body and lifted her up.

Luna was mystified as she realized that she was rising and was now looking down upon the Earth and her bedroom window. She looked at her chest, which appeared to be glowing, Luna looked side to side for her arms, but there were no arms. There was only light coming from her non-existent body. In that moment she realized she had become the Moon, high above and far away. It was wonderful. The star voices spoke and welcomed her. Embracing the Moon's light and wisdom implanted in her the gift to interpret the dream world. Understanding and interpreting dreams would become part of her gift.

"Someday, you will tell the teachings that you have received from our light. You will remember the story of integrating the Earth and Sky with body and spirit."

Luna was delighted and at home, bathing in the beauty of the light and becoming one with it. The stars and their beings were her brothers and sisters. It was a connectedness that could only be understood in this overwhelming feeling of unconditional love, at one with all of creation in the universe. She again remembered why she had chosen this mission, to experience the being of spirit placed in the physical form of a human. The stars were grateful for all she would do in this lifetime to help the Earth's people understand.

From far away, she heard a faint voice calling to her. It sounded familiar, but she could barely hear it. Then it became louder and recognizable.

"Luna, Luna!" her mother shouted.

It was morning and Luna was back in her room, in bed. As she opened her bedroom door and peeked out, her mother spoke.

"Luna, I have been calling you for fifteen minutes. Why didn't you answer?"

You really don't want to know, Luna thought.

"You're going to be late for school."

"Sorry Mom, I'll hurry," Luna replied.

Luna decided to talk about her body's changes with her mother. She didn't realize that Claire was well aware of the changes in her physical body. Claire knew it was time for her daughter's first brassiere.

"Mom, did you notice that my body is changing?" she asked.

"Yes, dear, and I think it's time you and I had a talk, woman to young woman."

Luna's mother explained how children were conceived and born, and the changes a girl goes through to become a woman. Although Claire never called it Moon time, the idea was similar. Claire talked about the things Luna should use when the time appeared, and where they were kept in the house. She alerted Luna that it would be happening pretty soon. It did not sound as wonderful and magical as the woman in the Moon portrayed, but it was the same idea. Claire decided that they would go shopping for Luna's first brassiere on Saturday, right after they bought the groceries.

Saturday arrived and they went food shopping. Luna walked the cart up and down the aisles, gathering up what was on the list, while Claire waited her turn for service at the deli counter. As Luna turned the cart into the spice aisle, she saw an elderly blue-haired, hump-backed woman standing in the middle of the aisle looking dazed and confused. Luna walked over to her, reached up, pulled down a bottle of garlic salt and handed it to her.

"Here you go," Luna said.

The woman looked down at the bottle surprisingly, and spoke.

"How did you know I was looking for the garlic salt? Are you psychic or something?" she joked.

Luna smiled without speaking, and kept moving down the aisle. Luna had heard the woman thinking over and over about finding the garlic salt. The woman's thinking was so loud that it annoyed Luna. So, she figured she would just get it for her.

Luna was impatient with humans. It was one of her greatest flaws. Hearing their thoughts distracted her. These experiences would help her to become compassionate and helpful to many humans in later years.

When the grocery shopping was done, Claire took Luna to the women's clothing store to choose two new brassieres. The lady in the store was very helpful. In fact, Luna thought she was too helpful. She was measuring Luna and it embarrassed her. Finally, the saleslady brought her two to try on in the dressing room. Claire came into the dressing room with Luna to make sure they fit correctly.

"It feels tight," Luna complained. "I can't breathe."

"No, it's the right size. It fits well," her mother confirmed.

"But it hurts me. I feel like a stuffed turkey," Luna argued.

"Luna, women have to make some real sacrifices to look good," she replied.

How will my breasts grow if they are tightened down like this she thought? *Maybe that is the point: wear the brassiere so they won't move and grow. This doesn't make any sense. This isn't comfortable. Well... at least I'm allowed to pick two that have pretty butterflies on the front of them.*

Within two months, Luna experienced her first Moon time. Although she was a little excited, her mother told her to be discreet.

"We don't advertise when we're having our period cycle. We make no mention of it. We take care of ourselves. We drink plenty of fluids and we get lots of rest."

This was something Claire's mother taught her and that she always tried to honor. Luna thought this made sense.

Moon time was another subject she was unable to discuss; Luna was becoming quite good at keeping secrets. The woman in the Moon had told her to be quiet, to rest, and pay close attention to her dreams. Luna did just that by starting a dream journal.

Luna's grandmother Anna was also aware of the changes in Luna's body. She had told Claire to let her know when Luna had her first cycle. Claire informed her mother that Luna's cycle as a woman had begun. Anna waited for the first cycle to end, and then invited Luna over for something special. With Grandpa Joe visiting at a neighbor's house, Anna had Luna all to herself.

Anna's salt-and-pepper hair was always neatly coiffed. She had bi-focal glasses with pointed rims. She never wore pants. Only dresses, even when she worked in her herb garden. Grandma Anna had a small slender frame and a bright smile, and she usually smelled like freshly cut roses. She was the most beautiful, loving human that Luna had in her life.

"Luna, your mother told me you have just had your first Moon cycle," Grandma proudly stated.

"Yes, Grandma. You called it Moon cycle, Mom called it a *period.*"

"Yes, well a period of time is a cycle. You will find that many people will call it different things, but it's still something to celebrate. It is a time when a girl becomes a young woman," Grandma said.

"Grandma, I've already heard it called Moon time."

"Oh? From whom did you hear this?" Grandma quizzed.

"Well, I was looking up at the Moon two months ago, and a voice began telling me about it. It was the woman in the Moon. It was magical, Grandma. I rose up and became the Moon! The light was my body. I was shimmering. No hands or feet! It felt good to be in the night Sky among the stars."

"Well, that was quite an adventure," Grandma said.

"Grandma, it was *real*. I could feel the weightlessness of my body."

"Luna, our native ancestors honored their Moon time. They were quiet and reflective, and did not work or take care of anyone or anything except themselves during that time. It was their sacred power time. The women would get together to rest, in a camp away from the men and children. They knew it was a time when their bodies needed to release, reflect, and renew. The older women would care for the younger women who were on their Moon cycle. Women supported and celebrated the powerful cycle, for only a woman's body was able to grow a child. A woman is a special and creative life-giving being. There is no creation without the feminine. These are the teachings from my mother. So today, we will celebrate you becoming one of us," Grandma smiled. "Long ago, our relatives had special ceremonies when a girl became a woman. The girls would have to learn how to bead, make clothing and moccasins, and cook. A girl would spend time alone on a small hill until she had a vision of who she was and what role she played within the tribe. Upon having this vision, the young woman would remember the connections between her spirit within and to all external beings in the natural and celestial worlds. The young women of the tribe were often given new names as part of the ceremony, as well."

Grandma lit the cedar in the shell and fanned the smoke over Luna to bless her. She sprinkled sage into the mixture and lit the sweet-grass braid. The smoke was now sweet smelling.

"Luna, my dear, you have told me of your visions and some of your journeys. I think you are ready for a new name, one that is unique to you, one that only you and the spirits will know and is never to be shared with anyone else."

As Grandma placed one of her shawls around Luna, she spoke, "The spirits name you, *Shining Moon Star Helper.*"

"Thank you, Grandma," Luna replied as she hugged her.

Grandma brought out a lovely cake filled with strawberry jam. It was topped with whipped cream and fresh strawberries that spelled *Luna*. Grandma gifted Luna a special twelve-inch leather necklace. The necklace had a pouch dangling from it, with a crescent-shaped Moon made of turquoise stone stitched onto it.

"This is called a medicine bag. My mother made one like this for me when I had my first Moon time."

"Thank you, Grandma. It's very pretty. But what's in it? What do you put in it?"

"Only objects that will keep you in balance. I have given you the four sacred herbs of tobacco, cedar, sage, and sweet grass. They're in a small piece of red cloth, tied with a strand of buffalo fur. I made a prayer over them for your protection and health. These are the first things to place in your pouch, and they will provide you with protection and strength. I wore mine underneath my clothes until it no longer fit around my neck. Then I made a larger one when I found more things to place in the pouch. When my mother stitched the pouch together, she prayed for my health and well-being with a pinch of tobacco, and I have done the same for you. As you get older, only special things told and shown to you in a vision should be placed in the pouch: gifts from the Earth, like an herb, root, stone, or animal medicine. You'll know when the time is right, I am sure. I hope you will cherish and honor it the same way I did," Grandma said with emotion. "I'm happy to pass on a small piece of your culture to you."

"Thank you, Grandma. I will cherish it." Luna hugged her Grandma and gave her a gentle kiss on the cheek. "I love you, Grandma."

"I love you too, dear," she smiled.

"Did you give one to my Mom at her Moon time?" Luna asked.

"No, dear. Since our Native heritage was a secret, I never made one for her. Many of our traditions were lost over the years. But I will pass what little teachings I have on to you."

They devoured the small cake celebrating Luna's first steps into womanhood.

Little People

Cyrus' next visit came months later.

"Luna, there is one more place I need to take you. I must complete your teachings before you turn twelve."

"Why?" Luna asked.

"It has to do with cycles. You will go through an eleven-year cycle. You have experienced ten years of learning. Your eleventh year, or master year, is for mastering and applying what you have learned in the prior ten years. You will then start a new eleven-year cycle of learning at twelve. The master years like eleven, twenty-two, thirty-three, forty-four, and so on may be the toughest years, for you must apply the mastery of your newfound gifts and then be ready for the changes that will begin in your new cycle the following year," he replied.

"Cyrus, can I ask you something?"

"Yes, dear one."

"Grandma asked me to ask you how to shut it off."

"Shut what off, Luna?"

"Shut off hearing everyone's thoughts," she replied.

"Luna, your gifts will always be there for you, but when you want to stop hearing, just focus on something else to lower your hearing. If you hear thoughts you don't want to hear, you must focus your mind on another scene. Allow your mind to focus on your own breath and the stillness inside you."

From that time forward, when people's thoughts became so overwhelming that she didn't want to know or hear them, Luna would focus on her breath and the stillness within her, and this would give her peace of mind.

"Come, it's time," he said.

Once again, a craft with a beam of light came to her window. This one was shaped like a saucer. They stepped into the beam and were immediately inside the beautiful disc-shaped craft. This, however, was the first time there were other beings inside the craft. There were some very small greenish-gray Sky Beings with large balloon-shaped heads. They had long, thin, frail monkey-like arms that almost hung to the ground. They were small, like children, and had large black eyes that appeared slightly slanted. Their mirror-like eyes reflected Luna's image back to her. The beings were able to change the shape of each of their four fingers into an instrument or tool. They laid Luna on a metallic table of energy.

Small static shocks came from their fingers when they touched Luna. They touched her forehead and stomach. It was uncomfortable at first, and made her heart beat faster. The energy was different from the beings from Merope, intense curiosity. These beings were interested in analytical facts and data. Foreign symbols and geometric shapes were engraved on every surface in the craft. The brilliance of a rainbow of lights shone on the ceiling. The beings surrounded her, tapped her all over, and communicated telepathically with her. They asked many questions.

"What is it like to be human? Are humans intelligent beings? What have you learned?" they asked.

They flooded her mind with questions. They said they had encountered many humans in their previous visits, but found most of them to be very fearful. Luna was puzzled by these beings. They were different, very busy, and active. Their rapid movements and thoughts exhausted her. She wasn't sure if she liked being with them and could understand why other humans might be afraid of them.

"We call these beings the *little people*," Cyrus spoke. "They have been coming to your Earth Star since ancient times. The human race has advanced through the knowledge and technology brought by these beings. Their crafts enter the great waters deep within the caves of the oceans. They hide in the Earth Star below the sea. Some humans have been escorted to the crafts during dream-like states, and are given medicinal and technical knowledge. The little people are trying to help the humans advance in medicine, mathematics, science and technology. But every time they pass on this knowledge, the humans use it to gain power, and harm the Earth and its beings. It is very disheartening to them. They have come to visit with you tonight. You must remember this night clearly."

The craft landed with little impact on their star. They were all beamed outside, where it was dark and cold. A type of vegetation in the shape of large oval seeds grew in pools of water, which they called pods.

"This is the world of Centaurus. We are on the star Alpha Centauri. I am Ekar. We are born here, but mostly travel on crafts. Our crafts are our home for most of our life. The energy to recharge our crafts comes from within the ground waters of this star. The pools are composed of molecularly charged altered water. Some pools are for fuel and some are for birthing. Particles within the water have an ionic charge, and when altered with the temperature of the atmosphere, it becomes our fuel. The cold fusion of the frozen fluid then flies the craft. It is free, sustainable energy. The pods with ionic charged water are seeded, heated by propelled movement, and then new beings are birthed within the pod."

Ekar continued, "Watch as they enter the pod in a circular formation and surround the seed. The force of the circular electrical charges heats and alters the water, allowing the large seed to gestate and grow. Eventually the seed will open and a new little one will be born."

Luna was taken back inside the craft by the little people. Ekar came forward and asked her to lie again on a table surrounded by the magnificent lights. He placed one finger on her temple. Initially she felt a slight static charge, and then she felt relaxed.

The being transferred its ideas and thoughts. Ekar was tired of humans killing the Earth Star. The beings were trying to help, but the humans had become greedy and cruel. They had taught the humans how to build pyramids, underground caves, and tunnels on the Earth Star. They had even taught humans how to survive underground when cataclysmic events destroyed the land of the Earth Star. Luna could feel the emotion that Ekar was transferring. He explained how they had already helped the humans on Earth survive and rebuild four separate times. They hoped that eventually humankind would get it right.

The vast majority of them really wanted to help. However, there was a militant minority of them that had become disenfranchised with the humans and had decided not to help them anymore. Instead, they wanted to breed with the humans and repopulate the Earth Star with beings of a superior intelligence.

"We will not destroy the Earth Star or hurt its races. Humans have already started that process. If they repeat their own annihilation, we will come to help the few evolved humans who are willing to start over," Ekar replied.

Luna was shown what the destruction would look like. She hoped it was something she would never have to live through. But those images would remain with her throughout her lifetime on Earth. The fires were terrible; screaming humans and animals engulfed in flames, buildings collapsing, and ocean waves washing away what was left with tremendous force. Luna shuddered at the horrific sights.

The little people returned Luna and Cyrus back to Earth in their craft. They came to visit and brought her inside the craft one more time before her twelfth year. They imparted more information to her on their race and intelligence.

Futuristic visions that the little people had implanted in her mind were not very pleasant. Trees and plants would die. Rivers and lakes would dry up. The Sun would scorch the Earth, creating great winds and fire. Humans would fight and kill each other for bits of food. Clean water would be scarce. As the Earth dried up, quakes would rattle and shift the land. Oceans would be displaced and flood the Earth with tidal waves. The images were very frightening.

It was too much for a young girl to see. Luna wondered how she could help humans avoid the fate she had seen.

Star Seed

Her final childhood visit from Cyrus came the night before her twelfth birthday.

Luna had been sad during the majority of her time on the Earth Star and Cyrus knew it was hard for her to live here. Her sparse moments of happiness occurred only when she was outdoors, communing with the plants, rocks, trees, insects, and animals.

Luna still wanted to go Home because life was so hard. All that she could see, feel, and hear overwhelmed her young mind, body, and spirit. Even though she had learned how to turn it off, it was still tiring.

"Luna, this will be our last visit. Look, Luna, see who is here. Your grandma Anna is here with me," said Cyrus.

Luna focused intently and saw her grandma in a silvery mist. She looked beautiful and at peace.

She spoke softly. "My dear Luna, I have left my body tonight and I'm going back to the Sky now. Don't be sad or afraid. We all go back to the Sky and stars when our body is no longer of use. Your grandpa and mother will be sad. Try to be strong for them and make them smile. They won't understand that my spirit will live on. Someday we will meet again. I am going to the Center of Oneness. You're a special child who has many gifts. Don't be afraid of what you see, hear, and know. Use these gifts to help others when you're older. I love you, dear."

Grandma smiled, and Luna watched her little spirit light fly up and away. Cyrus came close to her.

"Luna, we've been friends for a long time, and we'll always be connected, for you are me, and I am you. Our spirit is connected to the Center's source of light. Remember, there is no separation. You have met beings from our travels to Alpha Centauri, Etamin, Vega, and Merope. There are thirteen stars with intelligent life, including Earth. You have visited only four of them during your training. My mission with you is complete. I must say goodbye now, but we will meet again at the Center one day," Cyrus said.

"Oh Cyrus, please don't go. Please don't leave me here," she said with panic.

His ghostly face and body seemed to melt away and shift. The light became so bright that she had to look at him out of the corners of her eyes. He was beautiful and breathtaking. No body or form, just a five-pointed star that melded into a twinkling, elongated column of light. He had embodied the human ghost form for the sake of Luna's teaching. Now he was once again a being of eternal light and able to return to the Center's Portal.

Overwhelmed by his beauty, she wept, feeling his presence. The light engulfed her like a loving embrace. The warm glow had touched her heart and the very core of her spirit. This memory would remain with her throughout her lifetime on Earth.

Tears were streaming down her face as she embraced the purity of unconditional love, the sort of love that every human heart has the potential to reach and become. Absorbed in this light, Luna found no words that could ever truly describe it.

Cyrus telepathically spoke to her, "Luna, we have taught other children. A few remember us, but are afraid, and many do not remember us at all. You are our first Star Seed. We need you to grow, blossom, and plant the seed of the stars here on the Earth Star. We will continue to teach the young humans upon their entry. We have come to help humans to help themselves before they destroy all life on Earth, as you know it. By communicating with all life forms, the human race can once again remember their connection to the Center."

"Remember the faces of your native spirit ancestors. They will help you when you need it most. Now you will learn the road of the ancient humans who knew the way to live in harmony on Earth. Those of your own native ancestry will balance you to the Earth. One day, you will balance the Earth and Sky in your own being."

"Remember each Sky Being race: the insects, the reptilians, the little people, and the metallic humanoids. In a few years, you will reunite with the three Sky Beings from Merope and they will teach you more. I will come for you when your mission is completed. Goodbye, Star Child. You are loved," he said.

"Goodbye, Cyrus, I will miss you. I love you, too," she sobbed.

His light disappeared. Luna cried in the dark of her bedroom. Her only friend and her grandma were both gone. She felt abandoned, and more alone than she had ever felt before. *What do I have to look forward to? Who will I talk to about my secrets?*

She experienced a wave of despair and emptiness within.

How will I ever be happy?

"I am alone now. Rastaban rarely visits. Cyrus said Alcor, Matar, and Chara will visit. I wonder when they will come. I hope it won't be too long," she sighed.

She wiped her tears, jumped out of bed, and ran into the living room where Claire and Tom were watching television.

"Mom, Grandma just came to visit me. She had a heart attack and died. But it's okay. She's going to the Center and she said..."

"Whaaat?" her mother gasped. "Luna, you had a bad dream. Grandma is not dead."

"But she came to me and said not to be sad or afraid and that we'll see each other again."

"Look, it was a *dream*. That's all," Claire said as her body started to tremble.

The telephone rang. Luna watched as her mother's expression changed from shock to sadness all in one moment. Claire dropped the phone from her hand and started to scream. Tears flowed from her eyes as she sank to the kitchen floor. Luna knew it was *the call*. Grandma was dead, a heart attack. Claire was in denial. Her hands cupped over her eyes in grief to catch her tears. She hysterically grabbed Luna by the shoulders and looked into her eyes and made her swear never to tell anyone that she knew Grandma had died. Seeing her mother's hysterical grief, Luna reluctantly promised.

Tom held Claire all night as she cried and grieved for her mother. She did not want to dwell on the fact that Luna knew about the death.

Did she really visit the child? Was it possible? It made her shudder in fear. *What does my child possess to know these unknown things?*

In the morning, Claire's body felt like it had been run over by a truck. Her eyes were bloodshot and there were dark circles under her eyes from a lack of sleep. Her mother was now gone from this world. She would never see her again. There was so much more she wanted to talk to her about. Claire had just started to rebuild the relationship with her mother. She had begun to realize her mother did love her after all. There were many more cookouts and family events that would now happen without her. Sadness engulfed her. Her father Joe would be just as devastated.

As Claire sat at the table slowly sipping her morning coffee, Luna appeared from her bedroom and slowly approached her mother.

"Mom, I'm sorry," Luna said as she stood by her side.

"Sorry? What are you sorry for?" she asked.

"I am sorry Grandma's body died. I am sorry that she came to see me and not you. She said you and Grandpa Joe would be very sad. But Mom, we *will* see her again, one day."

Claire just stared at Luna, and saw the sincerity in her daughter's eyes. She wanted to scream at her over this nonsense. But she wanted, in fact needed, to believe in the truth of these words.

Her own child was frightening to her. Claire had feared for years that she was either a liar or mentally disturbed. Now, in this moment, she almost believed in her gifts. Luna comforted her and made her feel better. That gift might have been her most precious one.

"Luna, I don't know what to believe. But I want you to never speak about this to anyone. Okay?" she said softly. "Grandma's visit to you was something special and you must keep that to yourself. Okay?"

"Yes, sure Mom," Luna replied.

Luna withdrew even further, holding all of her past experiences inside her heart, mind, and soul. Luna decided from then on to never speak of Cyrus' teachings, the Sky Beings, dead spirits, hearing other's thoughts, or seeing the spirit inside of all living beings.

Luna wanted to be a good daughter; one that her mom and dad could be proud of and she desperately wanted her mother's love and acceptance. Luna tried to turn off hearing other's thoughts. When dead spirits appeared, she ignored them and told them to go away. They did go away most of the time. She tried to adapt to a *normal* life like other humans: school, study, homework, watch TV, eat and sleep. But turning off her gifts for the duration of the next few years, made for an unfulfilled life.

Mutant Teenager

Junior high school was quiet for the most part, but trying to be normal as a mutant teenager wasn't easy. Once Luna entered freshman year of high school, life became difficult. She had to adjust to a much less disciplined school.

There was more freedom to speak, share ideas and ask questions. It took her the entire year to adjust. Eventually, she came to enjoy the freedom of working on group projects with other students and expressing her creative ideas and thoughts in her writing class.

There were times when she heard the over-stimulated minds of the adolescent boys and their preoccupation with sex and thoughts of touching the girls' bodies. The crazy fantasies of the boys touching the large breasts of the well-endowed girls disgusted her. After awhile, she was able to tune them out.

Many of the boys were attracted to Luna, who was overly developed for her age. At fourteen, she was well endowed with a bust of a twenty-one year old woman.

The class she least enjoyed was Physical Education. Being co-ed, the girls and boys played sports together. The boys were aggressive and often bruised or injured the girls. Luna and the other girls would frequently try to act sick to get out of gym class, particularly if they were playing floor hockey.

Luna watched as the boys hit the hard, small ball across the floor and into the net. She didn't like the energy of competition and the anger that filled the boys' heads when they played. The teacher, Mr. Donnelly, said that competition was good for a person, but Luna sensed it was egotistical and rageful energy. As Luna watched the boys play, she had a vision of Doug getting hit in the mouth with the ball and having his teeth bloodied and broken. Mr. Donnelly blew the whistle and awoke her from the vision.

"Luna, you're in," he yelled.

"No thanks, I don't want to play. I don't feel well today," she replied.

"Luna, get in the game or else you will fail this class for the semester."

Luna picked up her hockey stick and entered the game. She stayed as far away from the ball and Doug as possible. She just ran up and down the floor. Then it happened. The ball came to her. The boys on her team started to yell and taunt her.

"Just hit it! Hit the ball, stupid!"

Stupid, I'll show you stupid, she thought.

Luna approached the ball and cradled it with the stick. She pushed it a few yards, then as the boys on the other team approached her to steal the ball, she smashed the ball toward the goal. Doug came flying forward and caught the ball in the mouth. It broke his two front teeth. Blood began to spill out of his mouth. The ball then bounced off him and into the net for a goal.

Luna didn't care about scoring a goal. Frozen with disbelief, she had seen this happen in advance. She knew she should not have played. Shaken, she went over to Doug to say she was sorry.

"Get away from me, you crazy bitch!" he screamed in pain.

Doug was taken to the hospital and released. The swelling in his mouth went down, but he did not have his teeth fixed until he was out of school. The sight tormented Luna for the rest of high school. Doug eventually forgave her. But they never became friends.

Luna and the other girls asked Mr. Donnelly if they could run on the track for the next few weeks of class. He agreed after the accident.

Luna would start out running and then finish walking. The other girls did the same. They all walked and chatted. The girls started to tell Luna their problems on these walks, and Luna always had insightful advice for them. Luna soon became a trusted friend and counselor. Luna was much wiser than the other students her age. She was a good listener and could keep secrets. Eventually the boys started to ask her for advice, especially about girls. While the others viewed her as insightful, Luna simply saw her advice as common sense. She didn't understand why they couldn't figure out these things themselves. But she was happy to help them and it allowed her to socialize.

Luna made many friends and felt her best when she could make other people feel better. Luna didn't feel smarter or wiser. She understood what she knew to be true. As the years passed, she realized it was a little more than just common sense. It must have come from experiences in previous lifetimes. The wisdom and understanding within her mind was well beyond her Earth years. Luna intrinsically knew what people's issues were, where they were imbalanced and what caused those imbalances.

Luna befriended many of the boys that she helped tutor in Science. Luna became known as the kindest and most trustworthy person in her class. Even the older senior students talked to Luna, and she became a trusted friend and ally to many of them. But Luna could not trust others with her own secrets and the stories from her childhood.

It had been three years since she had seen Cyrus, and she still missed him at times. Rastaban, the mater, came each year to reconnect and fill her energy. Luna still gazed through the window at the stars every night before going to bed. And every night, her eyes filled with tears, waiting for the day she could go Home forever.

Luna adjusted to high school by her sophomore year. Schoolwork was easy and she had little interest in boys and dating.

Burt Johnson, a senior, had taken an interest in Luna. He found her attractive, intelligent, honest and mature, much different than the other girls. Luna didn't play mind games with boys.

Burt had blonde curly hair and green eyes. He was tall and slender, and was interested in space and science. He loved the outdoors and camping. One day, he decided to sit at the same lunch table as Luna.

"Hi, my name is Burt. You're Luna, right?" he asked.

"Yes," she answered.

He started to share his interest in camping and science, and his love of nature with Luna. By the end of lunch he had piqued Luna's interest. He explained he had a telescope and looked at the stars at night. Burt knew all the names and locations of the stars. After sitting at lunch with Luna for a week, Burt finally asked her to hang out after school.

Luna and Burt sparked a friendship and spent the next month eating lunch together. One day, Burt brought his telescope to school.

"So what do you think?" Burt asked.

"Wow. I sure would like to look through it at night. I bet the stars look so close you could touch them," Luna imagined.

"Yeah, they're awesome. The planets are stellar. You can see Saturn's rings. The Moon is incredible. Would you like to go to the lake and I will set up the scope Saturday night? I know a great place on the shore where there's a clearing with no trees in the way. And we can get a pizza before going to the lake," Burt suggested.

"I'll have to ask my parents first, because it'll be after dark. I'll let you know."

"Since I don't have my license yet, I can have my mother drop us off and pick us up. Is that okay?" he asked.

"Sure."

Later that evening, Luna asked Claire about Saturday night.

"Mom, my friend Burt wants to go to the lake on Saturday night and set up his telescope. His mother is going to take us. Is it okay?" she asked.

"Burt?" Claire asked.

"Burt Johnson. He's a senior at my school. He's got a telescope. He wants to set it up at the lake so we can check out the night Sky. He wants to be an astronomer. We'll go for a pizza and then to the lake," she said nonchalantly.

"Luna, I've never heard you talk about him. Is he a nice boy? You're too young for a boyfriend. Well...do you like him?" she pried.

"Jeez Mom, he's a *friend*. Yes, I like him as a friend. He's interested in the same things I am. He's not creepy like the other boys who are always trying to touch your breasts or butt. He's a nice guy. Please, can I go? I really want to use his telescope," she pleaded.

"Okay, but be home by ten-thirty."

"Great. Thanks, Mom."

Luna went to her bedroom and called Burt to tell him Saturday was on. Claire was intrigued. This was the first boy Luna had shown interest in. She wanted her to have friends but knew Tom would be less excited about Luna's first date. Tom still saw Luna as his little girl, and was happy that Luna wasn't interested in boys yet. Claire assumed it was a date. However, to Luna, it was a night of looking at the stars and that's all. But, Burt *was* kind of cute. Their conversations and his knowledge of the stars is what really interested Luna. Maybe she could trust him at some point, and share some of her knowledge from the stars.

Saturday evening came. Burt's mother dropped them off at the restaurant and said she would be back in an hour to bring them to the lake.

"Your mom seems nice," Luna said.

"Yeah, I think she'll be happy when she doesn't have to cart me around. I can't wait to graduate and get my license," he replied.

Burt always ordered a veggie pizza. He and his family were vegetarians. No meat or animal products. Pizza without cheese was different for Luna. She loved cheese, but the conversations they had were worth its loss.

They talked about science-fiction books and movies. Burt talked about his camping experiences and the animals he saw in the woods, building a campfire and sleeping under the stars.

"Luna, there is so much outside of our little Earth. The Sky is limitless, don't you think?" he asked.

"Of course, how can you look at the Sky and not believe there is something more beyond here," Luna said confidently. "Burt, do you believe in life on other planets and stars?"

"Sure. With all the planets and stars, there has to be more than just us," he replied.

"I believe that, too. In fact," Luna paused. "I have seen them. Some look like large insects. There are different races. They are called *Sky Beings*. Some are metallic humanoids with..."

Burt interrupted her. "What? Luna, are you saying you've seen them?"

"When I was small, I had a guide that was from the Center. He took me to a few different stars and showed me many things."

"Luna, you're kidding, right? You are pulling my leg, aren't you? That would be crazy," he scoffed.

"No, it's not a joke," she stated.

"Luna, maybe you've had dreams that you thought were real as a kid. You better not talk about it as it being real. People will think you're crazy," Burt said laughing.

Luna lowered her eyes. They started to well with tears, but she held the tears back.

"I guess you're right, Burt. Maybe they were dreams that seemed real," she concluded.

Luna knew they were real but she decided to drop the conversation. She was disappointed in Burt. He continued to talk about the night Sky and the telescope. Luna listened politely, but barely responded.

When Burt's mother came to bring them to the lake, Luna asked to go home instead. She said she wasn't feeling well. She would skip the telescope at the lake.

"Luna, are you sure? The stars will be spectacular tonight. It's a clear night," he begged.

"No, my stomach feels sick. I think the pizza didn't agree with me. Sorry."

As she returned home and left the car, Burt said, "See you Monday at school, Luna."

"Yeah sure," she replied.

Luna entered the house and ran to her bedroom.

"Luna? You're home early. Is everything okay?" her mother called to her.

"Sure, Mom. I guess I got a stomach ache from the pizza. I'm going to bed," she called back.

Claire knew something was wrong, but Luna didn't want to share. Claire felt helpless at times when it came to Luna. She decided to just let her be. Luna was not okay. She was hurt, angry and disappointed. She cried for a few minutes and then picked up the journal she had started after her first moon cycle. Writing down her private thoughts and dreams allowed Luna to process her feelings and experiences.

Saturday May 1st
Tonight over pizza, Burt did not believe I could have seen and been to other stars. He thought I was dreaming. I thought I

would share one of my secrets. I thought he would understand. He thought it was a joke. When will I learn! He said people will think I am crazy. He advised me not to believe it was real. I am so tired of being alone here. I HATE IT HERE! I hate keeping these secrets. I hate remembering. I don't fit in here. I am an outsider. Matar said I would know when it was time to share and teach. I don't think I will ever know when or if I will have the courage to complete this mission. It all seems so useless and hopeless. I hope Rastaban comes to visit tonight. His protection makes me feel better. He understands.

That evening Rastaban did visit. In her sleep, Luna began her usual breathing pattern before he arrived. As she opened her eyes he was above her and lifted her. His energy melded around her. The energy was intense and warm. She was emotionally and mentally fulfilled. Her body was always tired after his visits, however.

"Luna, I came to your aid. I heard your thoughts and needs," he vibrated in communication.

"Thank you, Rastaban," she replied.

"You will always have me. You don't need anyone else. I love and protect you. No mere human can protect you like I can. We have a special bond."

Rastaban did not encourage Luna to have relationships with others, especially not with boys. Luna remembered Cyrus' warning about the reptilians and their possessiveness. She also remembered the warnings and teachings of the insect race about disengaging the reptilian energy. Luna hoped she would never have to release Rastaban, because he gave her an unusual comfort.

Luna avoided Burt at school on Monday, and began to speak to him less. He eventually got the hint that Luna was no longer interested and left her alone.

Luna became friends with a girl in her school named Samantha. She was a nice girl who was a year younger than Luna. Samantha was a petite blonde, blue-eyed girl. During Luna's junior year, Samantha had become quiet, depressed and withdrawn. Luna decided to talk to her after school one day.

"Sam!" Luna shouted.

Samantha quietly walked towards Luna.

"Hi," she replied.

"Sam, is everything okay? You seem sad," said Luna.

"I'm okay."

"I know how bad I feel inside when I'm sad or troubled. It's like the world is going to end. It's an awful feeling," Luna said.

"Yeah, well what do you do about it?" Sam asked.

"I usually just sit in silence and picture something happy in my mind. Maybe a dream or a wish I'd like to see happen, a type of meditation or visualization. Do you want to try to do that together right now?"

Luna knew that if Sam became quiet, she'd be able to see what was going on more clearly, and maybe even help her.

"Okay. But what do I have to do?" she asked.

"Let's close our eyes and we'll take a couple of long deep breaths to relax ourselves. Then visualize a picture that makes you happy," Luna replied.

"Okay. I'll try."

Luna led them both through the breathing and then they became silent. Luna saw very clearly what the problem was. Luna entered Sam's energy field with her mind. Sam was being verbally abused by her father. He was going into rageful fits and yelling at her. Next, in a vision, she saw him hitting her and giving her a fat lip. It bled and left a bruise. Luna had not seen this injury on Sam. Perhaps it was to come in the future. Luna felt very sad for her friend. A tear silently fell down her cheek.

Luna composed herself and said, "Okay, let's breathe again, one more time. Now let's open our eyes."

"How do you feel, Sam?" Luna asked.

"I do feel better. I feel calmer. Thanks, Luna," replied Samantha.

Luna was very concerned for her friend's safety and decided to talk to her father that night. She stayed awake and waited for him to come home from his night shift.

"Dad," Luna called to her father.

"Luna, what are you doing up?" he asked.

"Dad, you said we should always try to help another person if we can, right?"

"Yes, if it's possible," he replied.

"Well Dad, I have a friend in school. Her father yells at her and says cruel things to her. She's afraid he's going to hurt her."

"Has she told you that he has hurt her?" he asked.

"Well, in a way yes. She's afraid of him. He gets angry and throws things at her."

"You have to get her to tell your counselors at school. They can help her," Tom assured.

"Okay. I'll talk to her tomorrow." With that, Luna went to bed.

Luna looked for Samantha on the next day at school, but Samantha was at home sick. Luna felt a bad feeling in her stomach. She called her house at lunchtime, but no one answered. Luna was distracted the rest of the day. She tried to call that night after dinner, but still no one answered. Luna was worried. She sat in her bed and went into a silent vision. She saw it again. Samantha had a bleeding fat lip and was bruised. She was crying in her bedroom. Her father was out of the house, at least for the moment. Luna secretly put a circle of light energy around Samantha to protect her.

When Luna arrived at school the next day, the other students were gossiping about Samantha. It seems she had a swollen lip from walking into a door. Luna sat with Sam at lunch.

"Luna, everyone is staring at me," she cried.

"Sam, I had a dream last night. I saw that your father hit you in your lip with his fist. He was yelling and saying awful things to you, making you cry. Why do you think I had this dream?"

Sam just froze. *How could she have known or seen this?*

"Maybe, someone is trying to help you, like a guardian angel. Is it true? Does your father hurt you? If he does, it's wrong," Luna added.

Samantha started to cry.

"Let's go outside for some air. We still have time before lunch ends." They left the cafeteria and went outside.

"It started about two years ago when my sister left home. He became mean and angry. But this was the first time he has ever hit me," Samantha said.

"You need to get help. You need to see Mr. Charles, the guidance counselor. I'll come with you. You need to report this," Luna stated firmly. Sam resisted at first, but then finally agreed.

They went to see Mr. Charles. Luna, as promised, stood by her side. Once all the details were known, the police went to her house and arrested her father. Luna called home and asked her mother if Sam could stay overnight. Claire immediately agreed.

The next day, social service made arrangements for Samantha to stay with a foster family. Eventually, Sam was happy again and walked the halls of the school with joy and laughter. Samantha stayed with the foster family for a couple years, until she was ready to be on her own. She was always grateful to Luna for helping her.

Luna's junior year went by quickly and summer was soon upon her. Claire switched to a night shift position at the local manufacturing plant at the beginning of the summer. The pay increase was good and the family needed the income. Luna was now her sister's babysitter, from after school until bedtime.

Leana was five years old. She adored Luna and wanted to be with her all the time. She peppered Luna with many questions. Where did trees come from? Where did clouds come from? Luna sometimes had a hard time knowing how to give good explanations to a five-year-old child.

Leana loved her dolls. She dreamed of being a mommy one day, just like Claire. She wanted to have a boy and a girl. Luna played with Leana for an hour each day. Then she'd make her dinner, bathe her, and put her to bed every evening. Luna sang to her until her sleepy eyes closed and she drifted away. Luna sang the native lullaby that Grandma had taught her just before she died.

Although Tom had a day job working as a mechanic, he continued a part-time night shift stocking shelves at a local grocery store. They were hoping to buy a house in the near future.

Luna would sit outside the apartment on the screened-in porch, while Leana was asleep in bed. Luna would watch the night Sky in all its beauty. It was calm, peaceful and magical. When she spoke to the night Sky, the stars far away twinkled at her as if they had heard her voice.

While observing the Sky one summer evening, three stars started to fall and streak columns of light to the ground. Out of them appeared the three familiar metallic beings. Luna left the porch and approached them after she recognized them. Her heart was racing fast. Her head and body felt faint.

"Luna dearest, do you remember us? It's Chara, Matar and Alcor," Alcor spoke.

"Yes," she replied slowly. "You... are... from Merope."

Her body was frozen with excitement and disbelief.

"When Cyrus left, did he not tell you that we would come to you?"

"Yes, but that was almost five years ago. Are you going to take me Home now? I can't leave Leana. She's sleeping inside. I have to wait until my parents come home from work. Can you wait until then?" she begged.

"Dearest, we have not come to take you Home. We have come to visit with you. We will visit you from time to time. We will replenish your energy and pass on our wisdom, knowledge and prophecies for your Earth. We will know when you need us, and you'll know when we will come. Be well, be at peace and we will be with you again soon," Alcor said.

The three gently reached out to Luna and placed their energy into her head, heart and hands. Luna was teary and basking in the moment as the familiar energy filled her being. When she opened her eyes, they were gone. They would replenish her energy the same way on their future visits.

Luna was excited and wondered what would happen next. As her mind wandered, a slight pang of fear started to creep in.

What if it made life harder again? For the last five years, I've adjusted to not having visits and trying to be a normal teenager. I still don't have anyone I can share my secrets with. Would there be more secrets? How much more do they expect from me? Her wandering mind came to a halt as her parents arrived home. Luna said good night and went to bed.

Their next visit came at the end of that summer. Luna was in bed and was very restless. Her vision was blurry, and she was a bit lightheaded. She knew this feeling. She went to the window. The columns of light came in through the wall and the three beings appeared.

"Dear one, you will come with us tonight. We will show you visions for the future. You will store all of this in your memory and recall it when you need it. There will be times we will take you with us during your sleep. We may not always wake you. It takes a lot of energy to cross the third dimension into the fourth and fifth dimension. Your breathing will change automatically to create a field of energy that forms a portal to travel the planes. But tonight we will take you in your waking state. Do you remember the breathing cycle that Cyrus taught you?" Alcor asked.

Luna nodded her head.

"Good. Now let's begin," Alcor stated.

Luna started the shallow quick breaths.

"Luna, your physical body is denser than it was years ago. You must breathe faster," encouraged Matar.

Luna started to take quicker breaths. She felt heaviness in her chest. She felt incredible heat and started to perspire. Sweat cascaded down her face. Her body became weightless and then she lifted off into the bluish-green sphere. Once again in the celestial night Sky, she spiraled up until she was on Merope, mesmerized again like she had been as a child.

Matar led her to a shimmering room with a black screen. She was inside a large crystal pyramid. There was a deep crevice inside the crystal, and that was where the screen began to download information to her very quickly. It told her of the very beginnings of the existence of the stars, and their birth from the large galaxies, each with their own center Sun star. The light and gases of energy traveled through explosions and created other stars. The true spirit light essence and creative thought from the Super Galactic Center of Oneness created all life forms. It was the power of a Great Cosmic Intelligence of spirit energy. It has many names of devotion on the Earth Star. *God*, was one in particular she would hear a lot. The family she was born into had an ancestry of native people termed Native American Indian. They called this creator *The Great Spirit* or *The Great Mystery*. There were many names, but it is the same Oneness. She was shown the expansiveness of other galaxies all under the same creative life force. She was shown that this life force of light created and contained within it unconditional love, perfection and peace. It was the true Source of all life.

Luna was overwhelmed with the magnificence of the creation of spirit life in the universe. This download was a wonderful experience. Future downloads of information would not always be so wonderful.

She would return to this place several times during the next year. The downloading of information was easier when she was brought during her sleep. Her body was not as tired.

Luna would know when they came to replenish her energy. During the times it was performed in her sleep, she noticed in the morning she would have little red burns on her chest and on the top of her hands. She would have a slight headache until the energy transfer was completely assimilated into her body. Each time, more energy had to be transferred to her, and this caused the burning spots on her skin.

On one of her visits, the screen revealed an unimaginable scene. Missiles created by power hungry human beings created explosions. Huge fires, floods and winds destroying buildings and the landscape of the Earth Star. Destruction was everywhere. Humans were dying in large masses. Their bodies had exploded into microscopic pieces, never to be found. There was a lack of clean water. Humans were dying of hunger and thirst. This scene was unbearable for Luna to watch. She wondered what could be done to prevent it. Alcor came forward.

"Humans must have a change of heart and mind. They must learn to live in balance with each other and with all beings. They must stop destroying and depleting the Earth. They are over-using the land, water and air. Imbalances cannot be fixed or regenerated easily or quickly. The races of the stars have been contacting your civilization for many years. We have helped in the healing arts and technologies to create a wonderful, peaceful life of perfection and balance, but they have misused this knowledge. We are here for them still, and we will help guide those that wish to believe. We have taught four worlds to survive and start again. This star is destroying itself quickly, but its life can be extended if the human race unites with all beings on the Earth Star. Otherwise, it will self-destruct. The Earth will only protect the balance of nature, not its people. She will shake hard and regenerate to balance. Humans are destroying themselves by abusing the Earth's balance. She will turn against them. The Earth Star will survive and eventually regenerate, but it will take many thousands of years. Humans will not be able to survive. It will be hard beyond belief," Alcor confirmed.

As with the same vision from the little people, Luna hoped she would not have to live through this. She wanted the Earth Star and its beings to reunite in love and peace. Returning to her bed, she cried until morning.

From that day forward, Luna felt an incredible heaviness within her. Knowing the possible future was a huge burden, wondering how she was going to live with this knowledge. She remembered Alcor speaking of hope.

"There is hope, Luna. Human beings have the power of the mind, heart and spirit. Remember the light within each being will live on no matter what happens. Help create a healing within you and help others to learn and create it within their minds, hearts and spirits. Let it spread on the Earth Star and beings will physically manifest the reality of love and peace, releasing greed and the power to control. Hope is never lost. Remember this," he said.

Luna carried this in her heart and mind throughout the years, but never shared her secret burden with anyone. Their return visitations would always happen on the eve of the full Moon.

During her senior year, a young man named Justin was very interested in Luna. He was mesmerized by her dark hair and eyes. Justin sat with Luna at lunch and they talked about sports and school subjects. It was just friendly conversation. Luna thought he was a nice boy.

The girls in her class started to tease Luna and told her that Justin liked her and had a crush on her. They thought that he might ask her on a date to the next dance. Luna became agitated. Justin was a nice boy, but she was not interested in dating. She didn't see boys like the other girls her age did. She understood outward appearances change on humans all the time. It was the inside spirit that counted most to her.

Finally, Justin mustered up enough courage to ask Luna to a Friday night dance in the school's gymnasium. Luna politely declined, even though she loved to dance. She would rather have gone with a group of her friends from school. The girls thought she was crazy to have a boy like her so much and not go out with him. Luna had two other suitors during her senior year. Each of them was politely rejected. Eventually the boys stopped asking her out on dates. They believed she must have been dating some older college man. But in truth, Luna was just not interested.

Luna believed that playing mind games and teasing each other was silly to do in human relationships. Trying to make each other jealous because of insecurities seemed ridiculous to her. Rastaban's bond left Luna no room or interest for anyone else.

On one of the triad's visits, Luna decided to ask about her indifference to human courtship.

"Alcor, why do the beings on Earth put so much emphasis and effort into courtship and dating? Why don't I have any interest in this? I am seventeen and have no interest in kissing, dating, marriage or babies."

"Well dear one, you see beyond the physical and into the spiritual. To you, it seems like a waste of time. However, it is how humans learn to interact and grow into adults. It is how they procreate human life. They learn to grow emotionally, mentally and spiritually through relationships. That is why the Earth Star was created, to gain spiritual, emotional, mental and physical wisdom through all types of relationships. Your merge with Rastaban keeps you connected with the stars and the spiritual world. In order to be grounded and have your desire to stay here on the Earth Star and complete your mission, you will have to disconnect from Rastaban. Someday in the future, you will use the knowledge you have been shown on Vega to disconnect from the corded energies. Perhaps one day, you will even help disconnect other humans that need it as well. You see Luna, human bonding and relationships are necessary. They allow one to grow and evolve. They will also help you take your mind off of the star realm and the Center. When you choose a person that feels right to be with here, you will know when to disconnect from Rastaban. But know dear one, you are always loved. The experiences with other human beings in this life are required, and with those experiences will come relationships."

Luna took Alcor's words and reflected on them for the next year as she watched and observed the courtships in high school.

Overall, Luna had enjoyed high school and knowledge came easily to her. Science and History were her favorite subjects. She loved to read about ancient times and cultures, anatomy and biology. Longing to learn more about the Native American Indian culture, she decided that she would travel after graduation.

As graduation day approached, her senior English teacher, Mr. Anderson, encouraged her to write. Luna had kept journals of her life experiences, thoughts and emotions for the last six years. Although her teacher encouraged her to share them, she did not share all of her journal writings. Those were secret and spiritual. The writings she shared were stories that helped her mask her personal journey thus far. Her stories were vivid and colorful.

In a discussion one day, Mr. Anderson told her that he was surprised she was not going to college, because her grades were worthy of any school. Luna explained that her family didn't have the money for college. She went home and discussed this with her mother.

"Mom, Mr. Anderson thinks I should go to college. He said I have great academic grades. I'm in the top five of my class of two hundred students. He said I should take the SAT," Luna said excitedly.

"Luna, I know you are smart. But Mr. Anderson is not going to pay for it. We just don't have the money to send you. I'm sorry," she said sadly.

Luna remembered that day. Claire and Tom had given her everything that they could. She knew and appreciated that they worked hard to provide the necessities and a good life for her. But she would have liked to experience college and further her education.

Mr. Anderson encouraged her to continue to write after high school.

"One day, I hope to see your name on a book, Luna. You have great imagination and spirit in your writings," he said.

Luna liked the encouragement. In her journal she wrote her thoughts.

Senior year April 10th
Today, Mr. Anderson encouraged me to write a book of poetry or
a short novel. He said that I have talent and great imagination.

He likes the stories that I've written in class. Maybe one day I will write. He also likes the poetry that I have composed in class. Maybe I'll publish this poem:
"In the night, the Sky is dark,
The life beyond for us to embark,
A journey begins that has no end,
Remember the Oneness within to tend."

As graduation day finally came, she still remembered the teachings from Cyrus and the other beings. Luna wondered if she would ever share all her secrets and gifts with anyone. At nearly eighteen, the words were buried deep.

As she sat in her seat on the high school's athletic field awaiting her diploma, she daydreamed and remembered all the people she had met in high school. She hoped they would keep in contact in the years to come. She was especially grateful for her friend Samantha, who was now doing very well and still living with a loving foster family.

Suddenly she was pulled out of her daydream.

"Luna Belliveau! Luna Belliveau!" bellowed the loud speaker.

"Hey, that's you," her classmate Josh said as he tapped her on the shoulder.

Luna arose from her chair and proceeded to the stage. People were cheering. She looked at the seats where Claire, Tom and Leana were. They were now standing, cheering and waving madly. The Superintendent of the high school handed her an award.

"She has a 98.9 point average for four years in History. Never in the school's history has an average been so high!" He presented the award to Luna. She thanked him quietly and started to leave the stage.

"Now wait just a minute, Luna. The next award is for the highest average in Science. I again present it to Luna Belliveau with a 96.4 average. Ladies and Gentlemen, this is the highest average in the school's history and never has anyone earned both awards in the same year. This is quite a feat, Luna."

Luna politely thanked him and slowly walked off the stage to roaring cheers and applause. Her classmates congratulated her as she walked to her seat. Collapsing into her seat, she lowered her eyes to the ground. Claire had trained her to blend in and begged for her to go unnoticed, to not draw attention to herself and her peculiarities. The pain of people staring and looking at her brought an uncomfortable anxiety that she had never felt before. Luna wished that her Grandma Anna could have been there.

Just then, she felt a tender brush on her shoulder.

"I am here, dear."

"Grandma," Luna whispered.

Anna floated in front of Luna. She smiled, put her hand over her heart and then disappeared.

"Luna, who are you talking to? You must be in shock winning both awards," snickered Josh who was sitting beside her.

Luna just smiled.

"Thanks, Grandma," she whispered.

The rest of the graduation was long. Luna received her diploma with the other students and the commencement was finally over. Her parents had a small party for her and invited a couple of relatives.

"We are so proud of you and your awards!" her father beamed. "I didn't realize your grades were exceptional."

Luna's favorite memory of the day was the visit from Grandma. What more could she have asked for? As she got ready to crawl into bed at the end of the day, she sighed as she stopped and peered out the window into the starry night Sky. The same longing was still upon her since she entered the Earth's realm and remembered her true Home. *Yes, one day I will return,* she thought. *One day.*

Spirit Guides

That evening, Luna had a lucid dream. She was in a beautiful canyon with layers of brilliant copper, bronze and gold coloring. The mountainous rock formed the familiar ancient faces of Indian elders. They were the same ones that came in the form of the clouds years earlier. Looking up, she greeted them with a smile. Two of the faces were male and two were female. As each one spoke, the ground beneath her shook and their voices echoed in her ears. They spoke of the powers of the elements. Each of them specialized in an elemental power and would be teaching her in the coming years. Red Burning Sky, White Running Trail, Sweet Willow Woman and Smooth Clay Face introduced themselves and their powers. They told her to remember, honor and give thanks for their teachings and the elements of their power.

"We will teach you about Earth, Air, Fire and Water. But you will need to physically travel to places away from where you live. Your teachings will be done on the Earth with us as your spirit guides. You will learn your earthly ancestral ways through an elder of your tribe," White Running Trail rattled. "For now, just rest on the blanket of your Grandmother Earth."

Luna saw the beautiful woven wool blanket of many colors on the ground before her. She laid down on it and felt the gentle breeze on her face, the Sun's glow on her body and the slow rocking vibration of the ground beneath her. It relaxed her quickly. After a few minutes, light sprinkles of rain from a passing cloud awakened her from her resting place.

She awoke and realized she was in her own bed on the morning after her graduation party. *Could this have been a dream?* Luna asked herself. *But it was so real.*

Luna started her day intrigued by the canyon. It was the first day of her new job. She had taken a part-time night position at a local diner and a full-time day position at a glass filter plant.

Since Claire and Tom only had one vehicle that they needed for work, Luna had to walk to work. Walking kept her grounded and connected with nature. It gave her great peace and time to reflect. As she trekked, insights flooded her mind.

The urge from the vision from the previous night, had her mind on thoughts of traveling, not to the stars, but to the canyons and mountains on the Earth. It was an urgent calling.

Her first day of work at the manufacturing plant was easy. The job was to inspect parts that were used to filter light. She was a natural and learned the job with ease. In future months, Luna became proficient at many different positions. The supervisor noticed how easily she could be trained in new positions and thought she was a valuable employee. He offered her extra hours and Luna agreed to work the overtime. She was saving for a car and possibly a trip to the canyon lands. Washing pots and pans and dishes at the diner on weekends was not as interesting as the filter manufacturing technology. Once she was earning enough at the plant, with the extra hours, she quit her job at the diner.

Luna enjoyed working with the crystallized glass filters. It reminded her of star places she had been to. She could see the rainbow prisms in the glass filters. They were cool and delicate to the touch. It reminded her of the Pleiades and the silver dome with the crystals and light. She remembered Cyrus' teachings.

"Luna, light can heal. Each color in the prism has a frequency of energy. It can mend the mortal physical body, the mental mind, emotional heart and the broken spirit. The light contains waves of energy that can't always be seen with the human eye. But it can heal. Technology on your Earth Star will develop and use laser light for healing many health issues in the body. Sound, light and electromagnetic waves create energetic vibrations that alter the energy pathways to repair the human body. It can penetrate tissues and organs of the human body.

Other stars and its beings already have this technology. However, I fear humans may find a way to misuse it."

Luna reflected on these words and then decided to question engineers and knowledgeable people in the company about the application of the filters. Luna's understanding grew as the months went by. Some filters were used for medical applications. Imaging scopes were used inside the body for performing surgeries. And others applications were used for military and satellite telescopes. Her days were filled with technological learning, and her knowledge broadened.

One night before Luna fell asleep she asked her guides, "Where is this canyon I need to see? Where do I need to go?"

Luna relaxed with the breath that Cyrus had taught her and kept her eyes open, not closed. She saw the canyon clearly with the blanket. An elder appeared as she walked to the blanket.

"Where am I? Where is this place?" she asked.

"We are in the Southwest canyons. There once were great waters that flowed through here. Now only large dry beds of stone from the Earth's body remain. Sit here on the blanket. I am Red Burning Sky."

Luna obeyed and sat down. The elder sat beside her. He pulled out a beautifully decorated long-stemmed smoking pipe.

"This is a Sacred Ceremonial Pipe. The ancestors have used this way to pray and honor the Great Mystery in all things. The fire that burns in the bowl is the connection to all fires of spirit in each being of life. It is the universe itself. It is the eternal Sky connection in each life. It is our connection to the Great Spirit of Creation. It is the connection to all of our sacred ceremonial fires past, present and future," he said.

"I have seen the spirit fire in things before. I was shown this on my visits to the stars," Luna said.

"Yes, the Sky Beings are helpers. They have helped humans and guided them for many generations. Many people do not believe in them because they live in fear. For many years, they have taught technology, science, healing and the mysteries of the Cosmos. They are powerful and honorable beings," he said. "Now you will experience the element of fire in ceremony like your ancestors have done for many generations. Fire is the energy of warmth and heat. It consumes what it touches. Fire transforms physical matter through its heat. It needs to be approached with respect. The first teaching is learning how to build a Sacred Fire. We will build it together. Observe and learn. I will teach you," he said.

The elder placed the pieces of wood in a specific circular manner, working clockwise, and honoring the wood and the circle with prayer. He chanted and invited the great fire to enter and ignite the wood. The wood ignited and began to smoke as the flames built. The elder continued to gently feed the fire with wood as they sat in silent admiration. The elder told her to watch the flame of the fire because it all had meaning.

"It is the way it speaks to us. Watch the direction of the fire and the smoke as it begins to burn. The direction talks to us about releasing, healing wisdom, beginnings and relationships. Many things can be learned and understood from the direction that the fire and smoke will take," he explained.

Luna paid careful attention. The smoke and fire were billowing East. The elder explained a new beginning was upon her.

"Now let us fill the Sacred Pipe. The fire in the bowl is the same fire and spirit connected to the universe and Great Spirit. We place our prayers in the bowl of clay from the Earth, the feminine. We inhale the smoke through the wooden stem, the masculine, raising it up to the Sky and connecting ourselves through a bridge to the source of the Great Spirit fire that is in every living thing. It is then that we are at one with everything. It reminds us that there is no separation. We are all related and connected to each other. What we do to other life forms, we do to ourselves. Everything has cause and effect."

He instructed her to relax and hold her mind in an honoring space of gratitude. Luna sat there mesmerized by this small fire of wood he had built. She could see blue-tipped flames. He continued to pray as they added wood to the fire.

Once the lesson of the Sacred Fire was complete, the elder started to prepare for the Sacred Pipe ceremony. Luna watched him as he carefully and respectfully handled the Sacred Pipe, cleaning it with the smoke from the sage he had lit in a shell. He sang a song and prayed as he filled the Sacred Pipe with a special mixture of tobacco that he called *sacred*.

He smoked it in an honoring way and then passed it to Luna to smoke in a similar manner.

Luna gently inhaled the smoke into her mouth and then released it. It tasted sweet, but left a slight burning sensation on her tongue. As she puffed, a vision appeared before her. Luna saw a round structure of animal skins with a fire outside. She saw herself crawl into the structure on her hands and knees. It was dark inside. There was an older Native American Indian man pouring water onto red-hot stones. The steam rose and heated her body. The Native American man spoke in a language that she did not understand. The structure was welcoming her in the darkness of its heat. The top of the low structure looked like the night Sky. It was lit with pinpoints of light that looked like stars. Her eyes began to well up with tears as she returned to smoke the Sacred Pipe. She passed it back for Red Burning Sky to finish and complete the ceremony.

Once the ceremony ended and the Sacred Pipe was put away, Red Burning Sky spoke. "You have seen the way for you to bring the Earth and the Sky world together. Ancestral spirits and Sky Beings will be your guides and they will show you many things. I will be one of them. You will also have a human being to teach you. Go to this canyon and begin your journey to learn how to live here with other humans bridging the Earth and the whole in the Sky."

With that he disappeared. Luna was wide-awake in her bed in the darkness. Her search for this canyon in the Southwest would begin at the library the next day. Luna finally drifted off to sleep with a new purpose and excitement.

At work the next morning, she asked co-workers if they knew of any canyons in the Southwest. A woman named Collette, a religious traveler, answered.

"The Southwest has quite a few canyon areas. We have traveled extensively throughout the West and Southwest. I can show you pictures and brochures from places we've been to. Why are you interested in the Southwest?" Collette inquired.

"Well, I want to travel and would love to see the canyon lands. They seem to be calling to me," Luna replied.

"I will bring in the pictures and brochures for you tomorrow."

"Great," Luna said happily.

Luna finished her shift at work and headed to the library. She looked for books and maps with the librarian's help. Luna paged through many books of maps and pictures of Utah, New Mexico and Colorado, but didn't find what she was looking for. She hoped Collette's vacation pictures would offer a clue.

The next day, Luna approached Collette on her mid-morning work break.

"Hi Collette, did you have a chance to find your pictures?" Luna asked.

"Not all of them, but I brought in a few for you to look at," she replied.

Luna excitedly thumbed through the pictures, searching for the shots of mountains or canyons. She quickly went through over a hundred pictures and didn't find anything that resembled her dream place.

"These are beautiful pictures, Collette. The places in Utah and New Mexico are wonderful. Thanks for bringing them in. Please bring in more when you can," she said.

Luna went back to her shift disappointed. She decided to ask her Grandpa Joe to take her to the bookstore to look through more picture books. Grandpa agreed. Since Claire had now switched to the night shift, and Luna was taking care of Leana, the trip to the bookstore would have to include Leana. Hopefully, Grandpa would take Leana for an ice cream or keep her occupied for a couple of hours. Luna had her license to drive but had not yet saved enough money to buy a dependable car. She thought about the trip to the bookstore throughout the walk home from work.

Leana loved being with her big sister Luna. She was so attached to her that she cried whenever Luna would go someplace without her. She wanted to be with her all the time. Once the school year started, Luna walked her home from school everyday after work. Leana would run to Luna and give her a big hug and smile. The walk home was filled with excitement as Leana recounted her entire school day. Upon returning home, Leana would show her crayon colored pictures and prized work papers with little stars and happy faces. Luna helped her to print the alphabet letters and learn to read. Then they would share Leana's favorite snack of peanut butter crackers.

Luna would usually prepare dinner in the afternoon so her father could eat before leaving for his night job. After dinner, she'd play with Leana and her dolls until Leana's bedtime. But on this night, she would be going to the bookstore after dinner. It would be a nice break for her. Oh how she looked forward to getting her own car and more independence.

Grandpa dropped her off at the bookstore and said he'd come back for her in two hours. He left and took Leana to the local diner for ice cream. Luna went to the information desk and asked where the books on canyons could be found. The woman led her to the appropriate aisle and section. Luna was off and running, flipping through pictures at a feverish pace. She knew she would recognize the picture as soon as she saw it. She went through book after book and placed each of them back on the shelf with disappointment.

She found a book on Arizona and she paged through the pictures. Halfway through the book, she found the scenery that matched exactly what she had seen in her dream vision. It was called Oak Creek Canyon. The book had pictures of many tourist places, but Oak Creek was definitely the place. Luna purchased the book, anxious to immerse herself in it.

Luna fell asleep that evening with the book on her chest. The pictures of Oak Creek were amazing. The canyon had deep engraved formations of red rock. The area had been described as dry, hot and somewhat barren.

Still, she thought, *just to be able to sit and walk in the presence of this place could be majestic. Or to at least bring me closer to what is calling me forward in my mission.*

Luna shared her findings in the book with Collette at work the next day.

"Oh yes. I have been there. It's beautiful, especially in May when the prickly pear cactus plants start to bloom. But it's too hot in the summer months. It can reach over 115 degrees."

"Well, I think I'm going to save and make the trip in early spring next year. Can you recommend a comfortable place to stay that's fairly inexpensive?" Luna asked.

"Sure. They have a couple of lovely motels and camping facilities in the area. But you'll have to rent a car. It's a couple of hours drive from the Phoenix Airport. Once there, you will find Jeep tours that can take you into the canyons," Collette replied.

Luna realized that she would have to work many extra hours at the plant in the following months. And the used car she hoped to buy might have to be put on hold for a little while longer. Luna gave part of every paycheck to Claire and Tom to help with the household, and it also gave her a sense of responsibility for herself. Luna knew how hard her parents had worked over the years. She had lived in a small apartment all her life, but her parents had now saved almost enough to buy a house.

When Leana was born, Tom and Claire sacrificed their own privacy and slept on a pullout sofa so that Luna and Leana could each have their own bedroom.

At only eighteen years old, Luna had become a very responsible adult. She was now working at least six days every week to earn enough for her trip to Arizona. She worked almost seventy hours per week during November and December, and was exhausted by Christmas. Grandpa was babysitting Leana so Luna could work extra shifts. The plant shutdown for the week between Christmas and New Year's Day gave Luna some much needed rest.

Leana and Luna spent time together during the Christmas holiday. They walked to the park in the snow, and stopped by the local candy store for a treat. Luna's conversations with Leana were like mother-daughter rather than sister-to-sister. Since there was an eleven year difference in age, Luna developed a nurturing and protective relationship with Leana.

One day when Leana was in the second grade, a boy in her school started to pick on her and punched her in the stomach. Since Leana had been born prematurely, she was a small and underweight child. The punching lasted for a couple of days until finally Leana broke down in tears and told Luna. The next day Luna asked Leana to point out the older boy. They waited for the boy named Todd in the schoolyard.

Leana pointed to him and said, "That's him, Luna. He's the one who hurts me."

And with that, Leana hid behind Luna, clenching her hand. Luna motioned to the boy to come to her. The boy's eyes filled with fear as he slowly approached Luna.

"Is your name Todd?" Luna asked.

"Uh huh," he gulped.

"How old are you, Todd?" she asked.

"I'm uh, I'm nine," he replied.

"Well, I'm eighteen. And I am Leana's big sister. She told me that you've been punching her and hurting her. I can't let someone hurt my little sister. So you're going to stop ... right?"

"Yeah... I mean, right," he agreed.

Using her gift, Luna looked deeply into the young boy. She could see he was an only child and lonely. His parents were wealthy, but spent little to no time with him. He was acting out. He wanted to make friends but didn't know how. His parents were too involved with their business meetings and local politics. Todd was left with an elderly aunt who could barely keep an eye on herself, much less her nephew. With his heart full of frustration, he walked home from school and stayed with his elderly aunt until seven or eight o'clock at night.

"Todd, I know you don't have a big brother or sister to take care of you or play with. I know you are lonely and angry that your parents work a lot. And I know that your aunt is too old to play with you. But you have to be nice to make friends," Luna stated.

"How do you know this?" he asked, bewildered.

"My sister Luna is real smart. I mean real smart. She knows a lot of things," Leana beamed proudly.

"Would you like to be our friend?" asked Luna.

"Sure," the boy replied.

"On our walk home, we'll go to the store and get a candy bar to celebrate our new friendship," Luna suggested.

Both children yelled at the same time, "Yay!"

After that, Leana did not have anymore issues with Todd. He slowly began to make other friends in school.

Although she loved her sibling, Luna sometimes found it hard not having time alone. When Luna was not working, Luna's alone time would only come after Leana fell asleep. It was the only time she had to read or relax. She looked forward to her vacation in the canyon.

The first day of the new year brought some friendly company. At two o'clock in the morning Luna was awakened by someone whispering her name.

"Luna... Luna." It was Matar, Alcor and Chara.

"Dearest, you are depleting your earth energy. We need to recharge you. You aren't resting enough," Alcor said gently.

They placed energy in her head and heart, but the third energy was placed in her stomach instead of in her hands. This time Luna felt a static charge that actually jolted her in bed. Her heart skipped a beat and her belly burned inside. It hurt for a moment then the pain subsided.

"Luna, this vehicle you are in, is mortal. You must take care of it properly. You cannot leave before your time. The body must rest, eat proper food, move, and have the mind and spirit in balance. Otherwise, the spirit light will leave your body too soon and you will not complete your mission," Alcor said sadly.

"When you go to the canyon in your vision, there is another place to visit. It is a red rock formation filled with a lot of energy. You will know it when you see it. It is a portal that vibrates and opens up a space for Sky Beings to enter the Earth unseen. You will learn about vortexes that connect this star to other dimensions. Search for it and spend time there. It will energize you."

And then they disappeared. The three were always quick about their business and didn't waste much time. However, they once explained that there really is no time outside of the Earth Star.

"Outside the Earth, on other stars and galaxies, there is no measure of time. It is all cosmic energy and light. It may take weeks or months to travel distances on Earth, while in other dimensions one can travel great distances in the blink of an eye. Light can go in one direction forever or it can be warped and bent to move to a past time. It is so expansive that it can't be measured. It is futile to even try," Alcor said. "Time is measured on Earth because human beings have the need to set limits, control with ego, and squeeze as much into a life as possible. This is how they believe they can experience a full life. Luna, the understanding is misguided. Being in the present moment is what matters most. To look further than that is time wasted. You can never get the precious current moment back. Too may humans put their life on hold until they reach a goal relating to money and success. Happiness can only be found, recognized and enjoyed in the present moment. Luna, you have a mission, but don't let the moments pass you by. Remind humans of the source of spirit life. Remind them of their connection to all beings. Help them connect the Earth and the Sky."

Luna took great solace in these words. She realized that during the last few months, she had worked so hard to earn money for her trip that she had forgotten to enjoy the things she really loved: reading, walking, being outside in nature, observing, and listening to music.

Luna cut back on her overtime hours in the new year to give herself more time every day for earth life. Luna worked less each day and still made enough money for her trip.

Her intuitive abilities were very helpful in her work. When there was a problem with a non-functioning filter product or with one of the machines used to test them, she was quick to see the problem and come up with ideas to help the engineers. Many of the engineers did not pay attention to Luna's ideas and suggestions. They didn't believe that a young, uneducated girl could or should tell them how to fix a problem.

So, Luna waited until the problem was bad enough to shut down the production floor and higher management had to have a meeting. It seemed crazy to Luna that because of ego, problems weren't solved and much energy, time, and product was wasted. Luna knew energy was precious and she had little patience with wasting it. It was one of her greatest cosmic understandings, but impatience with humans was also one of her greatest flaws.

Luna would sit silently with a problem and determine the cause and solution to the situation. At other times, she would sit with her eyes closed and look inside a machine to see what needed repair. A vision would appear, or a voice would tell her what was wrong and how to fix it. Of course, she could never reveal how she received this information.

One problem had been that the filters weren't conducting properly. Luna was shown that the chemical baths used to clean the filters were actually harming the filters. The chemicals had become contaminated at the vendor's manufacturing plant. Luna understood it clearly. Now if she could just get someone to listen. She knew the engineers and the supervisor would not listen, so she decided to talk to the chemical waste maintenance person whose job was to order and then reclaim the chemicals. They spoke about contacting the chemical company. In two days, he found that there was a problem with a certain inventory lot. The vendor thought they had reclaimed all the contaminated chemicals but they missed the fifty cases that were already shipped before they realized they had a problem.

The problem was solved and the chemical waste supervisor received all the credit. Luna did not want the praise or the attention. She just wanted the problem to be fixed. Besides, how would she explain the information she was given to fix the problem?

Well, you see I just ask and sit quietly, and I hear a voice or see a picture, Luna thought. *Yes, I'm sure they will believe that.*

The plant subsequently experienced more problems, and each time Luna found a way to anonymously help, though it became harder each time to help without being noticed.

Luna later received teachings from another ancestor guide. Not every guide would come to her at night. One appeared in her quiet time at the lake. The town's lake was a spiritual place and she frequently went there during winter, spring and fall. Summer brought many swimmers and picnickers to the lake and it was too crowded and busy for Luna. Any summertime visits to the lake usually occurred after sunset, after most of the public had left.

On one Sunday morning in April, at the lake, she sat in her favorite place, in the crook of a cedar tree that was about three feet off the ground. Luna gazed at the stillness of the lake. The lake was mostly thawed. As Luna focused her eyes and quieted her mind, she felt the peacefulness of the slight breeze coming to the circle of cedars where she was sitting. She smelled the sweet fragrance of the trees. They were standing tall and their strength comforted her. Luna noticed a figure floating across the water. She heard noises that sounded like rhythmic rattling. The rattles seemed to chime together and propel the floating figure forward.

The figure stepped in front of her. It became clear that it was an elderly woman. She had bronze weathered skin and wore a beaded buckskin dress. Her skin was very old, and deeply wrinkled from where the Sun had kissed her many times.

"I am Sweet Willow Woman," she sang in an old worn voice. "I will teach you about the waters. When you wash and bathe, water cleans the impure things off the outside of your body. But it can also clean and nourish the insides of your body, mind and your spirit. Water can relax and nurture. It has a power that is both gentle and forceful. The gentleness of it can nurture and give us sustenance when we drink it and bathe in it. A gentle rain can lift the spirit. Tears can release the burdens you carry, and bring renewal. Water mirrors our reflection when we look deep into a pool. We see who we truly are and we can not hide from that. The forceful water from the oceans and storms clears out the old and replenishes our energy to begin anew. It can carve an impenetrable stone with its rapid flow, as well as transform the body, spirit and mind. The waters are powerful. It is a gift to all. It is needed to survive in the earth body. It is needed to renew and heal. Human beings become life and grow in the womb of water and blood. It cradles and comforts. It forces one out into nature's world of existence. Learn the powers of the waters, by being in lakes, rivers and oceans, by standing in the rain and storms, and by bathing in water. Release the waters of our bodies to cleanse and purify through excretion of sweat and tears."

Sweet Willow Woman provided teachings of how to use and connect to the waters in Luna's mind's eye. Once again the same vision came to her; she saw a round structure with a fire outside, and herself crawling into the structure on her hands and knees. The same older Native American Indian man was pouring water on some red-hot stones. The steam rose and heated her body. This time she truly felt the steam cleaning her body, releasing the confusion in her mind, and gently lifting her spirit. The water spoke as he poured it on the hot stones. She heard the sizzle, and as the water pooled over the stones, they sang a melody. The song was beautiful and it brought tears to her eyes, releasing countless emotions. The elder spoke again in a language she did not understand. The darkness of the structure felt like Home, blanketed with pinpoints of light overhead that appeared as stars. Luna felt herself rising to the night Sky and again felt comforted.

Luna's vision ended and the woman was gone. Only the silent lake remained. Luna quietly said thank you to this woman spirit in her heart and mind, hoping she would hear her. Luna recounted the vision and then walked home. She journaled the woman's words and all she had experienced that morning. She memorized the stones' melody as it was a song to release sadness and grief. It was a song she would later hear again.

Luna returned to work the next day. She had booked her flight and made reservations at the campground. Camping was much less expensive than staying in a hotel or motel. She bought maps to plan her travel and rented a four-wheel drive vehicle to get to and from the canyon on her own. Her trip was creeping closer. Luna needed to be in the canyon and find the rock formation vortex that the beings had shown her. She couldn't wait.

Although she shared her plans with her mother and father, she could not share the truth of why and how she was led to go there. All that she could say was that she was going there for a vacation because it looked like a fun place. When Luna told her parents, Claire was not happy that she was traveling that far from home by herself. Claire wasn't much of a traveler herself. She felt very comfortable being at home and being a mother, and had no great desire to search or venture out. When Luna expressed her desire to travel, Claire tried to discourage her.

"You want to go where?"

"Arizona," Luna replied.

"Why do you want to travel to Arizona? It's a desert and it's hot, with lots of snakes and poisonous creatures. I don't like the idea of you traveling by yourself, a young girl all alone. It's very dangerous," Claire sighed.

"But Mom, I have everything all mapped out and planned. It'll be fine. I'd like to see that part of the country. It's different from here, a change of scenery, something new and exciting, and a chance to meet new people. Dad understands. He used to travel when he was in the Air Force."

Tom did understand. He was enlisted for four years in the service and was stationed all over the country. He did like to fly and travel. If he had not met Claire and settled down to marry and have a family, he might have continued to travel. Tom did not regret his decision to marry. He adored Claire and loved both of his children. But he had to come to Luna's defense when it came to encouraging her to travel.

"It'll be a good experience for her. Claire, she needs to travel now while she's young, before she falls in love and gets married and starts a family. Let's not give her a hard time. I know you worry and so do I, but I believe she's smart, capable and mature enough to do this," he said.

"I guess you're right. Luna is responsible and mature even if she is only eighteen. She has always been wise beyond her years. I guess it's just my own fears of flying and worries of bad people out there in the world. I guess I just don't understand her, and how she has no interest in wanting a boyfriend, having children or getting married. Luna wants to be somewhere else, anywhere but here in this home. She takes walks to the lake and spends a lot of time in her room. She spends too much time by herself. That's not normal," Claire replied.

"Claire, she works and baby-sits for Leana after work and helps with other chores. She's a good girl. I don't think it's strange for her to want alone time and to go out by herself. In becoming an adult she needs to have a break from home responsibilities and have fun. Maybe that'll be fun for her. We need to let her be. Why are you so hard on her?" he asked.

"Well, she has always been different and I fear that she won't have someone in her life to take care of her and have a family with children. I don't want her to be old and alone someday. It's abnormal to not talk about or want those things," Claire answered.

"Maybe she doesn't want those things or isn't ready for those things. Hell, I'm not ready to see her have those things. She's too young for marriage or kids. Let her enjoy her life and have her own experiences," he said.

"But she is not enjoying her life. Luna is always sad. Oh, I know she smiles, but there is something wrong down deep. A mother knows her child. I just don't understand her. It's hard to relate to my own daughter. I hope I'm doing a better job with Leana. She loves her dolls and wants to be a mommy. She has had little boy crushes at school. You know the normal things that little girls talk about," she added.

"Well, maybe Luna will be happier if we just accept her for who she is," Tom suggested.

Claire shrugged. She really did want to be close to her daughter and for her daughter to love her. It was hard for Claire to express that to Luna. Luna was so distant.

Claire had been thinking all day that she needed to find peace with Luna before she left on this trip. Claire had a fearful mother's instinct that Luna's life would change after this trip. Maybe she would become more independent. She did not want to wait until late in life to mend fences with her daughter, like she had done with her own mother. Tom was right: she had always been hard on her. Her own fears, concerns and desires shaped what she wanted Luna to be. She now needed to accept Luna's decision for this trip.

"Luna, I would like to talk to you," Claire said calmly.

"Mom, I am going on this trip. Please don't try to change my mind," Luna said firmly.

"No, Luna. That's not what I want to talk about," Claire paused. Her voice grew shaky, her eyes filled with tears. "I am worried, but if it is important to you, go and have fun. But be careful, Luna."

Luna had not expected this.

"Thanks, Mom. That means a lot to me. Don't worry. I'll be careful in Arizona, and I'll take lots of pictures to show you when I get back."

Luna received an awkward hug from her mother. It was the first hug between them in a few years.

The Journey

The month of May arrived and Luna was ready for her adventure. Her suitcase was packed with comfortable clothes, sneakers, toiletries and a camera.

Luna had a hard time relaxing the night before her departure, barely getting any sleep, but just enough for a quick dream. Again the scenery of red rocks surrounded her. The red formation stood tall above her, but this time she wasn't in a canyon. She was at the base of a large bell-shaped red rock. As she peered above, she noticed a white trail of clouds moving over the top of the red rock. The clouds floated over the top and landed on the other side in back of the structure. As she started to walk toward it, she felt the ground beneath her start to vibrate and shake, and she heard a loud hum as well. Her head was light and her stomach felt queasy. She looked down to the red dirt to catch her balance for a moment. As she lifted her head, a Native American Indian elder approached her. His hair was long, white, and flowing loosely. He wore a buckskin shirt and around his neck hung a claw of some kind, wrapped in leather. He was thin and had dark eyes. His dark skin was weathered and tough like leather. He looked older than Red Burning Sky. She had seen his face before. He was one of the former faces in the clouds from childhood.

"I am White Running Trail. I am one of your spirit guides. I will teach you about the air. You cannot see it. But it fills every space and being. It brings life through the breath. It cleans and regenerates the blood, tissues and organs in each being. It brings calmness and relaxation when it is used as nourishment for the soul. It fills the mighty spirit winds of each Grandfather of the directions. It gives direction to the snow and rain. It moves the waters on the land. It is the invisible power of the Sky," he said.

Luna paid attention to his words. He closed his eyes and was silent for a moment. Then he cupped his hands and blew into them ever so gently, creating a whirlwind of breeze. Red dirt flew into a dust funnel around them. The funnel grew higher and lifted them up onto the bell-shaped structure. When the dust settled, they were standing high on the ridge of the bell-shaped red rock. The view was magnificent and she could not believe they were lifted by such force.

"The wind will help to blow away the old to lay ground for the new. It can destroy what comes into its path if it's not respected. You must learn to respect the air and the wind, even if you can't always see it. You cannot live and breathe without the air."

Luna was on top of this structure and felt the vibration of the rock as she breathed in and out. She closed her eyes to feel its rhythm, and when she opened them again, she was back in her bed. She lay there for a few moments to reflect on the dream before journaling. When she finished writing, she took a quick shower and was out the door to the airport. Her father drove her to the airport, remembering his traveling days.

"Well Luna, are you excited? Your big day has arrived," he said.

"Yeah Dad, I am," she replied.

"Do you have everything, your tickets, emergency numbers, money, car rental information, maps?"

"Yes. I have it all. I have triple checked everything," she reassured him.

"I want you to have fun, but I also want you to be safe. Don't pick up any strangers when you're driving. Keep your money in a place other than your wallet, like maybe in your shoe. Did you take travelers checks?" he asked.

"Dad, don't worry," she replied.

"Are you excited about flying? I remember how nervous I was at first, but then I really enjoyed it."

"I expect it'll be like what I've experienced before," she said.

"Experienced before? When have you flown before?" he asked with a raised eyebrow.

"I guess… when I had dreams of flying. You know, how I imagined it," she replied quickly.

"Okay," he nodded in understanding.

After a kiss and a hug, Tom left her at the airport terminal to begin her journey. Tom worried as they parted, but knew the trip would be good for her. They both had tears in their eyes. As far as he knew, it was the first time that Luna had been away from home. As they parted, Luna thought to herself: *At last, I can begin my journey.*

Luna boarded the airplane and found her window seat. She realized now that the aisle seat might have had more room, but at least she would have the window to look out of and rest her head on.

All the seats on the flight were filled. The woman who sat next to her started a conversation and asked all the usual questions. Where are you from? Where are you going? How long will you be there? Do you have relatives there who will pick you up? Luna was polite, mostly giving one-word answers and then listened to the woman's story. On the second flight, connecting to Arizona, she pretended to sleep against the window so that she wouldn't have to engage in conversation. Luna looked through the window at the majestic billowing clouds. As the airplane started its descent, she noticed the land below and how the Earth was raped and pillaged with roads and covered with hot tar. It made her body feel like she, too, had been torn and ripped apart. Emotionally and physically experiencing the pain of Earth's land made her eyes mist with empathy. It was the beginning of her connection to the Earth. It would stay with her for the rest of her life.

Luna found her way to the car rental agency in the airport. She rented a new red Jeep, believing it would be able to navigate the terrain in the canyons. The clerk at the rental counter gave her a map and highlighted the route to Oak Creek Canyon.

The highway outside Phoenix was through desert land. The saguaro cacti on the sides of the road looked like tall people waving to each passer-by. The prickly pear cactus bushes and their yellow flowers were in bloom. The landscape didn't change much during the next two hours of the drive.

She was traveling in early afternoon, the hottest time of day. Luna cranked the air conditioner in the Jeep to the maximum. The last temperature reading in Phoenix was 114 degrees. Luna had never experienced heat like this. Most summers in New England, the temperatures were in the low 90s. It was a good thing she heeded travel book recommendations to pack water and snacks for the drive, and to wear light long-sleeved clothing for sun protection. The road seemed endless and there were few rest stops. Time passed quickly as she sang with the radio.

Soon she began a slight uphill climb and noticed the sign for Sedona. Upon her descent from the top of the hill, she saw the beautifully carved ruby red mounds of rock formations on either side of the road. They took her breath away, placing her in an ancient land. The minerals in the clay shimmered colors of cinnamon touched by the Sun. Tears welled up in her eyes as she pulled the Jeep off the road. She snapped pictures, as witness to her arrival. Luna felt the sacredness, a place on Earth that had been carefully carved by the elements of wind, rain and the great waters. It was inspiring. She drank in the tranquility as she sat on the dusty pavement and breathed deeply to ground herself.

The campsite cabin in Oak Creek Canyon was a few minutes away. She hurried back into the vehicle, down the road into Sedona, taking in all of the distinct formations. Ahead of her, a huge bell-shaped red rock became visible. It was mesmerizing and drew her closer.

"This is it! This is the place I have seen in my dream, the place of vibration, the vortex," she spoke to herself.

Luna heard chanting in a foreign language in her head. The land was speaking to her. While pulling over to the side of the road she realized it would be quite a hike to get to the bell formation. She would have to come back the next day and snap some pictures at sunrise.

Luna proceeded down the main street and found a shop that offered sightseeing tours and information. She purchased a book of the vortexes and energy sites in Sedona. Many of them had a specific name. The bell-shaped formation was actually called Bell Rock. Others were Chimney Rock, Coffee Pot, Cathedral Rock and the Courthouse. All were named appropriately for their shape and appearance. Although she wanted to venture and explore, she needed to travel a few more miles and settle in. Check in time was 3:00 p.m.

As she traveled through Oak Creek Canyon, there was a stream that flowed parallel to the road. There were many large boulders lying in the stream. People were fishing, others were swimming. The water looked clear and refreshing. Finally she approached the small rental cabins and went to the main house to check in.

The cabin was rustic. It was one large room with a single bed, a lantern, a small table with two chairs, an old rocking chair, a small ice chest and one clean but small sink. There was a small butane camping stove and a modest supply of pans, dishes, coffee cups and silverware. Luna brought her own sleeping bag, flashlight, matches and Swiss army knife. The campground had a separate building for bathrooms and showers, on a first-come first-served basis. This would be interesting. At least the stalls were private and clean. Tomorrow, she would return to town for more ice, water, fruit and snacks.

The camp manager advised Luna of a local park named Slide Rock State Park just a couple of miles away. It had great hiking and a picnic area nestled in the canyon. It also had a small area for swimming.

Inside the main building was a sign up sheet for a lecture on Friday night featuring a well-known Native American Indian elder, named Red Eagle. The camp asked for a small donation for the evening lecture. Luna was excited. She signed up and made a generous donation. While unexpected, the lecture seemed to fit the journey and schedule perfectly.

Luna awakened the next morning to greet the stillness of the Sun rising in the desert. It was interesting to feel how cold it was in the early morning compared to how hot it was in the afternoon. Luna packed her knapsack and rode back to the red rock formations in Sedona. She especially wanted to visit Bell Rock. She hopped in the Jeep and was racing with the Sun as it quickly rose. After pulling the Jeep onto the road's soft shoulder, she proceeded to hike on her own trail to Bell Rock. She climbed the formation in a sideways circular pattern before she sat down to rest. Looking down, she realized that she had barely made a dent on the trail. As she looked out to the scenery below, she was searching. Not knowing exactly what she was searching for, but trusting she was being guided. Luna resumed climbing for another two hours before deciding to rest. She unrolled her light blanket and backpack and sipped on some water.

This mystical place made her light-headed. The buzzing energy of this place was familiar, the same as when her childhood friend Cyrus would visit her. Chara, Alcor and Matar had spoke of this place and that she needed to come here. Luna made herself comfortable and lay in silence with her eyes wide open. The peace and tranquility was unbelievable. Luna meditated in silence for four hours, into the early afternoon. The Sun crept overhead and made it unbearably hot. She climbed up a little further to a small mesquite tree that gave her a little shade. Luna covered the tree's branch with the blanket and sat under it. Luna planned to stay a while with the help of the water bottles and snacks that she packed.

Luna scribbled her feelings and insights.

> *The red rocks appear to be sad ancient faces crying. I hear native chanting and singing. It touches my soul. I feel connected to this place and to the energy here. It feels so serene and comforting. I am so alive and consciously aware. The rock faces are filling my heart with emotions. I feel privileged and honored.*

She looked at her watch for the time and saw that it had stopped. She decided to return to the Jeep. As she gathered her things and put them into the backpack, she turned around and saw a coyote in front of her path down from the rock. She quickly sat down and started to worry. *How am I going to get by it? Will it attack me? It looks pretty frail and hungry.*

She remembered the teachings of communication from her Sky friends, to search inside and see the spirit light in the coyote. As she did this, the coyote sat down as well. Luna heard its mind communicate.

"You must stay the night. I will protect you and keep you company."

Luna agreed to stay the night hoping the blanket would be enough to keep her warm. As sunset started to approach, the Sky was amazing. It was filled with hues of violet, turquoise and pink. She bathed in the wonder of this beauty that most people do not get to see or appreciate. The Sun rose and set everyday with most people taking it for granted.

Luna made a silent prayer of gratitude for the Sun and for this day. She asked for help and courage to make it through the night, knowing she was alone here and no one knew exactly where she was. She thought about her mother, father and Leana, and being alone in this moment, remembering her family she realized how much she loved them.

The coyote eyed her every move. His stare was intense. Luna wondered what he had come to teach her. Grandma Anna told stories about animals coming to teach the people and bring them wisdom for balance. He kept his distance, about twenty feet away. Luna did not dare make any sudden movements that would startle him. The coyote sat upright on his hind legs.

The solitude she felt was not loneliness, for she had felt that most of her life. The silence gave her peace within, without having to endure conversations of mindless chatter with people who did not understand her. She felt empathy for the world and everyone in it, and she felt disheartened from the visions Alcor had shown her for the future. Luna carried the world on her shoulders.

Why is it my responsibility to send a message to people to bring them back into balance? Who am I? I was not born into a prominent leadership family. Who will believe me? Will any human ever really understand or believe me? Will I ever find someone on this planet I can share my life mission with? Someone who will be able to love and understand me unconditionally? Or do I have to accomplish the mission alone?

She sat and thought with silent tears.

Why am I having thoughts about sharing my mission with someone? Do I want to have a relationship with someone? Am I starting to want a connection with another human more deeply?

Luna was confused. This place gave her a different perspective, stirring up emotions from deep within her.

The coyote had laid its body down to rest. Suddenly, it arose to stand erect on all four legs as if it heard her heart. It came to within a foot of her and whimpered. She listened deeply to his wisdom. He brought out in her an awareness of her feelings, admitting to herself that she wanted a human connection, a partner. It would be too hard to complete her mission without one. Humans long for interaction. That is their nature. But she lacked the trust to accept herself and others. These feelings were tough to admit.

Embracing her human self was uncomfortable. Luna took the last few pieces of beef jerky from her backpack and kindly tossed it over to the animal. It scoffed it down quickly and looked for more.

As the night Sky darkened, a large raven appeared overhead and cawed. It circled overhead and then suddenly dived down, in attack mode. Luna jumped up to her feet and ran off of the blanket. Turning around, three feet behind where she had been sitting, a large snake was ascending from its hole in the ground. Snakes, she had read, hid in the ground during the heat and came out after sunset when it was cooler. The snake slithered around through the brush and left the area.

Luna was intrigued. Had the raven come to warn and protect her? The bird had come out of nowhere. Nature was beautiful. Why did the raven help her? Maybe it heard Luna's prayer. Luna wanted to coexist with nature. Now, she was reaping the rewards of honoring her connection to all beings.

I know that I am guided to stay here tonight, she thought. Just thinking about this gave her goose bumps. *I must pay attention. Nature is sending me messages and helping me.*

Luna went through the night with the blanket wrapped around her and kept an eye out for snakes, scorpions and spiders. Making a prayer, she asked all the creatures to share their space with her.

The stars were brilliant. They seemed close enough for her to just reach out and touch them. Like diamonds sparkling on a black velvet blanket, comforting her.

As the hours went by, she heard a loud hum. The vibration shook the ground and her entire body. She surveyed the Sky. Out of the cloud lit by the Moon, a large silver elliptical craft with red, blue and green lights on its underside emerged overhead. It was a different shape than what she had seen when she was a child. And it was much larger. It was massive. It covered the entire night Sky, like a world within itself. Luna was startled as she watched with wonderment. As it hovered above her, three columns of light in a triangular formation descended to the ground where she stood. As the beams of light surrounded her, Chara, Alcor and Matar appeared. They floated to her as she greeted them.

"Dearest, you have followed the plan we set for you. This is what we call the Mother Ship. It sustains the energy of smaller crafts and gives regenerating technology through sound and light from the celestial realm. Tonight you will feel the full force of the power, not merely through the three of us, but from her endless generator. After almost nineteen years on this Earth Star, you still long for your Home in the Sky. You will receive the necessary energy and life force to open your heart further. Your insights and knowledge will become more advanced once you are attuned to this level tonight," Alcor spoke.

"But why now?" she asked.

"Here, you are in an inter-dimensional vortex. This vortex can allow the ship to go undetected and will draw no attention on the grid. There are other places all over the Earth that have this same frequency. Look to the places of great temples and structures and you will find a secret vortex. The ship cannot be detected."

"Smaller crafts can land under your seawalls in the great oceans. They are shaped in spheres. Someday, all humans will be allowed to see the crafts and Sky Beings as well. With our union, we can help the Earth Star to become an enlightened place. Now stand here between the three of us," he commanded.

"It is such a huge ship. Will this beam of light energy hurt?" she asked.

"No. It will feel like an implant of endless energy," he answered.

Luna stood between the three beings. They formed a large triad around her. The light emerged from the center of the underneath of the ship above. She was in a massive spotlight. The beam changed colors: white, violet, purple, blue, turquoise, green, yellow, orange and red. The beam had little particles that floated around her like swirling dust. Luna felt her body get cold, freezing until numb, in fact, as if suspended in time. Her body was shaking uncontrollably and then lifted off the ground at her chest. She twirled around very quickly in a spiral motion, suspending her in the air. Luna could not move. As she relaxed and immersed herself in the freezing temperature, her mind drifted. There was comfort now and a sense of calm fulfillment and contentment.

When she was completely regenerated, she was transported inside the universal craft. Bright lights were everywhere, a galaxy within itself.

The metallic beings shrouded in light, floated inside the weightless gravity. Several planetary Moons in the Sky of the great craft could be seen. It was a gateway into other dimensions that expanded beyond her eyesight. Astral music and soothing tones surrounded her. Advanced knowledge of invisible vehicles for flight and healing therapies of light and sound were imparted into her mind through her vision as she entered the craft with the beings. Her mind received it so quickly that it nearly appeared as a blur. Banded colors of light were served as the food that nourished each being, a consciousness that spoke telepathically, using telekinesis for movement. Knowledge levels beyond what human minds could comprehend. Luna closed her eyes but her mind could still see.

That was the last feeling Luna could remember. The howl of the coyote called her body back. She had been gently placed on the ground and the Sun was rising. As she looked around, the coyote had left. He had completed his task. After making a silent prayer of gratitude, she quickly wrote in her journal.

> *The light lifted me up by my chest. It paralyzed my body as I twirled in a spiral motion. I saw the lights transforming the energy within my body, the bands of color rebuilding and energizing me. It was cold at first. Then it became extremely warm, radiating and pulsating. The universe inside the Mother Ship was incredible technology. Was it the future for humans? Will they teach us?*

Luna put her journal away and started her descent to the Jeep. What took her hours to climb would only take half the time on the way down. She floated with each step. As she neared the Jeep, she realized she was ravenously hungry. A nice breakfast was in order. The little café she had noticed on Main Street seemed appropriate.

Her energy was high all day. She went back to the campsite, took an invigorating cold shower in the main building and changed her clothes. The shower felt good, cleaning the red dust off her skin and face. Once refreshed, she relaxed and journaled in her cabin for the rest of the day.

The following day, Luna took a picnic lunch to Slide Rock State Park. Since the park was open until sunset, she had plenty a time to explore. There were many tourists when Luna arrived. It was a well known swimming place. Luna removed her hiking boots and dipped her feet into the cool water, wiggling her toes and swishing the water between them.

Luna noticed a group gathered off in the distance away from the picnic area. As she looked closer, she realized they were dressed in Indian and western fashions. Her father would have said they looked like hippies. Luna decided to walk toward them. A Native American Indian man in his fifties, seemingly the leader, asked if she wanted to join them.

"I am Grey Coyote and we are going to have an Earth honoring prayer circle. We have gathered to honor Grandmother Earth and all of her creatures. We will sing and pray and create a circle of unity and love for all beings. The Grandmother is weeping. We are destroying her by the minute. We tear into her heart by mining uranium and other metals with greed. We will pray to the Great Spirit to end the mining that is shaking and depleting her," he said.

Grey Coyote. Isn't that interesting?

Luna thought about the gray colored coyote that stayed with her through the night. She joined the circle and prayed for three hours. It was peaceful. When it was over, people said, "Hau" and hugged. Grey Coyote approached Luna and thanked her for joining the circle and praying. He said he and a few of his students and friends would spend the summer traveling across the United States to pray on the Grandmother for her healing, and that she was welcome to join the group. He also gave Luna his address in Oregon, and invited her to visit his small farm and community. He was on a mission to educate people and create a better world.

There was something about Grey Coyote that resonated with her. Luna took his address down and kept a copy of the small newspaper that he published himself. She thanked him for the invitation and experience. Little did she know she would meet him again.

The Eagle Lands

Luna left the park and found a local Mexican restaurant for dinner. She went unnoticed for a while before the waitress took her order. Luna was so immersed in writing in her journal that she hardly noticed the long wait.

> *Tuesday May 4th*
> *I met Grey Coyote, an Ojibway Indian today. He has a sacred connection to the Earth. His teachings are to live in balance with the Earth. He arranges gatherings to pray for the Earth and all its creatures. He reminds people to take only what is needed to survive and to leave the land for future generations. I believe he is a good man and teacher. I hope our paths will cross again.*

Luna hardly slept on this trip. An hour or two of naps was all that she required. She bought a couple of books to read at night from one of the stores in Sedona.

The next day Luna drove to the Grand Canyon. It was a few hours away by car and was supposed to be a spectacular sight. Luna planned to spend the entire day on this excursion.

As had become her custom on this trip, she rose with the Sun. She mapped out her trip and she packed water and snacks for her trek. She reached the canyon a little after noon. The Sun had come over the canyon and had washed out its colors. Luna was disappointed.

It just looks like a big hole in the Earth, she thought.

Noticing an advertisement at a restaurant for plane rides over the canyon, she found the agency and booked an early afternoon flight. The plane was a small Cessna. Luna felt the wind gust, playing ping-pong with the plane. As Luna and another couple and the pilot flew over the massive canyon, it was hard to believe that great waters once filled and shaped these crevices many thousands of years ago. The canyon appeared drab with brown and beige tones, with only a few small green areas. The pilot said the colors were magnificent at sunset. Luna couldn't wait to get off the plane. It was too cramped and she could not hold the camera steady enough to take any pictures.

Once back on the ground, Luna drove to the other side of the canyon. The canyon had many sights to see. She spent the rest of the day anticipating the sunset. And as it came, Luna was glad she stayed to see its beauty. It was as if the Creator had placed the Sun at just the right angle to cast the shadows of red, pink and golden hues.

This was the breadth of wonder that no human being could possibly have had a hand in creating. Luna took in the glorious sight and once again offered gratitude for the beauty and being able to be here to see it. She took many pictures before the hues disappeared.

Luna decided to stay overnight at a local motel that was more expensive than the campground cabin, thinking that driving back in the dark would not be a good idea.

Better to drive in the daylight when you can see the map. The roads are too narrow and winding, she thought.

Sleep still escaped her. She dozed on and off through the night.

When the Sun rose, Luna ate a hearty breakfast and drove back to Oak Creek, making a couple of gas and rest stops along the way. She was back by early afternoon and noticed an old dusty Volkswagen van as she pulled into the campground. Next to the van stood five longhaired men, two of whom were darker skinned Native American Indians. One man was gray haired and older, maybe seventy. He had a large presence. He was tall and thin, and wore a red plaid shirt, a buckskin vest, and old cowboy boots.

He must be Red Eagle.

They were unloading duffle bags, tents and backpacks. They checked in at the main cabin. Luna followed them into the building. The manager was not as polite to them as he had been to Luna when she first arrived. She had seen the distrust in the manager's eyes as he looked at the group. They were going to set up camp in tents, not in a cabin.

The tent fee must be more affordable, Luna surmised to herself.

"You have a small group for the lecture," the manager informed.

"Hau, that's good," Red Eagle replied.

The elder looked at Luna and smiled. Luna smiled back.

"Come to the talk tomorrow?" he asked.

"Oh, yes," Luna replied.

"Want to help out?" he asked.

"Sure," she said.

"Come by later," he added. And then he turned and walked into the woods with the small group.

Come by later? Luna wondered what that meant. *Did that mean in an hour or two? And what am I going to help with?*

She had agreed without even asking. Feeling like a child, questions filled her mind. She remembered Cyrus telling her numerous times to just listen and pay attention.

This is going to be interesting, she thought.

There was a knock on her cabin door late in the afternoon. She opened it. There he stood, with a big smile and twinkling eyes, seemingly full of mischief with an old cowboy hat on his head and his long braids wrapped in red cloth. He had a leather pouch around his neck. *It must be his medicine bag,* she thought. His jeans had worn thin at the knees. His smile revealed that he was missing his front teeth.

"You, come now?" he asked.

"Sure," Luna could not help smiling back.

"Look there and help. Find the Grandfathers," the elder was pointing to the ground.

"What? Find the Grandfathers?" Luna was confused.

"Yes, the stones are our Grandfathers. They are the bones of Grandmother Earth. They hold her together and support her. Here, take this tobacco, make a prayer for stone nation to come to you and offer themselves for the purification ceremony. Like this."

He offered the tobacco up to the Sky and to all the directions and below to the ground, and then let the wind take it. Luna repeated the process. Although she couldn't speak the foreign language he spoke, she made her own private prayer of gratitude.

"Okay, go now." He gave her a gentle push into the woods.

She came upon the other members of his group and watched them find stones the size of a human head. A young man named Max offered her assistance.

"Listen for them to speak to your heart. They will tell you where they are. Then ask them if they will give their life in ceremony for the people. You will know. If they lift easily from the ground, take them and offer a pinch of tobacco in gratitude. If they don't lift, leave the stone be. Gather them and put them in the pile that we started over there," he motioned.

"How many do we need?" she asked.

"Grandpa Red Eagle will let us know when we have enough. The spirits will tell him."

"Oh, okay," she said.

Luna's mind was racing with excitement.

Did he say spirits? Like dead spirits? He can see and talk to spirits?

It took a couple of hours to gather the stones. It was a silent process and one that brought Luna much joy. She *was* able to hear the stones clearly.

I wonder if Red Eagle is also on a mission.

The group walked in silence back to their camp area. Luna proceeded to turn back toward her cabin when Grandpa called to her.

"You come tomorrow. Help again," he said with a smile.

"Sure." Luna nodded her head and smiled back. She didn't worry about when she had to be there. Luna had a feeling he would find her.

Luna made drip coffee for the morning before she went to bed, with the intent of reheating the coffee in a metal pan at dawn.

Early morning, as the coffee was warming, there was a knock on the door. She opened the door and Red Eagle stood there smiling. His hair was again in braids with red cloth ties and wore his black cowboy hat.

"Time to pray to the Morning Star and Sun, we must build a lodge for purification. Come," he said, as he turned to start the walk into the woods.

Luna shut off the small burner and followed. Coffee would have to wait this morning. The group was gathered again. The elder lit a large ball of sage and set it aflame in a half shell. Everyone gathered in a circle. The smoke was fanned from the top of each person's head down to their feet and all around each person. Red Eagle explained that sage was used for purification and to put each person in a focused, sacred place and to clear one's thoughts and heart. Luna enjoyed the aroma and the ritual. It was similar to what her Grandma Anna used.

The elder offered a tobacco prayer to each of the directions and asked that, "The spirits be with us as we begin to build the Earth lodge for purification."

Careful attention was paid to select saplings of the right size and shape. The procedure was very loving and compassionate. The men in the group slowly bent the saplings into a round domelike structure. Luna was asked to tie them together in a specific way, which she did respectfully. The ground inside the dome had already been prepared. A hole was dug in the center of the structure and the soil was placed outside the structure in a special location and manner. Luna was amazed at how low the woven frame of saplings was to the ground. One would have to crawl on their hands and knees to go inside the dome. The structure was then covered with blankets and animal skins. Red Eagle explained that this was to keep the visible light out. It took most of the day to finish building the domed structure, which they called a *lodge*. When it was completed, Grandfather Red Eagle said that it was good and the spirits would approve.

Max offered Luna some of the beans and rice he was cooking on a small camping stove. Luna thanked him and said she was going to eat at the little café in town instead. Max reminded Luna that the lecture was around dusk that evening. The talk would be held outside, in front of a small camp fire that he and the other men would build. People could sit on the chairs that were provided by the campground or on the ground. He said the lecture would start when the spirits decided, possibly at dusk. The lesson of *spirit time* would be one for Luna to learn to embrace in future years.

Luna took a shower to freshen up and had a quick dinner in town. She was back early enough to help set up the chairs and blankets around the fire. The place chosen for the lecture was in a beautiful circle of large pine trees in the woods, not far from the secluded hidden spot where the lodge structure was built. The campers gathered early to find well-positioned and comfortable camp chairs.

A large drum and two chairs were stationed at the front of the circle. Luna guessed that was where the elder would sit. Luna was very much at ease with the outdoor seating and the fresh smell of pine and wood smoke. It was very relaxing. The thirty or so people who gathered in the circle were full of anticipation. Red Eagle and Max came down from the path in the woods. Max sat in the chair near the drum. Max started drumming and Red Eagle started to sing in his native tongue.

His voice was guttural, high pitched and melodious. The song was emotional and gave Luna goose bumps. It was moving and powerful. People clapped when the song was done. Red Eagle gave a look to everyone and started to laugh. He said it was a prayer to Spirit and they didn't have to clap for a prayer. It wasn't a show.

His lecture was full of joking and laughter, mostly at life and how people perceive him and the Indians. He said Spirit had told him that he needed to help all of the races of people to clean themselves up and learn how to be caretakers of the Earth. He talked of being born of spirit from the womb of the Grandmother Earth. Her clay and dirt is our body and our kinship. That is where the first breath we take comes from as we enter the world. We are all the same. We are all red people. We all have the same red blood inside, no matter what color our skin is on the outside. We all have male and female aspects inside of us. Man from the Sky and woman from the Earth. Just like the Sacred Pipe. The stem from the tree reaches to the Sky. That part is man. The bowl from the clay is from Earth. That part is woman. We all have the same spirit light inside us from the Great Spirit Mystery of the Sky and stars. Red Eagle talked about the stars and the races of other beings.

"They are real," he said. "They have been coming here for a long time trying to help us learn many things. They are trying to save us pitiful two-legged from destroying the Grandmother. The Indian way is to take only what you need and leave the rest for the future generations. Use all parts of the tree and the animals you hunt. Offer gratitude for the old ones who have passed on and to all life forms that help you in your life here. Live in balance with all creatures of the Earth and the Sky, not just the human two-legged. Folks take too much, want too much and are never happy. They always want more. Greed and power destroy. They want the green frogskin to make them happy. It is only paper, not real power like the wind, thunder or fire."

Max explained later to Luna that *frogskin* was the word Red Eagle used for money.

Luna understood this man's words and heart. It was the same teachings as the beings from the other stars. She felt a warm connection to this elder. He was simple with no frills and no ego. He seemed to genuinely love people. He was always smiling, joking and laughing.

He talked of growing up on a reservation. He revealed that spirits communicate with him. He made it seem very normal and mundane. But to Luna, those parts of her gifts seemed far from normal. The lecture lasted into the wee hours of the morning. The Sun had gone down. The Sky grew black. The stars danced and twinkled from far away. He talked on and on, and in between, he sang songs while Max drummed for him. The drumbeat was soothing. Luna rocked back and forth on the ground. As Luna looked around the circle, she noticed many people had closed their eyes and fallen asleep. Red Eagle paid no attention. He continued his talk and songs.

Hours later, he ended by saying, "Hau, that's all for now." He rose from the chair and walked down the path to his tent. As he passed Luna, he winked at her and said, "Tomorrow."

It was four in the morning. Luna couldn't believe how quickly the time had passed. He had talked for almost eight hours non-stop. Of course it was slow-paced and relaxed, but eight hours. The donation hardly felt like it was enough for all the elder had shared.

And what did he mean when he said *tomorrow* to her? The lecture was only for Friday night. Luna didn't know what was in store for tomorrow, but she knew she would like to talk to Red Eagle about the stars and the beings.

Luna arose at noon to some rustling outside the cabin. She peeked outside and saw Max.

"Hey there," he called to her with a wave.

"Hi," Luna waved back.

"Grandpa is having a purification ceremony later tonight. He asked me to invite you and six other campers who were at the lecture last night. Did you want to join us?"

"Oh, that was nice of him. But why did he ask me?" Luna asked.

"We never question him. The spirits tell him things and we do as he asks to honor him. You aren't on your Moon are you? You know your menses? I don't like to ask about those things. We usually have a woman around to ask, but none are traveling with us this trip. You can't be a part of ceremony if you are on your Moon," Max explained.

"Why not?" she asked.

"Well, I will try to explain. It has to do with a woman being in her own ceremony in her body. The two ceremonies don't mix; one goes up to the Great Spirit and the other goes down to the Earth Grandmother. Both are powerful. But they don't mix together. A woman's Moon releases and connects to the Earth power and purification connects to the Sky power. They go in opposite directions. That's the best I can explain it."

"Oh. Well, anyway, I am not on my Moon," she said.

"Great. Then join us late afternoon or so. Red Eagle will offer teachings on the ceremony and then we will light the fire. You will need to gift tobacco to him and to the firekeeper and the singer if you have some. It is out of respect and gratitude."

He turned and headed down the path in the woods to his tent.

Luna took a quick shower and headed to town for lunch and to buy some packages of tobacco. She met Max when she returned from lunch. Max explained to her what type of modest clothing she should wear for the purification ceremony.

Luna gathered the things she needed and headed down the trail to where the ceremony would be. She recognized faces from the lecture the night before. Five other people were sitting in the camp chairs. Luna sat on the ground. The elder explained why purification was necessary.

"Going back to Grandmother's womb inside the lodge, reminds us of when we came from our human mother. We go back to be reborn. We clean ourselves up from all body, mind and spirit messes that we make for ourselves. It makes us clean and whole again. We take the Grandfather stones and heat them with fire. Then we put a green herb on the stones to honor them. And last, we pour water on the stones and make the steam to breathe in. We get our breath of life back, clean from the inside out. It is a powerful prayer. We sing and ask for help. The spirits hear us and come in and help us like that, to be cleaned up and made new."

Red Eagle explained how to make prayer ties out of tobacco and cloth. He said that normally in the old days, he would not have ceremony with men and women together, but the spirits told him otherwise lately. He explained the appropriate dress for men and women that were needed so as not to distract each other. He gave teachings for about two hours while the Sacred Fire was built. Luna watched as the fire was being built. It was made in the same way as her vision teaching from Red Burning Sky, except the firekeeper was placing stones in the fire.

The firekeeper lit the fire in solemn prayer. After appropriate teaching and practice, each person sat quietly and made their prayer ties. Later, everyone changed clothes for the ceremony. Luna had to make do with a fairly new dress that she was planning to wear on the flight home. It would now get muddy from the water and the dirt inside the lodge, but she didn't care. She wanted to honor and respect what was required.

As the time to start ceremony neared, Luna started to get nervous. Her stomach was jumpy and a little queasy. What if she had to go to the bathroom? As a child, she was generally fearless. Now all of a sudden, every fear she could imagine came to her. *Will it be too hot? Max said it could get over 200 degrees in there. Will I be able to breathe? Could I die?*

Luna took a deep breath to calm herself. She never worried about death.

What is this emotional fear?

She trusted the gentleness of Red Eagle. It was no coincidence that she came upon him here this week. How better to learn about her Native American Indian ancestry than to pay attention to what was right here in front of her. Red Eagle had said he was from a Plains tribe that once hunted the buffalo but was then forced to live on a reservation.

The elder offered a prayer in his language and called the Great Spirit, the directions and his helper spirits. Each person then crawled in on their hands and knees, humbly honoring all their relations. Inside the lodge, the women sat on one side and the men sat together on the other. There were ten people squeezed inside. The firekeeper stayed outside and brought the stones in to the elder, one by one. Red Eagle placed them in a particular way in the center pit inside. Each stone was honored in a special way and greeted with a special herb that smelled sweet as it burned on the stone. A sacred bucket of water was handed in and then the door flap was closed.

Red Eagle began to sing as the stones glowed and the heat became like fire on the skin. He sang another song and poured water on the stones. It made so much steam that it was hard to breathe. The elder had said in his earlier teachings to keep your eyes open in the dark, because you might miss something if you didn't. Luna tried to do this but the steam was hard to see through. She crouched close to the ground and gently rocked herself back and forth, listening to the songs and the beat of the drum. It helped her endure the heat. Finally the door flap opened. Steam escaped from the lodge and the cooler outside air entered the enclosed space. After catching her breath for a moment, the door flap was closed again.

More water, more steam, more prayers, more song. Luna was starting to become a little more comfortable rocking back and forth on the ground, inhaling the steam in unison with the songs. The steam filled her lungs and slowly cleared them. Toxins released from the pores of her skin. Red Eagle spoke many prayers in his language. His voice cracked as if he were weeping. Luna started to fill up with tears. She didn't understand what he was saying, but she felt the emotion as he prayed for all of them in the lodge. He was filled with love and compassion, humbly asking the spirits to help all of them. Luna began to sob, releasing her tears. Surrendering all that ached in her heart, all of her secrets and fears. Before she realized it, the door flap was open and she was still sobbing on her hands and knees, with her head bent to the ground.

Luna finally lifted her head and saw Red Eagle looking at her through the dim light of the fire outside.

Red Eagle just smiled and said, "Good stuff, huh?"

Luna wiped her eyes and had to laugh, and everyone else inside chuckled too. Everyone was releasing laughter and tears. More hot stones were brought in, many more in fact. Then the door flap went down. Lots of water splashed onto the stones. The stones sizzled so loudly that it sounded like they were singing. Red Eagle was silent. He let the stones sing almost the entire time. Luna remembered the familiar song from her vision with Sweet Willow Woman.

Luna looked up to the top of the lodge, and saw a buffalo in the darkness. *Was it a ghost?* It started to charge at her from the air. Luna closed her eyes and then opened them. She was nose to nose with the buffalo and could feel his wet nose and heated breath on her face. Luna saw his front hooves lift up and offer her a stick of some kind. As she looked closer, it was a large smoking pipe covered with buffalo hair. He was offering it to her. As soon as she recognized this, the buffalo was gone.

The door flap was opened again and the steam from the inside was released. Luna sat there in silence wondering what to make of this.

Then Red Eagle said, "We had a spirit come to visit, one from the four-legged nation. It was good."

I wonder if he saw what I saw, she thought. *Maybe I'll ask him later.*

The door flap came down for the final time. More water was poured and more singing. And then it happened, just as in her vision. The top of the lodge became like the night Sky, filled with twinkling lights. It was a blanket of many tiny white lights. Luna could see everyone's face in the lodge as if there was a bright spotlight shining inside. She saw that most of the people inside had their eyes closed. Four of the blue lights started to enlarge until they became faces. Luna recognized them. They were the spirit guides; Red Burning Sky, Sweet Willow Woman, White Running Trail and another face who spoke.

"I am Smooth Clay Face, Granddaughter. You have now experienced the Earth element. She is part of your body. You come from her. You have laid on her and wept on her. She has cleaned you and made you new again. Walk gently on her and protect her. Here is where you find your Home on the Earth Star. Here in this lodge, inside your Grandmother's womb you will heal. You must bridge the Earth to the Sky. We can see you and hear you. This is where you find peace with your mission on this Earth Star. Search no more. Within this lodge is your Home. Come here and balance when it is too hard and you need help with being a human. Your Earth ancestors knew how to bridge where all life begins and returns. Live here and complete your mission," she said.

And in a flash they were gone. The door flap opened up for the last time. A Sacred Ceremonial Pipe was passed and everyone smoked. Luna again remembered her teachings from Red Burning Sky and knew what to do. When it was completed, everyone crawled out of the lodge and hugged each other. Red Eagle hugged everyone too. He came to Luna and smiled as he spoke.

"The spirits had a good time with you. The buffalo came and offered the path of the sacred to you, the way of your ancestors. Spirit wants you to walk the road of your ancestors. You have spirit helpers. Call on them for help. Sky helpers from the stars are real too," Red Eagle laughed.

Luna thought, *some people might think that Red Eagle is strange or weird. But he doesn't care and isn't afraid. He's an old warrior with many scars. Amazing, he saw what I had seen in the lodge. Finally, I know I am not alone here. Another person can see what I see.*

It was the first time someone else had confirmed her experiences as real. Luna was so happy she started to cry again, but this time, they were tears of joy. She had found someone who made her feel okay, not abnormal. Someone hopefully she could talk to, who would believe her and whom she could learn from here on the Earth. He was a real, human, spiritual being. Luna was happy she came to Arizona.

Since she had to leave for home the next day, she needed to ask Max how she could keep in touch with Red Eagle. As she started through the woods to her cabin to change into dry clothes, Max called to her.

"Grandpa wants to see you. After you change, come to his tent for some food. We will have a feast, a communal supper."

Luna changed her clothes and sat down with the group to eat some buffalo meat, corn, rice and beans, and berries. They offered a plate to the spirits first with a prayer. Grandpa motioned for her to come and sit by him. She carefully obliged.

"Spirit said you come on the road with us tomorrow. We will go to Utah for a couple of days," he commanded.

"But I'm leaving to go back home to New England tomorrow. That's on the east coast," she replied.

"No. Spirit said you are home now. This road takes you and keeps you home as a human being. You saw it in the lodge, a way to bridge the Grandmother Earth to the Sky. You need to purify. You will have many before you go back East."

Luna was dumbfounded. Her flight left tomorrow, on Sunday. She had to go back to work on Monday.

What did he not understand? She could not just take off and follow him on the road... or could she? She could not quit her job. No, that was irresponsible. Mom and Dad would have a fit. She sat in silence and pondered.

"No good thinking too much. It messes you up and ties you in a ball," Grandpa joked.

Luna returned to her cabin fully expecting to leave tomorrow.

Was this the beginning of a new journey, learning how to bridge the Earth and Sky world?

The stars didn't seem so far away any more. There was a way she had now seen, to be close to them while living in her human body. Although she knew it would take many years to fully understand her mission and hopefully complete it, tonight she felt less alone and forgotten. She had hope.

This man Red Eagle had vision and internal power. She knew he had many teachings for her.

Should I go with him? Quit my job? Is this why I was lead to come here?

Luna sat outside the cabin and looked up into the night Sky.

Luna thought, *I have met a man connected to the ancestors. I have much to learn from this elder, Red Eagle. Should I go with him*, she wondered as she looked into the beyond.

Three stars twinkled, catching her attention and shot across the night Sky one after the other. Luna knew it was an affirmation to go on this journey with Red Eagle. She would cancel her flight and change her ticket for when this traveling journey was over. She would call her supervisor and ask for a leave of absence and would quit if he didn't grant the leave. She would tell her parents that she was extending her trip and would keep in touch and hoped they would understand. Luna's mind was made up. Little did she know that this journey would last for seven years, with many purifications; at least three a week in different towns, ending each year in Montana.

On The Road

The next morning Luna drove to Sedona to find a pay phone to call her parents and cancel her afternoon flight. The call home was tense. Claire and Tom were frantic.

"Luna, you are going on the road with this unknown Indian man and his group?" Claire gasped. "Luna, talk to your father."

Claire handed the phone to Tom.

"Luna, you don't know who they are. They could be thieves, drifters or bums. Luna, come home," Tom demanded.

"Dad, I can't. I need to learn the way of the Indian ancestors. This man will teach me. Grandma taught me a few things, but I want to learn more. Dad, I'm old enough now. I'll be alright. I'll call you every week to tell you where I am. Don't worry," she assured him.

"But how will you eat? Where will you sleep? You'll be living poorly. You're not used to that," he cautioned.

Claire grabbed the phone from Tom and cried into the phone.

"Luna, come home. You hear me? Come home now!" she yelled.

"Sorry Mom, but I can't. I have to do this. I love you, Mom. It will work out okay. I know this in my heart. I'm not a child anymore. Please don't be upset. I'll call and write every week. Love you," Luna choked.

She hung up the phone with tears in her eyes. This was the right thing to do. But it was hard to detach from the only family she knew on Earth. Luna did not know how long this journey would be, but she had to follow her heart.

Luna pulled her emotions together and called the supervisor at work.

"Luna, I am sorry, but I cannot hold your job for you. I'm sorry you're not returning. You've been a great worker. Give me a call when you return and we'll see if we have any openings. Good luck," Mr. Williams replied.

Well it's done, Luna thought.

She had opened her life to who knows what. A small panic filled her stomach. She took several deep breaths to relax. *This is the right thing,* she told herself. *I'm just scared. It's normal to be anxious when your life is about to change, right?*

Luna rambled back and forth until calmness swept over her. It was as if all her guides surrounded her with love and assurance, and this comforted her.

She drove back to the campground to meet Red Eagle, Max and the others. They followed her to the next airport where she'd return her rental car. Luna became the sixth person in the van, and added her suitcase to the small trailer the van was towing.

She would now be on the road with five men of all ages and with many stories to tell.

Sam Butler was in his fifties, and was the oldest behind Grandpa Red Eagle. He was a recovering alcoholic. He had been sober for fifteen years and followed the Native American path, or the Red Road, as he put it. He had a long salt-and-pepper ponytail. He wore an old straw hat and worn cowboy boots. His thin tall frame disguised his well developed bicep muscles. He was the firekeeper in the purification ceremony. He built, maintained and was one with the fire. He handled the Grandfather stones and wood with great honor and reverence. He had been on the road with Red Eagle since his sobriety.

Clint Black Horn was a dark skinned man. He was a full-blood like Red Eagle. He was in his forties and was the set-up man. He set up the tents and camp and special ceremony altars for the elder. He also set the dates for the lectures. He was a handsome man with dark eyes and long black hair that he always wore in braids. He smoked hand rolled cigarettes and drank lots of black coffee. His tribe was Blackfoot, and he too was raised on the reservation. He was an alcoholic and had been sober for ten years. He hooked up with Red Eagle ten years ago and asked to help him get clean. He had been on the road ever since.

Willie Sturgis was in his late forties. He was a large, heavy-set man. He loved to eat and his body size proved it. He was the gentle giant. Willie looked like a mean bull but was a teddy bear of a man. His front teeth were crooked and his laugh was loud and infectious. His demeanor was easy-going and happy. He loaded and unloaded the van and trailer, and did the wood splitting. He was also the mechanic and handy man. He could fix and duct tape almost everything. His hairline was receding and his gray hair was thin. He tied it back in a ponytail. He had a rosy complexion and sweated profusely.

The last of the group was Max McKenzie. Max was in his late twenties. He had been with Red Eagle since graduating college. His mother had died and he was in a lot of grief. The elder took him on the road as his student. Max was a red-headed, freckle faced man, with clear blue eyes and wild, thick, wavy hair. He also tied it back in a ponytail, and wore a red bandana around his forehead. Max was serious and quiet. He was the singer and Red Eagle's right hand warrior. He saw to the elder's food and whatever he needed to be comfortable. Max had great love and respect for Red Eagle.

What a group these men were. How will I fit in? What will my role be in this small tribe of unique individuals? Only time will tell.

"Next stop Utah," Max announced.

The group laughed and shared stories of the road. Being on the road with these men and hearing their stories became the fondest experiences of her journey.

Luna quickly became part of the crew. Her role was to handle the domestics, washing laundry at the local laundromat or by hand in rest stop sinks. She hung the laundry on a line in the trees at the campground when they rested. Some nights they slept in the van sitting up when money was tight. She became efficient at cooking, but learning to cook over a campfire took some time. It took several attempts to keep from burning the beans and rice. The men never complained, but Luna was sure they choked on some of her early cooking disasters. Everyone lost weight during her first month on the road.

The toughest time for Luna was when meat was gifted to the group. Luna had to learn how to skin, gut and cook the animal without wasting much. Clint patiently taught her the process. They were given lamb, but more often deer. Chickens were tough too, with the feather plucking and boiling.

These men quickly became her uncles and protectors. She learned the Red Road by experiencing ceremony and living a simpler way. It was a life that involved hard work. But it had its rewards. Learning to appreciate everything and clearly seeing the beauty in everything as one and connected.

Lecture days were happy ones for Luna. She enjoyed Red Eagle's lectures. Each one was different. He talked about whatever came to his mind from the Great Spirit. He definitely followed, and was guided by, his connection to the spirit world. His teachings always involved connecting the Sacred Hoop. He reminded people that every living thing had the same breath of life, and connected to everything in the universe. It was Luna's favorite teaching.

The purification ceremonies lifted her spirit and mind. When the group was traveling, the elder held the purification ceremony three nights a week. Luna had personal time with Red Eagle once or twice every week. These were her most precious days. She listened closely. He always talked about whatever she had on her mind, without Luna ever having to ask the questions.

"Look and listen with your eyes and heart. It is how we go to school," he would say. "You can't learn if you're always talking. You need to be quiet."

Red Eagle asked Luna to call him *Grandpa*. It was an endearing name to him and he wanted Luna to feel as comfortable and at home as the others.

A couple of months later Luna asked about the stars.

"Grandpa, have you ever seen beings from other stars?" she asked.

"Hau, the little people," he grinned.

"When did you see them?" she asked again.

"They came when I was little, maybe three or four years old. They would teach me and show me things. They are *real*, Luna. But most folks don't believe. Someday, there will be many of them here to see and they won't be a secret. Folks will think they're going crazy," he laughed.

"Grandpa, I've seen them too. I have seen beings on other stars. Some are reptilian, some are metallic humanoids and others are like insects."

Luna waited for his response, biting her lip.

"Hau, there are many stars, many kinds of beings. But only one spirit fire connects them all from the same place as you and me," he added.

Luna sighed in relief. He believed her. She had just shared her deepest secret. And it was no big deal. It was accepted. No questions. No criticism. Nothing she had to keep quiet about. The weight of the world had just been lifted off her shoulders. The load was lighter.

"Luna, I will teach you the Earth way, the way of the ancestors. It is simple but hard to follow. It is a narrow road but a good one. I will teach you how to be a human being. Just learn to live and respect your relations. Finned ones, winged ones, four legged, creepy crawlers and the hardest of all, the two legged. Human beings are weak and the hardest to love. We make bad choices and always want more. We think we're smart because we have a brain. Sometimes we're just stupid. We look far ahead for what's next and we forget what is now right here. Learn to walk on the Earth with all of your relations," he stated.

Luna took those words to heart. It was hard to live and be human. She always felt separate and different. She had a body like them but her mind was different. *She* remembered the Center.

After four months of traveling through Arizona, Utah, New Mexico, and Colorado they finally came to Montana. The place for the lecture was a small bookstore with an outside patio that faced the mountains. The landscape surrounding the bookstore was gorgeous with the snow crest top against the clear blue Sky. There were twenty people seated outside this September afternoon.

Max unloaded the large drum. Willie and Sam set up a small display of crafts to sell. Bone chokers, deer skin pouches, antler necklaces, sweet grass braids and wrapped dried sage bundles that the group had gathered from the side roads and fields on their travels. The money helped with food and traveling expenses. The donation money was barely enough to get to the next town.

Red Eagle sang his opening prayer before starting the lecture. Max was on the drum beating it in rhythm. Luna was ready to take her seat among the people when a lady motioned to her, calling her away from the lecture. Luna quietly left and approached her. The woman was in her sixties and had her hair twisted in a bun. She wore heavy makeup and adorned herself with large stoned jewelry on her neck, ears, wrists and hands. She wore a long black dress with a flowered velvet shawl around her shoulders. Luna followed her into a tiny room that had a small table, two chairs, cards, incense and a white flamed candle.

"Here dear, have a seat. I would like to give you a reading. I have been reading for over forty years. I have never seen an aura such as yours. Your colors are so bright that they illuminate the room. My name is Olivia," she spoke.

"Thank you, but I don't really want a reading. I don't have the money to pay for one, but thank you anyways."

Luna began to stand but Olivia pulled her arm gently.

"No, please sit. I am called to do this. No payment is necessary. Take this deck of playing cards and shuffle them. You'll put your energy into the cards and then I'll read them."

Luna wondered why this woman needed cards. *Why can't she just see into my mind? Why does she need these props?*

"It is because people need to focus on something while I read their field of energy. It helps build the story and confirm what I see," Olivia answered.

Luna realized she had asked the question in her mind and not out loud, and yet Olivia answered her thoughts.

Luna smiled back, "Okay."

Luna shuffled and Olivia placed the cards in a pattern as she read.

"You have secrets that make you feel separate from others. You need to build relationships and be yourself at all times. Stop hiding. You came to do something. You must complete it. Do not forget that. You are among this group of people. They are good for you. You will learn much. You must use your gift of insight. You are a powerful being yet you hide who you really are. You need to be true to yourself. You will be with this group for a long time. You should be reading like me. You have the gift. Do you have any questions for me?" Olivia asked.

"Well, what is my gift? What is my secret? How long will I be with Grandpa?" Luna asked.

"Your gift is that you can see energy and you hear and understand things very clearly. You see other realms which most people fear. You struggle with life here. You struggle with human beings. You need to accept yourself as one of us. You are human. The Indian man will help you with that. You will be with him a few years."

Olivia took the cards and put them back in the deck. She began to shuffle them.

"Now you read me," she laughed.

Olivia placed the deck in a fan pattern in front of Luna and chose the cards for Luna to read.

"But I don't need these," Luna said firmly.

She closed her eyes and entered Olivia's energy field.

"Your mother was a reader. She taught you her craft. She is here now."

Luna opened her eyes and before her she saw an old face with a beautiful smile.

"She says her name is Adele."

Olivia almost lost her false dentures. She was shocked. Then a wave of emotion brought tears to her eyes.

"Is she really here?" Olivia asked.

"It is okay that you placed her in a nursing home. Do not feel guilty anymore. She is happy and wants you to be happy. You should retire from reading. She knows it doesn't bring you joy. You have used what she has taught you but you need to be painting again," Luna stated.

"Oh my, I did feel bad I could no longer take care of her. I loved painting when I was younger. I became a reader like my mother. But I always loved to paint," said Olivia choking on her words. "Thank you, dear. Thank you, Mother."

"She is gone now," Luna confirmed.

"Here, I want you to take my cards as a gift and work with them. You will know when to begin reading for others. I know you may not need to use them but it helps the client to focus their energy. Some people are not open enough and it helps them calm down. It will give their mind a place to focus," Olivia said gratefully.

Luna accepted the cards, hugged Olivia and returned to the lecture. She reflected on the cards and the meeting of Olivia.

Me, a reader? As if I don't have enough secrets. How will I explain this to my parents?

Olivia had said that Luna would know when it was time to read. She also stated that Luna would be on the road for several years. Luna certainly did not believe that. She figured she would go home for Christmas.

The lecture ended and they were back on the road. They camped an hour down the road. Everyone was busy with their chores. Luna boiled the water for coffee over a campfire. The drip process took a long time, but she became an expert at it. Grandpa greeted her at the fire. Luna made him a cup and as he sat down on a camp chair.

"Grandpa, I met a woman at the lecture today. She was an intuitive reader. Olivia said I had a gift of being able to read people and believed I could earn a living with it. What do you think?" she asked.

"Hau, you must use your gifts that Great Spirit gave you. But you must use them with love and honesty. You must be sure that people do not turn their power over to you. That is the black road of greed and ego. If you give guidance, help them empower themselves. You will know when the time is right. As for the frogskin, it is not wrong to earn a living if it is honest. Just make sure it is for the right reason and stay in balance," he replied.

Luna sat with the cards each night and asked for insights on what each card represented. She wrote it all down in a small notebook. It took two months to complete. She laid the cards out in several patterns until she found one that felt right. The cross of the four directions was the one she chose. North to South was the present situation or road. West represented the influences and things of the past, while the East was the future, the new beginning. It was all intuitively given to her until she had full knowledge of the cards. She worked alone with them for several months.

The winter months brought the group back to Grandpa's home in Montana. It was a small shack with two bedrooms, a large fireplace, and a small kitchen that had a gas stove. The outhouse was in the backyard. On the west side of the cabin was an uncovered willow framed lodge. He also had a couple of old trailers on the land that barely looked inhabitable.

Luna figured she would go back to New England, but Grandpa had other ideas.

"Luna, you need to go on the hill. You must prepare. Spirit wants to speak with you. Must know who you are, your direction for life, and what you can do for the People," he said seriously. "You stay here to prepare. Take the white trailer."

Luna never questioned Red Eagle.

Panicked, she ran outside to talk to Max. Clint, Sam and Willie lived in the yellow trailer, and Max lived in the house with Grandpa.

"Max, what does he mean *prepare*?" she asked.

She had heard about the stories of questing on the hill. It was another spiritual ceremony between the quester and the Great Spirit, or *Spirit* as Grandpa said. It was done from one to four days. It was usually done four times but Red Eagle had quested many times. It was a way a person could ask an important question about one's life and direction. It was not taken lightly. One would have to prepare for a year or longer with prayer and fasting.

"You must learn to fast from food and water slowly over the year. You start with a few hours at a time and then you gradually increase the fasting hours. You will learn how to prepare your altar prayer ties and you will be purifying a lot over the next year. Grandpa will teach you the prayers to sing to Spirit," Max explained.

"How long will I stay on the hill?" she asked.

"Grandpa will tell you. Spirit will tell him. It will probably be one night since you are new to this. But he will let you know. Don't worry, he will prepare you well," he replied.

Christmas came and went. Luna's family was disappointed she did not return home. They were emotional when she called Christmas Eve from a pay phone at a local food mart. Luna sent her love as always, and thanked them for the new sweater, scarf and mittens they sent her for Christmas. She greatly appreciated the small amount of cash they also sent. Of course, Luna spent it on food for the group for the winter months.

In the prior month before their arrival at Grandpa's home, it snowed heavily and they had to sleep in the van, taking shifts turning the heat on and off. There were plenty of times when the van broke down and they missed the scheduled lectures. But in those times, they would find people who were generous enough to fix the van, and provide them with meals and a place to stay for the night.

Luna's experiences on the road proved to her that there were many good human beings with generous hearts and minds. She became a firm believer that the human heart was caring and generous, even though she met a few not-so-kind humans who protested, ridiculed them and shut down the lectures because of their religious beliefs.

The campgrounds were the best place for lectures because Grandpa would run a purification ceremony that was not part of the lecture. It was for the traveling group and sometimes one or two invited guests.

An old trailer on Grandpa's land would be her home for many months of the preparation. Luna continued her domestic chores of cooking, laundry and cleaning. She mended shirts and pants and darned socks. But she also learned about being in ceremony and living simply. They arose every morning at dawn and faced the sunrise in prayer. And they faced the sunset every evening at dusk in prayer. Grandpa also taught her the prayer songs to sing when she would be on the hill.

Luna traveled locally with Grandpa when he was called upon to perform healing ceremonies. Sometimes a lodge would need to be built. At other times, he would only work from his bundle of sacred things. Luna observed healings from skin infections, stomach pain, mental problems and even cancer. Red Eagle explained that *he* did not heal anyone. Spirit did the healing. He just prayed on behalf of the person needing the healing and directed attention to that person. Spirit worked with him and through him.

Luna loved these ceremonies. She assisted Grandpa with herbal preparations and applications when they were required. They would stay up to four days with the patient needing his help. The family would feed and set up a place for Luna, Max and Grandpa to sleep. Luna was taught many healing mixtures. Each one was unique, because as Grandpa said, "Each person is different. Each needs a different medicine."

Grandpa explained that the body could heal itself but the mind could get in the way. The mind worries, has negative thoughts, gets sad and focuses on emotions like anger and resentment. The mind causes all the imbalances that create a loss of spirit that can eat away at the body and cause disease.

"We treat the spirit first, then we treat the mind and heart, then last we treat the body," he stated.

Luna wondered how one could keep one's balance.

"Grandpa, how do we keep our self in balance? Our minds cannot just shut off," she asked.

"We need fresh air, clean water, clean food, enough sleep, sunshine, moving the body to keep in shape and good thoughts. What we put in and around our bodies will become us. We must take care of it. Hate, jealousy, anger, sadness, and worry hurts the muscles, blood and nerves. It takes away our energy. When we feel tense we must rest and relax. Be quiet and breathe. Slow things down. Empty the mind and let the body do what it knows how to do naturally without thinking. Folks talk and think too much about tomorrow. Folks aren't grateful. They never say thank you to the Great Spirit for what they do have. They always want more and focus on what they don't have. They look outside for happiness and collect things to make them happy. Happy is in *here*," he said as he pointed to his heart.

Luna learned a lot from him. She learned to stay calm and laugh in tough times and how to be happy inside with very few possessions. The little rundown camper became her palace. She limited her personal belongings to only what would fit in a small suitcase. She wanted nothing more. She had seen poverty and tough circumstances on her healing trips with Grandpa. He never charged for the healings. People would generously gift him their possessions, coffee, tobacco, a blanket, food, whatever they had as gratitude to seal the healing. Grandpa's mission was to help and teach the people and he did it with grace and humility.

The Quest

Luna had been with Red Eagle for nearly two years. She had made preparations all year for her quest on the hill, through purification, fasting and prayer. The simple question was to ask the Great Spirit, *who am I and why am I here?* Luna remembered her mission but didn't really understand it and how she could accomplish it. Grandpa told her that she needed to know herself before she could know what she needed to do here and how to serve the People.

Luna was twenty-one. She was far away from her family. Although she wrote her family and called regularly, she wondered if she would ever go back to New England.

The fasting preparations were hard. No water or food for hours. In the beginning her stomach growled and made noises, reminding her of her hunger and thirst. Praying helped her focus her attention elsewhere, but it was a slow process. She fasted from only food at first, gradually increasing the fasts until they lasted for over twenty-four hours. Then she abstained from both food and water and increased the duration of her fasts until she completed twenty-four hours. Fasting from water was harder for her than fasting from food. She craved water. When she was thirsty, it became tougher to focus on prayers. Max told Luna she was lucky that Red Eagle had pity on her and was only putting her up on the hill for one day this time. Luna could not imagine four days and nights. She was grateful, very grateful.

The quest day came and Luna was as prepared as she could be. The Great Spirit would have to help her with the rest. She purified in the lodge and then Grandpa and Max escorted her up the high hill. Grandpa's people prayed on the same hill for many years. It was about a twenty minute walk straight up. Luna had climbed the hill, prayed on the spot, and offered tobacco to the land many times during her preparation. Grandpa sang to the spirits to let them know she was coming. As Luna prayed silently, time seemed to stand still. Luna was relaxed, her senses heightened.

When they arrived, the small area was already prepared in a sacred manner. Willie and Max set up her blankets and altar in a small space before the Sun rose. The place was only large enough to sit or stand. But it would be her home for the next day and night. It was beautiful, with colored prayer ties in every direction.

Luna stepped into the altar and Red Eagle closed her in with no communication. His final instructions were given when she was inside the purification lodge.

"Make your prayers and ask your question. Then listen and pay attention. Spirit may bring you an animal, insect or bird with a message. The wind or Sky may show you something. Stay awake. If you are lucky, the Great Spirit may give you a message. Cry for your vision," he said.

Max and Grandpa left and walked down the hill in silence with their backs to her. Luna became overwhelmed with emotion. She was now alone. No human contact for the day and night. It was now about eight o'clock in the morning, only a few hours after sunrise. Luna's emotion brought back memories of Cyrus and her feelings of abandonment when he left her. She missed her grandmother Anna, her parents and Leana. She hadn't told them about the quest because she didn't want them to worry. Here she was, alone and immersed in nature. Grandpa said that some people have died while seeking their vision.

What if I die? My parents wouldn't know where I am or understand this. I guess I didn't really prepare well enough.

Fear started to fill her mind. Luna did not fear death. She understood the transformation and the spirit living on. But being alone on this hill brought up many hidden fears. Luna worried that every noise was that of a bear, coyote or wolf. Max told her that bobcats had been seen in the area. Her mind was racing and her heart was beating so fast that she thought it would fly out of her chest. *Calm down,* she told herself. *Relax. Breathe.*

Luna had not expected to feel fear and abandonment. She continued to breathe and stop thinking, focusing only on her breath. Eventually she calmed down and the tears stopped flowing. With reverence she rose and faced the West and began her song to let it be known she was there and what her intention was. Luna asked her question and prayed for just about every person she knew in the world and then prayed for people that she had never met. She prayed for peace in every country and continent and for every issue in the world that she could remember. Luna prayed until she was exhausted and her mind could no longer find the words. Luna looked up to the Sun, realizing it had barely moved. Grandpa said to follow the Sun and the Moon to know how much time had passed. She remembered Max's words.

"You lose track of all time on the hill. You can become lost and disorientated. You slow down and become one with nature. You must remember to stay on the blanket inside your alter. There you will be safe."

From the looks of the Sun, it had probably been less than an hour. Luna started to laugh. She felt that she had prayed so hard and long and yet only a little time had passed. She sat down on the blanket and listened. Luna was serenaded by several bird calls. She smelled the sweetness of the grass. She watched the ants and spiders crawl on the ground. She became an observer and realized how insignificant she was. The world and life went on whether she was there or not. Bumble bees were pollinating the wild flowers in the distance, dancing from one flower to the next. All were doing what they needed to do to survive, living their life in the chain of creation. Hours eventually passed. The Sun was now overhead and it was becoming hotter.

Luna stood and prayed again to each of the directions, offering gratitude and asking her question. After she finished this round of prayers, she sat down and felt invigorated. Luna felt a strong life force flowing from the ground below into her veins. She was at one with and in peace with her surroundings. The wind began to pick up. Luna felt the wind in her hair and on her face. The air was comforting and cooled her in the heat of the Sun. Time passed. As the Sun was getting ready to set behind the trees, Luna began to feel an incredible thirst. She tried to swallow and bring saliva into her parched mouth. All she could think of was water: water to bathe in, water to swim in and water to drink. Her mind was tormenting her. She wrestled with it. The thirst became uncontrollable. It had probably only been ten or so hours, but it felt like several days. Luna stood and once again prayed for help. She prayed for those who had no water to drink who may be dying of thirst right now. As she prayed and moved around to each direction, her foot stumbled on a small pebble at the edge of her blanket. It jammed her toe and caused her to take notice. It was a small stone, about the size of a nickel. When she looked at it more closely, she noticed it was white in color, and shaped like the foam on a wave in the ocean. *Just great*, she thought. It reminded her more of water. She was trying not to think of water. The more she tried to push it out of her mind the more she thirsted.

Luna sat down, held it, inspected it and listened. The stone told her to place it in her mouth, for it would quench her thirst. Luna became one with the stone as she sucked its power. She entered into a vision, riding on top of a wave with her body. Luna felt coolness on her skin and the moisture of the wave around her body. She relaxed and suspended herself in the water as it nourished her. When she returned to the blanket in her mind, much time had passed. She was no longer thirsty and felt renewed. She removed the stone from her mouth and offered it gratitude. It would become a piece to place in her medicine bag in the future.

The Sky was now dark. She again stood and said her prayers. Then once again she became silent and still, observing the night Sky. The stars were starting to appear and the Moon was beginning to rise. As the night Sky became pitch black, the stars grew brighter. Luna was somber. She remembered Grandfather's teaching to stay alert and awake, especially during the early morning hours. That is when he said Spirit may bring a message.

Her eyes became heavy. She decided to stand and sing a prayer song. It gave her a burst of energy and woke her up. As she looked up into the blackness, several stars began to fall from the Sky. It looked like a small meteor shower dropping from the heavens. The stars were massive white balls, streaming to the Earth. As they got closer and headed towards her, she panicked. Luna threw herself to the ground face down, burying her head in the blanketed Earth. She began to cry.

"Great Spirit, Grandfathers of all directions, Grandmother Earth and Spirit helpers, protect me. Pity me, I am scared and having a hard time," she cried.

Luna felt a stillness around her that calmed her entire being. She noticed a luminous glow around her. When she lifted her head from the ground, she observed a circle of lighted spheres surrounding her. The individual shapes were full of white light. Luna counted them in the circle. There were twelve of them. Their voices were gentle and loving. They communicated telepathically.

"We are here to represent the thirteen stars of intelligent life. Remember this and keep to your mission. Share the stars with others. The Earth is only one star among thirteen with intelligent life."

But there are only twelve of you, and you said thirteen, Luna thought.

"*You,* in the center, represent the thirteenth, the Earth Star. In your childhood here, you have seen places with intelligent life in the Cosmos. You still remember your true Home, the light, the spirit soul, the eternal life from the Center."

The twelve spheres generated light toward Luna. She became the center with all of the rays connecting to her. The light became spokes of a wheel connecting to her. The wheel of light began to spin around. The energy and heat it created in Luna was intense. Luna felt her body levitate above the ground, releasing her consciousness. No longer could her eyes see. She could only sense expansion of heat.

Luna became one with the spokes in the wheel of light. All of the spheres had merged. She could not feel or see her hands, feet or body. Luna did not know how long this experience lasted. It could have been a moment or an eternity. Time stood still. The only thought she recalled was *remember becoming one with the light, of no separation and to share the teaching.* As she became the light inside the spheres, she found herself observing the blanket below on the hill and her body no longer upon it. She expanded once more and became a star in the distant night sky and aware of the Earth below. After a while, Luna heard a distant chant calling her back to the Earth. Red Eagle had been told by Spirit when it was time for her return.

When she came back to consciousness, it was morning. The Sun had been up for a while. Luna sat in silence and began to recall her time on the hill. She needed to recall her experience, and share with Grandpa, who would then interpret the quest for Luna.

Grandfather Red Eagle and Max returned to the hill in silence with their eyes lowered to the ground, making no eye contact with her. They escorted Luna down the hill and into the lodge to purify and complete her quest ceremony. Luna was tired and thirsty. The heat in the lodge was tough on her throat. Speaking was a struggle, but she managed to recount her experiences. She laid down on the coolness of the Earth where it was easier to breathe.

Spirit spoke through Red Eagle in a firm voice, "You've been reminded of your connection to all life on Grandmother Earth, observing you are just part of the whole. No one part is bigger than the other, bird, spider, or bee. But all are connected. Who are you? You are part of the whole. Why are you here? You are to remember the spirit within you and all beings in the universe. One day, you will share your secrets and connect the Earth to the Sky for its earth people. You have more years to learn how to be human. You need to learn to be grounded in the wheel of life. Live here. Love here. Pray here. Great Spirit has given you the sacred name, *She Falls to Earth*. You do not share or speak this name to others. Use it only in ceremony or in private prayer to Great Spirit. It is sacred, hau."

The purification lodge door flap was lifted and Luna crawled out. Willie, Clint, Max and Sam welcomed her back with huge hugs. Each gave her some water and food. Luna was surprised, for now she was no longer hungry. She had to force herself to eat. As she slowly ate, she thought about her new spirit name and what Spirit had spoken of in the lodge. She understood the essence of her name. But now she would have to learn how to become it.

Gratitude

Red Eagle told Luna that she would stay in quest preparation for the next three years. Each year the quest would be a day longer. Next spring she would stay two days and nights. The following year it would be three and the final year it would be four. He would help her train her body and mind with prayer and ceremony.

Luna greeted each sunrise in prayer and lived life in service to Grandpa Red Eagle and her communal brothers. At sunset every day, she raised her voice in prayer in gratitude for another day of life. Material possessions were few, just the necessities for survival. She fasted slowly and regularly. Her body learned to live on less.

From May to November Luna traveled with Grandpa and the crew. The early spring was set aside for quest. She bunkered down for the winter in Montana on Grandpa's land, where he did healing ceremonies for local people in need. Luna continued to accompany him on these trips and helped to prepare the tinctures, salves and compresses. Luna learned his ways over the years and kept notes on all of the preparations and experiences in her journal.

Traveling was hard and tiring work. On some days, Luna's body felt worn as her back and feet ached. The group comforted each other with backrubs and foot massages. Money was scarce, but thanks to donations from caring and grateful people, the crew never went hungry. Luna experienced many hardships over the next few years: the van breaking down on the road, canceled lectures, camping in the heavy rains and a broken windshield from baseball-sized hail during a tornado. But Luna noticed a few things through it all. Their human spirit was still high. They laughed a lot, and strangers showed up to help when needed. It was as if all were in sync with the universe and flow of life. Luna began to trust life and stay in balance under difficult circumstances.

When the van would break down, within an hour, someone with a tow truck who happened to be a mechanic would come along. This person often happened to have someone in his family who was sick and in need of help. Red Eagle would conduct a ceremony. The van would get fixed, and the crew would be provided with food and shelter by the grateful people. It became less about giving a lecture at a bookstore or campground and more about going out into the world and being of service to unknown people who needed Red Eagle's assistance. It was as if the Great Spirit guided the journey for them. They would always be in the right place at the right time, no matter what unfortunate circumstance occurred.

One evening, Luna had a conversation with Red Eagle. He was sitting in a worn camp chair, in solitude under the stars.

"Grandpa, can I sit with you?" Luna asked.

He slowly nodded his head, grinning slightly.

"Grandpa, I noticed that every hardship and every snag in our schedule when we are on the road seems to work out okay. People help us fix the van and give us shelter or food. Sometimes we never get to the scheduled lecture but it never seems to upset you. You just laugh and stay calm. Many times were tough. Having a road washed out after a flash flood, and having to turn around and miss the lecture, a tree falling across the road during a severe thunderstorm and having our camping equipment blown away from high winds during a tornado. It's hard being on the road. It can make you weary and depleted. Why do you continue at your age when it's so hard?" she asked.

Red Eagle just sat there in silence for a moment and his face became serious as he spoke.

"Life is not hard. Life is life. Life is how you see it. The Great Spirit's hand flows through all of it. The road washing out let us turn around and meet an old man whose wife needed our medicine salve for her ulcerated leg. Spirit led us to her. The downed tree gave us wood for the fire for a ceremony that helped the little boy with a stomach illness. The wind took our camping equipment so that we could be given new equipment by that young couple who had extra and in better condition.

It is all in how you see the big picture. We get what is needed. If we are in the flow, Spirit will guide us to where we are needed. My mission is to serve Spirit and to go to where that takes me."

He added, "We are here to help and share with each other. How you live and use the time should not be wasted. Your mind and heart need to be in balance to live a good life. The ego's wants make us unhappy and out of balance. Take and use only what you need to live on, and no more. More than that is wasteful. Having a grateful attitude for everything in your life keeps you in balance as an earth person."

After that night, Luna observed the road and life with more gratitude and excitement. If she remembered to embrace life as a gift, it was no longer hard, a struggle or disappointing.

Red Eagle offered another teaching before her two day, two night quest. Luna was worried about fasting. Red Eagle offered his wisdom.

"The Great Spirit requires us to sacrifice, to give of ourselves and of our time but it is only you who can choose to suffer. Suffering is not needed or asked of us by Spirit. You don't need to suffer to heal."

This teaching allowed Luna to experience the quest with a new perspective. She did not have to struggle. She had prepared well, and now she had to let Great Spirit take care of the rest.

It turned out to be an insightful time. She was visited by a small black bear on the second afternoon. Luna stayed calm and just observed his actions. He sniffed and approached her blanket. Luna stayed fearless and centered. The bear retreated. When the quest was over, Red Eagle explained that Great Spirit sent the black bear to be a medicine helper for Luna. It would give her strength, courage and help her to learn the healing ways. Months later, Red Eagle taught Luna the proper way to call upon the power of the medicine helper when it was needed.

Final Quest

As five years on the road passed, Luna was ready to complete her fourth and final quest with Red Eagle. It would be the longest, four days and four nights. Luna had prepared like she had in previous years. The last question for her to ask was *how she could serve the People?* It held bigger energy and focus.

"If you ask and are lucky enough for Spirit to give you answers, then you're responsible to do what Spirit says," Red Eagle warned. "Don't ask and waste Spirit's time if you are not going to carry it out."

The time came for Luna to be alone on her blanket. The Sky grew dark and black clouds started to gather around her. She had only been there a few hours that morning or so she thought. Luna was disorientated because of the lack of sunlight. She could no longer follow its trail in the Sky to determine the time of day. Luna stood and prayed for protection and for the storm to pass. The wind picked up and the Sky suddenly opened. Large hail, the size of half dollars fell to the ground. In a matter of a few minutes the blanket was covered with two inches of small crystallized chunks of ice. Her feet were cold, Luna began to shiver. As she prayed, she felt her consciousness escape her and was transported to a realm of light. As the light dimmed, she realized she was with Matar, Chara and Alcor.

"Welcome, dear one. It's nice to see you. We have come to remind you about the Center, the place of light. You have asked the question about how to serve the People in your quest. You need to remember this place and tell them about it. Use all that you have seen and have been taught. Be one with them. Tell them about the light within. Accept yourself as a human. You are one of the few that remembers the cosmos and believes. Help them balance the spirit and the body, the Earth and the Sky," Alcor spoke.

"But how can I do that?" she asked.

"Use your talent of words and expression. Take your memories and your experiences and share them for all to see and hear. You will have more to experience in the human body. Someday when the time is right, you will write a book because you have something to teach. You will share your secrets as you accept the human part of yourself. You will no longer feel different or separate from these human beings, for you are one of them. The Center of light, spirit and creation connects all beings from everywhere in the universe. Take care of your body. You will need it for many more years to complete your mission. It is time now for you to return to Earth. Farewell, dear one. We will see you again," he said.

Luna was brought back to consciousness by a tingling sensation on her face. When she opened her eyes there was a large black spider crawling on her face. She gently lifted the spider onto her finger and placed it on her blanket on the ground. It lifted its two front legs and wiggled them. Luna observed it for a while and then heard it sing in her head. She slowly chanted the melody with the spider. It was gifting a song to Luna. Luna would remember to ask Grandpa and Spirit about it in the lodge when she was brought down from the hill.

Luna was told that the spider connects and weaves things together. It was a creator. It would help her weave her story into a book someday, years down the road. Its medicine was powerful. It would help her to connect herself to the human race. It would take her a couple of years to truly understand.

A few weeks after Luna's quest, Max had decided to leave Red Eagle and move to California. He was going to work in an alcohol abuse rehabilitation program.

Luna was to become Red Eagle's singer and drummer. It was an honor granted by Great Spirit and sanctioned by Red Eagle. Red Eagle had asked the spirits who the singer would be and was told, *She Falls to Earth*. He was told that she needed to learn to use her voice and connect with the heartbeat of Grandmother Earth. It was a little unsettling for him. At first he resisted. The protocol was that only men worked with the drum. He was given his confirmation when Luna came to him with a dream.

"Grandpa, I had a dream. There were four elder native women and they were teaching me to sing. Then four elder native men were teaching me how to make a two sided drum. I had this dream four nights in a row. Can you tell me what it means?" Luna quizzed.

"It means that Spirit knows best and is just reminding me," he laughed.

Luna still did not understand his comment in the moment, but she would later. Max taught and passed on the sacred songs to Luna before he left. It took her a couple of months to make a drum in the old way. Luna immersed herself in the sacred ways for the next two years and was at his right hand. She moved from the small trailer into Grandpa's cabin. The other men did not seem to mind. They knew Red Eagle was guided by Spirit. They were not jealous of Luna. They knew it would be hard for her to take on that responsibility.

There were times when Grandpa awakened her in the middle of the night, to drive somewhere unknown, guided only by Spirit's voice. Luna took cat naps whenever possible to catch up on sleep.

Luna had grown so much and had learned a few things about the Native American Red Road of her ancestors. Grandpa said it would take many lifetimes to fully learn the old ways.

He told Luna, "You never stop learning. No one knows enough. Only the Great Spirit has all wisdom."

One morning she shared her experience from the Center with Grandpa.

"Grandpa, is the Center Light of Oneness different from Great Spirit the Creator?" she asked.

"No, I believe it's the same. Just a different name. To my people, we call the place where life is given and the power that flows through everything, the Great Mystery, Great Spirit. It is where the spark of light is given to a being. It is made of energy that is placed into form. The Center is a place that gives life and where the spirit light will go back to. It is the same. My spirit will go back to the Great Mystery of Spirit, to the center in the Sky to reunite and become one again," he replied.

"But do you believe we come back in form many times?" Luna asked.

"Hau," he chuckled. "We can't learn everything one time around. We have a brain, mind, heart and body. We take baby steps each lifetime. When we finally complete, then we can remain in spirit with the whole. Until then, we are just babies learning to crawl and need to live here with all of our relations."

As two more years passed, Luna had been with Grandpa for seven years. The years had flown by.

Within the last month, Grandpa had become distant with Luna. Grandpa's heart was heavy. He did not eat or talk much, and spent most of the time alone and in prayer in the cabin. Luna sensed the separation and became very emotional. She was worried he was sick or upset with her. During her prayers, her parents came to mind often. She remembered the letters and pictures they had sent each year at Christmas. Her heart missed them, especially her mother, Claire. She didn't understand why she was feeling these emotions now. She shared her sadness with Clint and Willie, of feeling abandoned by Grandpa, and losing the connection with him. His solitude did not allow Luna the time to talk with him. She felt displaced.

A month later, Grandpa asked Luna to sit with him. He brought out the Sacred Pipe and said, "Let's pray."

Luna was excited to be in ceremony with him.

He said gently, "It is time for you to go home. I have taught you what you need to know. You need to be a human being. I have tried to help you learn this. Have a relationship with a human being and someday share your experiences and write a book. Your time with me is done. It is time to disconnect you and turn you over to Spirit and your helpers. This is no longer the place for you to be."

"But Grandpa, I am scared. I still don't know enough. I don't know how to live. I can't think of leaving you," she cried.

"You have started to miss your family. Spirit has shown this to me. You need to make things right with your mother. You need to accept your humanness. Use your gifts. Release your secrets. Spirit gives each of us talents, and to honor Spirit we must use them. You cannot hide here. It is time to use what you have learned. I turn you over to Great Spirit. I have nothing more. Our time is complete. Hau," he said.

He opened his bundle and began the ceremony in his sacred way. Luna had seen him perform this many times. She watched closely and with more reverence this time. This could be the last time she prayed with him for a long time. Her eyes welled up with tears. She choked back her sobs and let the tears roll silently down her face. Her heart was being torn from her chest and split in two. Through the smoke, she saw the four ancient familiar faces. They were smiling. Sweet Willow Woman, White Running Trail, Red Burning Sky and Smooth Clay Face began to chant. As Grandpa blew the smoke into the air, the four of them received it. They were accepting their responsibility to guide her for the next part of her journey. The pressure in her chest and tears began to subside. The sadness left her. The disconnection was complete. When the ceremony ended, Luna hugged and thanked Red Eagle.

"I have something for you," he smiled.

A long beaded deer skin bag lay underneath his bundle. He handed her the bag.

"Open it. Spirit said it is what you need to have. It is the same one Spirit showed to you in your first purification," he added.

Luna opened the bag. She retrieved a long stem covered with buffalo fur and a large red stone bowl with four carved rings around it. It was a Sacred Pipe. Red Eagle made both the stem and bowl for Luna. Once again, Luna filled with tears. She had forgotten the vision of the buffalo handing the Sacred Pipe to her in that first purification. Grandpa's gift was dressed exactly in the same way.

"We will bless it, open it in ceremony and connect it to you tomorrow. You will be responsible for its care and safety. I will give you further teachings tomorrow. You will pray with it for the rest of your life. It will send your prayers from the Earth to the Sky, where Great Spirit will answer."

True to Red Eagle's promise, Luna and the Sacred Pipe were blessed and connected in ceremony the next day.

Willie, Clint, Sam and Grandpa Red Eagle pooled their monies for a bus ticket home for Luna. It would take Luna four days to reach her New England town. Luna took the next two days to say goodbye to her native family and the land. She revisited the hill where she had spent her four quests, and offered tobacco in gratitude and then smoked the Sacred Pipe alone. This mountain of wilderness had served her well and allowed her to discover herself and her path.

Luna returned to the cabin for her final meal with Grandpa and her brothers. It was bittersweet, remembering life on the road: living in Montana, eight foot snow drifts to dig out from and healing and crossing ceremonies for people who were put in their path. As Luna looked out the glass window she barely recognized her own reflection. Her face was worn from the Sun. Her dark hair was now below her waist and in braids. Her plain worn white t-shirt was covered with a long sleeve denim shirt. Her long flowing paisley skirt covered the top of her scuffed, ankle high, work boots. She had aged.

Luna was uneasy at the thought of starting over. Where would she work and live? How would she honor and live the teachings Red Eagle had given her? Fear arose in her belly as she wondered. Grandpa placed his hand on her shoulder gently.

"Hau, don't worry. Spirit will guide you the same as you had been guided to me. Just trust. Thinking too much hurts the brain. Give it a rest," he laughed. "Spirit will let me know how your doing."

"I'll miss you," she said as she embraced him.

Clint drove Luna to the bus terminal early the next morning. Waving goodbye, a tear escaped down her right cheek and Luna wiped it away quickly.

Will this be my last time in Montana? Will it be the last time I see Red Eagle? Am I a different person than I was seven years ago? Will I be accepted any better for who I am than before I had left?

One thing had to change: she could no longer hide and she had to accept herself as a human being.

Back to Reality

The bus trip to Massachusetts was long, marked with lots of napping and changing of buses. She ate light: dried fruit, assorted nuts, granola bars and lots of water. The landscape changed from mountains, to prairie grass, to bustling highways and finally to her last stop. Luna called her parents and asked them to meet her at the bus terminal on Saturday afternoon. Luna exited the bus in her hippy-looking attire with a red bandana around her forehead, and searched for the familiar faces.

"Oh... my... God," Claire gasped. "Tom, look at her. She is so skinny. She looks like a homeless person."

"Now Claire, calm down, she's home now. We don't have to worry anymore. Let's just welcome her home. Okay?" he nudged her.

"Okay," she responded.

"Luna! Luna! Over here," Leana screamed as she was waving her arms.

Luna approached slowly and gave her sister a hug. Leana crushed her with excitement.

"Luna, I missed you. You have to tell us all about your adventures," she squealed.

Tom and Claire also gave Luna a hug. Luna tightened her grip around her mother.

"I've missed you, Mom," she whispered.

"Let's go home. Grandpa Joe is waiting for us. I have a nice dinner planned for us; browned beef with potatoes and chocolate cake."

Luna remembered the dinner well. She had given up sweets long ago, having grown accustomed to eating soups, stews, corn, wild berries and nuts. But she would eat a small bite of cake for her mother's sake.

Luna returned to the new house her parents had purchased. It seemed like life had changed for them as well. Grandpa Joe had really aged and was now living with them. He had suffered a stroke and was confined to a wheelchair. At seventy years old, he looked like he was a hundred.

"Hi, Grandpa," Luna said as she kissed his forehead. He tried to speak but his speech was slurred.

"Hi, Woona," he responded.

The meal was delicious. Everyone was excited and talking at the same time. Luna said very little. Once again, the emotion of feeling out of place surfaced.

"Luna, we'll have to take you to the store tomorrow to get you some proper clothes," her mother suggested. "You won't find a decent job wearing those clothes."

Luna twitched inside, "These clothes are fine. I bought them at a slightly used clothing store for a good price."

"No one will hire you looking like that," she snapped.

"Okay now, let's forget about the clothes. Luna, what are your plans? Do you have any ideas?" her father asked.

"Well Dad, I'll look for work and would like to get an apartment and a cheap car. I guess I'll check the papers tomorrow."

"The filter plant is looking for quality control technicians. Maybe, they'll hire you back," her mother informed.

"We'll see."

Luna was in no mood to argue with her mother. She would wait and see what Spirit would put in her path in the days ahead.

Luna retreated to a new bedroom and unpacked her small suitcase and carefully removed her bundle containing the Sacred Pipe.

"What's that?" Leana asked standing in the doorway.

Leana had become a real beauty. But to Luna, she was still the inquisitive child.

"It is a Sacred Pipe. Grandpa Red Eagle gifted it to me to pray with. It is a very sacred thing. Please do not touch it, okay? It needs to be handled properly," Luna said gently.

"Okay, but you'd better not smoke it in the house or Mom will have a fit," Leana warned.

"Yeah, I know. That is why I need my own place soon," Luna sighed.

Once again she felt like a child. She needed to break the scores of secrets that she held inside for fear of conflict and ridicule.

Luna went to the filter manufacturing plant to apply for a job on Monday morning. She wore her long hair loose and borrowed a clean skirt and blouse from Leana. Luna had become used to wearing dresses and skirts for ceremony and now wore them all of the time, expressing her feminine side.

Luna was hired to inspect filters for the Quality Control department and would start the following week. Her old supervisor had become the new hiring manager and was willing to rehire her.

That evening, Luna read the newspaper and saw an advertisement for a Holistic Health Fair on the coming weekend, about an hour's drive away. Her mother had inherited Grandpa Joe's car after the stroke. Luna asked her father to borrow the car hoping he would agree since there were now two cars in the family. Her father agreed.

Luna arrived at the fair and found many things of interest. Meditation lectures, massage and energy sessions, astrology charts, health food exhibits and of course a long line for intuitive card readers. There were Rune readers, Animal card readers, Tarot readers, Palm readers and Pendulum readers. As she entered the large ballroom, she saw there were many readers sitting side by side at small tables. They were dressed in flashy and eccentric outfits. Many of the women wore heavy makeup and lipstick, and lots of large gaudy jewelry. It was as if each had a gimmick to attract and lure clients to their table.

Luna searched the room for an authentic reader by sensing their energies. She found a short, pudgy, jet-black haired woman in her sixties. She was sitting in a trance state, alone at her table. She lifted her eyes and locked eyes with Luna. Luna could hear her thoughts calling her over to her table. Though Luna felt no threat, she resisted. The woman then proceeded to leave her table and walk toward Luna. She handed Luna a specialized deck of cards from France that had astrological designs and a Star imprinted on the cover.

"It's time," she spoke. With that, the woman walked out of the room, and left the building.

Luna's mouth was open. What had just happened? The room began to slowly spin for Luna. Her mind returned to the book store in Montana and the reader Olivia, remembering her words: *You will know when to begin reading for others when the time presents itself.*

The woman had just said, "It's time."

Could it be? Am I supposed to begin now?

"Hi, my name is Peter," called a voice from behind.

Luna returned from her thoughts and turned around. Peter was a tall white-haired, blue-eyed, handsome man, early fifties at most.

"Are you a reader? That was my best reader Crystal who just handed you her cards. What did she say to you?" he asked.

"Uh... she said... she said, it's time," Luna stuttered.

"It's time?" Peter repeated. "It's time for what?"

"I believe, it's time to use my gift," replied Luna, bewildered in the moment.

"So, you *are* a reader. That's great. As you can see, I have a space available."

"Well, I don't really read cards. I read people's energy," Luna said honestly.

"Really, how would you like to read me, as an interview for the job? Let's go back there behind the desk, where I run the software for natal astrology charts."

Luna followed Peter as if she was in a trance and floating. The energy of the fair was of a high vibration and chaotic in certain places around the room.

As they sat down, Peter asked, "So what's your name?"

"Luna."

"Luna, how do you conduct your readings?"

"I just need you to relax and let me enter your energy field. So what would you like to know?" Luna asked.

"Just tell me what you see," he replied.

Luna closed her eyes, took her breaths and entered his energy field. She felt a lot of feminine energy. It was very unbalanced with the awkward masculine body. Then Luna began to speak.

"You have denied your true self. You hide your male lover. You pretend to be what you think you must," she spoke.

Peter gasped. "What?"

Luna continued, "It's okay to be partnered with anyone you choose. You ended your relationship with Danny because he no longer wished to hide who he was. Your heart is hurting. Someday you will have the courage to accept yourself. You used to help people in the past but now it has become a business. It will be your downfall if you don't correct it and balance the greed of money and truly serving people."

Peter was shocked. *Who was this young woman? How could she know this?* He had seen many readers. Luna was the real deal. This woman was very direct. She did not ask questions. She just supplied information.

Luna noticed an older woman materialize from the ethers. She was behind Peter.

"Tell him that he should not take his life. He needs to be happy and accept himself. I love him. He was thinking of taking some pills and booze to end it all. He is an alcoholic and he needs help," she spoke.

Oh, no. I can't say that, Luna thought.

"Tell him. Tell him," she pleaded. "I am his mother Emma."

Luna closed her eyes and relayed the message.

"Peter, your mother Emma is here. She loves you. She wants you to get help with the alcohol abuse. She was there the night you were going to take the pills and end your life. That's not the way. She helped you fall asleep before you could take them. She wants you to love and accept yourself and get help. She truly loves you."

Emma's apparition left as quickly as it came.

Peter's eyes filled with tears. "I can't believe this. How could you know? She really was here?"

Luna nodded.

"Thank you," he paused. "So would you like a job? We have fairs two weekends a month from April until Halloween. You could make a week's pay in a weekend. You could help people. Here's a contract. Look it over. Here is my phone number. Let me know soon."

Luna returned home with excitement in her heart. She was grateful for the synchronicity of the day's events. But the knot in her stomach held the fear of expressing her desires to her parents. At dinner that evening, inquiries about Luna's day consumed the conversation.

"Luna, did you have a nice day?" her father asked.

"Yes. It was good."

"Did you remember to put gas in the car before you came home?" he asked.

"Yes," she replied.

"Well, tell us about the fair. What did you do all day?" her mother asked.

Now was her moment. She needed the courage to speak.

"Well Mom, I had tofu and bean sprouts on whole grain bread. It was fabulous. I had a back massage for ten minutes. I attended a free hour-long astrology lecture that was fascinating. There also were holistic energy demonstrations like chakra balancing and Reiki. There was also a relaxation meditation."

Luna held back on the card reading and her experience.

"Well, that sounds like a bunch of nonsense to me. But if it was interesting and you had a good day, that's fine," her mother declared.

"Well, also...," Luna paused with her eyes lowered. "I met an interesting man named Peter. He offered me a job at the fair every other weekend until the end of October. The pay is really good."

"I thought you were going to take the job at the filter plant?" her father questioned.

"Yes, but this would be extra part-time work. It will help me save for a used car and an apartment. Do you think I can borrow the car on weekends for a couple of months until I have enough saved for a down payment and insurance?" Luna asked.

Tom and Claire glanced at each other. Tom was proud that Luna was ambitious enough to want to work hard like he did. Her parents both nodded in agreement.

"Your father will go with you when it's time to buy a car. What did you say this Peter does at the fair and what will you be helping him with?" she asked.

"Peter creates astrology charts on his computer program. Many people are interested in how the planets align in their birth chart. The work will be interesting and fun for me," Luna replied.

Luna did not lie. Peter *did* create charts. It *would* be interesting work for Luna. She just omitted the part about intuitive readings. She was taking one step at a time.

"Luna, I don't understand why people would pay for such nonsense, but if it's something you want to do, it's your choice," she agreed.

That evening before bed, Luna read the contract and signed it. She would work as a reader for Peter at the fairs for the next five months. Luna called him the next morning to confirm.

Luna wrote to Grandpa Red Eagle every two weeks to keep in touch. Luna continued to write to Max regularly since his move to California two years ago.

Luna knew at some point she needed to be in charge of her own life again. Money and material possessions were limited when she was on the road, but she was herself—the intuitive, conversing with spirits and Sky Beings, and assisting Red Eagle by telling him what she saw in the sick person's energy field. They worked together as a team. She was accepted and understood by Red Eagle and loved by his community and the people she met. Luna knew she had to completely accept herself; despite her fear of not being loved by her parents, especially Claire. She never wanted to disappoint Claire. Luna always felt guilty about not thinking and acting in ways that would make her mother proud. Claire, in turn, was often critical and judgmental. Luna felt she would never live up to what was expected of her. After being away for seven years, this feeling still burdened her heart.

The Plan

Luna reported to the filter plant on Monday morning to start her new position. The work was easy and boring. Luna memorized the defects found in the filters and could easily decipher the acceptable from the scrap. Luna did her job extremely well and became proficient in the production line.

Luna met a woman named Beth Simon who was ten years older than she was. Beth worked in the same quality department and on the same day shift. Beth was a plain Jane type: short red hair, small freckled cheeks and no makeup. She had blue eyes and was tall and slender. Beth was a vegetarian who lived on a small farm and grew her own cooking herbs and vegetables. She was very interested in nature and natural holistic techniques, especially yoga and meditation. Luna shared stories with Beth about life on the road with Red Eagle. She questioned Beth about her thoughts on intuitive abilities.

"I believe everyone has the ability, but may need to further develop it. There are some people who come in already developed and can use the ability easily," Beth said.

Luna and Beth became friends over the next months. Luna helped Beth with her garden and they spent time meditating and sharing experiences. One evening, Luna finally shared her reading abilities with Beth.

"Beth, have you ever been to a holistic fair?" Luna asked. "It is a place where they have intuitive readers and holistic lectures on astrology and things of a spiritual nature."

"Sure. I've been to a few and I really have enjoyed them. I had a couple of readings a few years ago. Although I believe in them, most of the readers were cold readers. They read body language. They weren't the real deal. Still, it was fun," Beth laughed.

Luna took a chance and shared her secret.

"Beth, I read at fairs twice a month, on weekends. I've been working as a reader for the last three months."

"Why haven't you told me before?" she asked.

"Well, a lot of people don't believe in it. They think it's odd. I don't want people at work to know. They may look at me as if I am weird. I just want to be known as a quality technician, that's all."

"Yeah, you're right. Don't worry, I won't tell. But I would love to have a reading with you. Is it easier or harder to read people you know?" Beth probed.

"Actually, I have only read for people I didn't know. But I've received insights and information all my life about people I do know. For me, it really doesn't matter just as long as their energy field is open to it. There is a fair next weekend. Why don't you come with me? I'm usually booked, but you could spend the day in lectures and demonstrations and we could have dinner in the evening. If I have an opening available I'll fit you in," she added.

"Great. Sounds like a plan," Beth agreed.

Claire and Tom were happy that Luna had found a friend to share her interests with. They met Beth several times and agreed she was a nice woman.

In three month's time, Luna had saved enough to buy a used car. Luna consulted with her father and got a two year loan on a four cylinder Ford Mustang. It had good tires, a clean engine and was only four years old. It had only 30,000 miles on the odometer. The car was white with a blue velour interior. It became her freedom, her pony. Red Eagle used to call the old van that they traveled in his *pony*. It gave them the means to travel to places where Spirit needed him to go. What more could she ask for than a Mustang pony. Luna vowed to herself to properly maintain it.

The next step was to save for a first month and last month deposit on an apartment. Luna checked the Sunday paper every week for the right place.

Luna and Beth went to the fair the following weekend. Luna scheduled Beth's reading for 6:30 p.m., her last appointment. Beth received the program for the day's activities and started to plan her day. Luna reported to her small table in the back of the ballroom. She liked to be in the back against the wall facing out. She had a separate table and kept at least four feet between her and another reader. It was more than an arm's length of space needed for herself. Luna explained to Peter that she required some personal space. Since Luna had become his top money maker, Peter let her have what she required.

Luna had become, through word of mouth, the most requested reader. Her ability as a medium for the dead was a novelty. Luna did not call herself a medium, nor did she promote it. She never promised that a dead relative would show up for the reading. Luna remembered her teaching from the Portal at the Center. The dead did not liked to be called back or requested. They would come on their own accord if they so desired. But word of mouth brought a lot of clients to Luna for help and resolution.

Peter had also begun to turn his life around. He had started a program and had been sober for a month. Peter and Luna would spend time talking about astrology at dinner after the fair ended for the day. Luna learned astrology and borrowed many of Peter's books. Astrology fascinated her.

Luna noticed on the program that a Native American author named Grey Coyote was scheduled to speak at 7:00 p.m. Luna booked off her scheduled and told Peter not to schedule anyone after her appointment with Beth. She wondered if it was the same Grey Coyote she met in Arizona. Either way, she wanted to attend. Beth's appointment was at 6:30 p.m. and that would be Luna's last appointment for the day.

Luna's day began with a woman in her late thirties, who had very dense energy. She had sadness in her heart. As soon as she sat down, a man her age appeared behind her. It was the first time Luna had seen a face appear with a rope around his neck. But interestingly enough, he was smiling.

"Tell her that I am sorry. I left her and the boys. I couldn't take it anymore. It had nothing to do with her. I was never happy in my body. I am free now. Please tell her I love her and that she needs to go on. She will find someone else to love and who will love her and the boys," he said.

"Your husband is here," Luna began. "He is sorry he hung himself and left you. He said it had nothing to do with you or the boys. He loved you. He hated being in his body all his life. He wants you to know he is at peace. He says that you will soon find someone to love you and whom you can love again."

The woman just sobbed. "Is he really here? How could he do this? If he loved us, he could not have done this."

"His pain was greater than anything else. He had a mental illness. What he fails to see is that he is only free for a while. But he'll have to come back in another lifetime to finish what he needs to do. However, he seems content now. You must find peace with this. He loved you the best he could. You need to understand and let him go," Luna explained.

"If it really is him, what is his name?" the woman asked.

Luna disliked having to prove herself and her ability. She hoped he would reveal his name to her.

"Martin," he replied. "They call me Marty."

"He said Marty. Martin is his birth name," Luna replied.

The woman dried her eyes with her hands. She composed herself and asked when she would meet someone else.

Luna closed her eyes and took some breaths. "You must first heal your heart and truly let Marty go. When you can open your heart again, it will happen. The man for you is much older than you and has his own business. He works with black tar. He has his own home. He has never married. The time line could be within the year. But your own free will determines your fate. Can you heal and let Marty go? The path is there if you choose."

Luna opened her eyes and the woman was smiling, for Luna gave her hope. She thanked Luna and left.

The readings after that were less eventful. Women came asking about their love life and children. Men came asking about their career and health. Only one dead spirit had shown up today. On most days, half the readings dealt with questions and half dealt with messages from dead spirits.

The time came for Beth's appointment with Luna.

Beth sat down with a smile on her face.

"So Luna, how do we do this? Tarot cards, using a piece of my jewelry, or holding my hands?" she asked.

"Just relax and take some deep breaths," Luna replied.

As soon as Beth relaxed, a young woman came through. She looked exactly like Beth.

"I am her twin. I died two hours after my birth. She has never known me, yet I am always with her. She knows of me and needs not to feel guilty because she survived. She carries this with her and needs to release this to move forward. She must heal and open her heart to a relationship. There is a wonderful man out there for her. I have seen him. My named is Elisa," she spoke.

Oh my, Luna thought, *this is huge. Beth had never mentioned anything about a twin. This will be healing for her.*

Luna spoke softly, "Your identical twin Elisa is here. Her body only lived two hours. She wants you to stop feeling guilty because you survived, and she wants you to open your heart to a relationship. You do not have to be alone. There is a man out there for you who is waiting to come in. She has seen him."

Beth was in shock. Her mouth opened wide and her eyes glazed over.

"There's no way you could know about her. No one knows. I have never spoken about it. Not ever. Yes, I do feel guilty. I wonder why I survived and she did not. Why me and not her? I have felt bad about this all my life and I have been trying to find peace with it," Beth confessed.

"It is time to let go and love yourself. You deserve to be happy and to find love. It is the next step for you. I am sure your sister will continue to watch over you as she chooses. She loves you and wants you to be happy," Luna confirmed.

"So tell me about this man," Beth said as she dried her eyes.

Luna closed her eyes and saw the face of a man that worked at the filter plant. He worked at extruding the glass fibers. Luna had seen him everyday. He sat at a table by himself. He was very shy and quiet. In her vision, Luna saw the man watching Beth. He had a secret crush on her, but was too shy to speak to her.

Luna described the man's features and said his name was Jack. He was quiet and shy.

"Where and when will I meet him?" Beth asked still giggling. She had made no connection to the Jack at work.

"He is closer than you think. Keep your eyes and heart open and it will happen," she replied. "But, both of you have free will and need to choose to make it happen."

Luna trusted what she had seen.

"Okay, I will. Thanks, Luna," said Beth.

When Luna completed the reading, she and Beth hurried to Grey Coyote's lecture.

Coyote's Tale

As soon as Luna had entered the room she realized it was the same man she met in Arizona. She was excited to see him again. Beth and Luna took their seats. The elder caught Luna's face in the crowd, recognized her and walked over to greet her.

"Hau, sister, we meet again. It's been a long time." He gave her a long, heartfelt bear hug.

"Hello. Yes, it has been a few years since Arizona. Grey Coyote, this is my friend Beth," Luna said.

"Hau, we better start now. Folks get restless. They live their life by the clock," he chuckled.

He walked to the podium and began his lecture.

"Hau, I am Grey Coyote. I am from the Ojibway people. I live on a farm in Oregon. I have come to talk about getting back to honoring and respecting the Grandmother Earth. We need to take only what we need and leave the rest for future generations. We must get back to honoring the Sacred Wheel of life. I lead prayer gatherings to honor all in the Sacred Hoop. The winged ones, the fish, the creepy crawlers, the four legged animals, the Moon, the Sun, the elements of air, earth, fire and water, the four winds of the directions and the seasons, everything that is above and below. Animals teach us how to live. Plants and trees give us medicines for any sickness we create through excess and imbalances of the mind, body and spirit."

Grey Coyote drew a circle on a large paper clipboard. He placed smaller circles inside the larger one. He made a diagram and labeled each smaller circle.

"This is the Sacred Hoop, the Circle of Life. At gatherings, stones are placed in a specific way with prayers and chants. We pray for all in the circle. It reminds us that we are all connected and dependent on each other to live."

Grey Coyote expressed his concern for the Earth. He spoke about recycling and growing your own food. Eating live food was a healthier way to live in balance. The lecture was only an hour long and went by quickly. Luna was glad she had the experience of the prayer gathering in Arizona. She understood his diagram of the stone placement because of the gathering she had attended. She thanked Grey Coyote when he finished the lecture.

"Come for a visit anytime. We have plenty of camping space in Oregon," he added.

Luna and Beth had a healthy dinner after the lecture. They stayed overnight and returned Sunday evening after Luna's appointments. Beth recounted the lectures she had attended during the weekend. Luna and Beth continued their friendship over the next several months.

Spring was back again and Luna had renegotiated her contract with Peter. She agreed to another seven months while continuing to work at the filter plant with Beth. Thanks to a one time invitation from Luna, Beth's secret admirer Jack had finally started to join Luna and Beth at breaks and at lunchtime. Jack overcame his shyness and asked Beth out for a date. The relationship flourished nicely. The pair became inseparable.

In the summer, on a free weekend from the fair, Luna decided to attend a Native American Indian Powwow. It was a social gathering with singing and dancing. There were also plenty of native crafts and herbal remedies for sale. Luna invited Beth and Jack to join her.

Beth was happy that thanks to Luna's reading and guidance, she had healed enough to open her heart to a relationship. Jack bought Beth a beautiful pair of turquoise earrings. They ate tasty buffalo burgers and succotash sold by one of the vendors at the Powwow.

Luna had eaten buffalo, venison, elk, lamb and duck while she was on the road with Red Eagle. She learned to eat what was donated and gifted. She also learned to honor the life of the animal that gave its life for her by offering a pinch of tobacco and a prayer of gratitude.

Luna watched the dancing and sat on the grass to feel the large drum vibrating in sync with the Earth's heartbeat. The drum filled her being. The chants and songs filled her heart. She was intoxicated by the vibrating sound grounding her to the Earth, while her spirit was flying in the Sky with the sound of the wind. What a beautiful space to hold. Luna closed her eyes and smiled, envisioning herself moving out of her parent's home and into her own place; a lovely old farm house with a vast open field. The drum and singers stopped and Luna awoke from her mind's eye.

It's time, Luna thought. *Spirit will guide me where to live.*

Luna asked one of the vendors to put her name on the mailing list so that she could receive the schedule of all the upcoming Powwows. She really looked forward to attending more of these social gatherings.

Moving Forward

It had been over a year since Luna was on the road with Red Eagle. Luna wrote to Red Eagle twice a month and sent him a small check to help with necessities.

Luna asked Beth to keep her eyes open for an apartment for her. She withheld her vision of the old farm house and trusted the opportunity would reveal itself if she was paying attention.

Luna's supervisor, Burton Ward, announced on the next day of work that he would be away for the next couple of days. His elderly mother was going to move in with him and his family. He was going to be cleaning and renting her old farm house until the she was ready to sell it. Luna perked up.

"Did you say an old farm house for rent?" she asked.

"Mr. Ward, when do you think the place will be ready and what will you charge for rent?" she questioned.

"Why? Are you looking for a place?" he asked.

"Sure, if the price is right," she replied.

"I suppose I can have it ready in a couple of weeks, certainly by the end of the month. The house is paid for, so I would just like someone to live there to keep it up. It's about twenty miles from here. About a thirty minute drive. I can show you the place next weekend. She has sold off farm acreage over the years. There are twenty-five acres left. It's not a farm any more, but it is a nice quiet place. We can talk about the dollars later," he said.

"Great," Luna said excitedly.

Now she had to break the news to her parents.

During dinner that evening Luna took a deep breath and told her parents.

"Mom, Dad? I have decided to get my own place. My supervisor at work has a house to rent about twenty miles from here. I'm going to see it next weekend," she announced.

"What? Why? Can you afford it?" her father asked.

"Why would you want to move out? You have it good here. How are you going to take care of everything? It'll be a lot of work, stress and worry. Living here, you can save your money," her mother argued.

"I have taken care of myself for a while now. I was away from home for seven years Mom, and I survived. It's time I'm on my own. I need to live my life and have privacy."

"But Luna, you should wait until you meet a nice man and are ready to get married," she said.

"Mom, I may never get married. I may never find the right person to be with. It's time to live the way I choose," Luna firmly stated.

"What do you mean by that?" her mother asked.

"Mom, you really don't know me. I have tried to please you, but I can't anymore. I need to be me. I have been making extra money at the fairs on the weekends by performing intuitive readings, not by printing astrology charts. I didn't tell you because I knew you'd say that it was foolish. But I'm good at it. I help people and give them guidance. I'm tired of keeping secrets for fear of being ridiculed by you. Just once, I wish you could love me, even if I think differently. I love you both, but I need my own place. It's time for you to stop worrying about me. This is what I want and need," Luna asserted.

"We do love you, sweetheart. We just worry that it will be hard for you. We want life to be easier for you, with less stress and struggle," her father added.

"Dad, life is to be experienced. I had that when I was on the road. I need to have my own life. Besides, I have two jobs and you hardly see me at home now anyway," she added. "I'd like your support, but if not, I'm doing it regardless. It's time."

"Well, I guess your mind is made up. I hope you'll still come to visit," her mother spoke sharply.

Luna, a psychic, Claire thought to herself. *What would people say about my daughter?*

Claire worried about her reputation. Luna was an adult, but Claire still wanted to protect her.

"Mom, of course I'll visit," Luna replied.

Luna moved into the old farmhouse. Mr. Ward had repainted a couple of the rooms. There were three bedrooms. She chose to make one room her meditation room, where she could pray with the Sacred Pipe, burn incense and meditate. Finally, she had freedom. She could burn sage anytime and pray, even during the night when most people were asleep. Luna relished the privacy. It was a place of tranquility in nature. She was so grateful that she was led there by Spirit and hoped that she'd be able to live there for a long time. Luna signed a one year lease with Mr. Ward, but would have gladly signed for five years if he had asked.

Luna enjoyed walking the acres of land, listening to the birds and observing all of nature. One morning she witnessed a fawn feeding from her mother. During the night, Luna heard the howl of the coyote and the hoot of the owl.

Luna enjoyed her time off from working. It was a nice balance to come home from the noisy fairs and chaotic energy. Luna had been working for Peter for almost two years. She decided not to renew her contract at the end of October. Instead, she would begin taking clients in her home. She prayed for help in making a good transition. Luna printed business cards and handed them out at the fairs over the next two months. Many clients began to refer new clients.

By November, Luna was taking clients in her home. It did not seem to matter that she was fifty or sixty miles away. Word of mouth brought them. Luna could now take as many or as few as she desired. She scheduled Friday evening and Saturday appointments.

It had been nearly two years since the Sky Beings had come to visit her. The four native spirits guided her when she smoked the Sacred Pipe and prayed daily.

Tonight she thought about her Sky friends. As she looked up into the star-scaped Sky, she was grateful and at peace with using her gift of insight to help people.

Luna had a soothing cup of chamomile and lavender tea before bed and fell into blissful regeneration. After a few hours of sleep, she heard her name being called from a distance. When she awoke she found Alcor, Matar and Chara at the foot of her bed.

"Greetings, dear one," Alcor said. "You are doing well. We heard your thoughts and gratitude. It is time for you to use the divine energy within. We infused you with the energy when you were a child. It is now time for you to share this with humans. Remember the bands of energy that you experienced with Cyrus? You will need to help human beings mend these bands, like when you helped your sibling Leana. Many need help because their mental, emotional and spiritual bodies have damaged their physical bodies. We will remind you."

Once again, as in the past, the three infused the divine universal energy into Luna's head, heart and hands. Luna initially felt the coldness within her body and then she felt the warmth. She could see into the human body like an x-ray. Her heart would feel another human's emotions. Her hands would feel the pulsing and sensation of life flowing through another human's body.

"Dearest, you must remember to prepare and attune yourself, and allow the energy to flow through you and into another being. You must also discontinue the flow, clear yourself and re-energize through rest once you have finished the energy exchange. Focus on the area needing attention and then release the energy. Allow the energy to expand into the form of the being, and to flow to where it is needed. Trust it. You will begin to use this very soon. You will know when the time is right," he explained.

"Dearest," announced Chara. "Do you remember the process of discharging energy? Remember the teachings on Vega? The insect race used the appropriate crystal circle formation."

"Yes, I remember. I have collected similar crystals from vendors at the fairs," she replied.

"Well, the time is approaching for you to disconnect from your reptilian mater. Your mission requires for you to engage in human relationship. You cannot fully accept your humanness without this form of relationship. The human heart demands such an experience. The relationship with the reptilian is both protective and possessive. It will not allow you to expand your humanness. You came here to express your mission in the human form. You must tell the story of the stars and the Center of Oneness. You still continue to separate yourself from your humanness. Every being has its own uniqueness. Accept this and the struggle within you will dissipate. Feel your connection to the Center and your spirit within. You have seen that all is connected to the Center in the same way. Yet, you still feel separate from your own kind, the human being. To tell the story you must accept your own humanness, and then lead through example. The disconnection from the reptilian will allow you to trust and accept relationships in your life," Chara said.

"But we only have contact a few times a year. What's the harm in that? I love him. He helps me and watches over me," she protested.

"As do we dear, yet you have your free will to choose to use the guidance we give or not. You have to live here among human beings. You struggle with keeping your secrets. Sooner or later you must fully embrace all of yourself, the spirit and the body. You are always protected because of the spirit within. It never dies. It is eternal. Only the human form transforms and fades away. You know this. You still remember how you came to the Earth. Why do you need the reptilian to protect you?" Chara asked.

Chara is right, Luna thought. *There should be no fear. The spirit light will eventually transcend and continue to move on. I have to disconnect. I have become too comfortable and dependent on Rastaban.*

The being's energy did bring euphoria to Luna. Rastaban would awaken Luna from her sleep, and immerse her in the melding energy for a few moments before leaving. In the beginning he would take her to Etamin. In the last several years, the visits had become brief interludes. Luna was beginning to understand, with Chara's help, that Rastaban was possessive and keeping her connected to his energy. Realizing that she was trapped, she agreed to perform the disconnection soon.

"In the future, you will help other humans disconnect from the reptilian maters as well. Again, it is part of your gift to serve the spirit and help the Earth Star," Chara said.

"Chara, I have started to learn from the Native American Indian ancestors. The native spirit guides speak with me. I pray and communicate with them. Is this still part of the mission?" she asked.

"Communication is important. They are spirits connected to the Center that have lived in human form before. They will serve you well. They will help you to live as a human being. They have chosen their mission to be of service to you and not return to the Center. Each being with or without form is a teacher filled with spirit energy from the Center."

The beings faded and disappeared.

In the following days, she prepared for the disconnection. She purchased white candles to use with the crystals. She would perform the ritual when the Moon was growing dark and in the time of release.

Time of Gifts

Luna's reading appointments were filled for Saturday. The downstairs bedroom became the reading room. Luna decorated the room with Native American Indian artifacts that she bought at Powwows over the summer. A lovely hand woven rug made by a Pueblo woman was used as a table scarf for her reading altar. She filled the room with gemstones, river rocks and crystals. Scented candles and sage bundles that were used to clear the energy were placed on the shelf beside the door's entrance. Luna lit the sage stick and carefully fanned the smoke to clear each client, when they entered the sacred space.

This morning's client, Molly, arrived on time.

"Welcome, Molly. I am Luna."

After clearing Molly, Luna added, "Please, have a seat."

"Thank you," Molly replied.

"So how can I help you? What would you like to know?" Luna asked.

As Molly relaxed into the chair, a face appeared over her shoulder. It was a young woman in her early twenties. She was smiling and had long blonde hair and vibrant energy.

"I am her sister. She misses me terribly. Tell her I'm okay. We did everything together. Tell her I'm okay. Tell her please," the young woman repeated.

Luna realized that Molly could not have been much older than her sister.

"Molly, your sister is here. She is okay. You miss her very much. The two of you were very close. You are a couple of years older than her."

Molly started to cry, "I don't believe you. How did she die?"

"She died on impact a few months ago, in a car accident. She is showing me her head. Her head was injured when it went through the windshield," Luna replied.

"What is her name? If it really is her, what is her name?" Molly cried.

The young woman replied, "Missy, Melissa."

"You called her Missy. Her name was Melissa," Luna answered.

"If it really is her, what is her favorite song?" Molly pressed.

"Look, this is not a dog and pony show. I do not need to prove to you it is her. I just need to relay the message," Luna lashed back.

Luna realized that some people did not want to believe her. They were in denial and Luna would not waste her energy trying to convince them. Her role was to listen and relay the message to appease the spirit, so they could rest and move on.

Missy started to softly sing *Happy Birthday* over and over.

"Molly, she is singing *Happy Birthday*," Luna said.

"No, that was not her favorite song," she snapped.

"Molly, she is singing *Happy Birthday*. Is today the time around her birthday?" Luna asked.

"No." Molly was confused, blocking the message from Missy.

"Happy Birthday, dear Molly," Missy sang.

"Molly, it's *your* birthday," Luna informed.

Molly froze. "Tomorrow is my birthday! I didn't get that. *She's* wishing *me* a happy birthday. When we couldn't spend my birthday together, she would call by phone and sing, *Happy Birthday*. Oh my God. I can't believe she is here," Molly sobbed.

"Missy is okay. She wants you to move on and to be happy," Luna confirmed.

Luna continued the reading and provided Molly with information about other areas of her life. Molly embraced Luna as she left.

"Thank you, I feel my heart has been freed. I would love to recommend you to my friends."

"Thank you, I would appreciate that," Luna said gratefully as she handed a business card to her.

Luna's early afternoon appointment was a little frustrating. Jonathan was a handsome man in his late thirties, with reserved energy. His face held a smirk that looked like a cat that caught a mouse. Luna felt this man was not a believer and wondered why he wanted a reading at all. If he wasn't going to open himself up, Luna was not going to perform the reading. It would take too much energy and she did not want to waste her time.

"You need to relax. Take a few deep breaths. I feel you are not a believer," Luna said.

"Well, you're right. I am not sure I believe in this, but I will try to be open."

Jonathan relaxed and took a few deep breaths.

"Now, what would you like to know about? What questions do you have?" she asked.

"I have no questions. Just tell me whatever you see," he smirked.

Luna relaxed and closed her eyes. Luna went into the vision.

"I see two of you. You have a twin. You look alike, only he parts his hair on the opposite side as you. It's something your mother used to do when you were both little. You have a small family restaurant together. He is getting married soon. You are worried about the business. Save your money. You will buy him out. He will open his own business in another town. All will be well between the two of you. By the winter you will need a new cook. I see a woman. If you are open to it, it could eventually become a lasting relationship."

Luna opened her eyes. Jonathan was astonished.

"You must be the real deal. No one has ever been able to read me," he implied.

"Well, no wonder. You block the energy when you doubt and are not open," Luna confirmed.

"Okay," Jonathan smiled. "I have a few more questions."

Luna had won him over. Luna never tried to sell herself. She trusted what she saw, heard and felt. The information was always correct. She took her time to understand the information clear and concisely. When the dead spirits could not communicate clearly, they would use pictures, symbols or music to produce feelings and thoughts. Luna needed to relax and open herself up like a vessel and set aside her ego to understand the information.

Luna regularly visited her parents on Sunday mornings. Reading for clients was a topic she didn't discuss unless Leana was home. Leana had a lot of questions, while Claire and Tom were not nearly as interested. They would change the subject. Luna knew it was because they did not understand, and it made them a little uncomfortable. Luna did share her experiences from the Powwows.

Leana was eighteen years old and had a new boyfriend. Working part-time at a local diner on weekends, Leana waited tables and made good tips. She was a social butterfly. Her boyfriend was a sophomore in college. Leana had hoped to attend the same college as her boyfriend, Rick, next year. Luna had only met Rick twice before, at the holidays. He seemed to be a nice person with good energy.

Luna experienced people through their energy field. She was very sensitive, and would leave if the energy was not good. Sometimes just standing by a person with negative, dense energy would drive Luna to escape. It would feel like she was drowning in quicksand. Sometimes it was hard to breathe and other times she would feel sick to her stomach. Many times, she would feel emotions like anger and sadness. Luna had learned to distinguish the energy of others from what she would personally feel, so that she could release and remove it from her energy field. Luna had learned from Cyrus to distinguish between the two, by going within to check her energy bands and seeing if it was within her, or just an imprint of energy from another person or room. Clear and clean energy was absolutely necessary for Luna to use her gifts. She cleared herself with the sage smoke every day she left her house and returned home. It was a ritual that kept her centered, grounded and balanced.

Luna wrote to Red Eagle and asked if she could visit. He asked her to visit the week of the vision quest in the spring. He could use the support. Luna would help with the cooking duties and whatever else was needed. Two young men would be sequestered during the week. Luna scheduled to stay for two weeks, one for quest and one to visit Grandpa.

Luna planned her trip and wrote to Max. She kept in touch with him every month. Max was still living in California, and was also planning to help with the quest. It had been four years since he had left Red Eagle and was now a teacher of Social Economics at the University of California. His years on the road with Red Eagle allowed him to see the real world. He looked forward to reuniting with the crew in Montana. Sam and Willie still lived with Red Eagle. Both Luna and Max were excited to be in ceremony again.

Mater Cord

Luna kept busy. She remained at the filter plant and increased her clientele by working on Thursday evenings. She had no trouble filling her schedule with clients. Word of mouth made her very popular. Although Luna had made many male friends, she was still not open to courtship. She knew the time to disconnect from Rastaban had come.

Chara's words rang true in her mind, "*The disconnection from the reptilian will help you to trust other humans and embrace your own humanness.*"

It was cold in late November. Luna prepared her altar with the white candles and crystals in the circular formation on the blanket outside in the backyard. She knew when she opened up to fourth and fifth dimensions that she would need protection from the dark negative energies. So she brought the Sacred Pipe to hold her prayers. Luna understood the gentle balance of dark and light. Both had power. Though Rastaban was her friend, he would fight to remain with her. Luna had seen the reptilians struggle with disconnections when she was on Vega.

Antic had explained the experience quite thoroughly.

"The reptilian feeds off of the human's energy. Although they have their own life force, they enjoy entwining themselves with humans. It allows them to experience the full physical and emotional sensations of a human. They do not like to part. Their intent is not to harm, but when separation becomes a threat, they fight like a demon to remain and conquer."

Luna knew that she must prepare her mind, body and spirit for this task. She smoked the Sacred Pipe and called upon all her spirit helpers including the animal and winged nations. She prayed for the courage and strength to do what was best for her life and her mission. Offering smoke to the Great Spirit and her spiritual helpers, Sweet Willow Woman, Smooth Clay Face, Red Burning Sky and White Running Trail, she asked for guidance and protection. When Luna completed smoking, she felt a peace surrounding her and within.

One by one, she lit the candles and started the high pitched vibrational humming chant. The hum grew louder and louder in the night. A crystallized web-like grid began to form above and around Luna. It was then she heard the sound, a loud piercing screech. It was a sound of frenzy and anger. Rastaban flew in from the Sky to force his way to the grid. The reptilian pushed and crashed, trying to demolish the grid. Luna continued the humming. The vibration encapsulated her. Rastaban thrashed back and forth, trying every angle to penetrate the grid. Rastaban wailed and screeched with anger and sadness. He knew what was happening and he didn't like it at all. He would lose Luna forever. Luna changed the humming tone. It was now a lower pitch, more of a rumbling. This would put Rastaban into a trance to sever the bond for good. As she hummed and held the vibration, tears fell slowly from her eyes. She felt Rastaban's pain, but was frightened to see his anger as he thrashed and charged against the grid. He was supposed to be her protector, not a wild animal. One whom she had thought loved her. But his actions were not love. They had become desperate and controlling. This was a side of aggression she had never before seen in him. Luna realized she was making the right choice. She had allowed herself to be held captive in his energy for too long.

Her low rumbling voice began to build voltages of energy until it finally discharged bolts and severed the cord between Rastaban and herself. It shot Rastaban dispersing back in a flash of light into his former dimension. Finally, it was over. She was disconnected. The grid above and around her had disappeared. The candles had melted and were barely flickering. Hours had passed. Luna was exhausted. She extinguished the candles and fell immediately into a deep sleep. The disconnection had depleted her. Rastaban's energy was no longer a part of her.

In her sleeping state, a man was coming towards her with his hand out to greet her. Luna could not see his face, only the image of his body.

He wore dark jeans and a flannel shirt. He had a leather vest. He wore a native bone beaded choker around his neck. His hair was dark and speckled with wisps of gray hair at the temples. He was standing by a lake and the Sun was shining so brightly that she could not see his face. Luna felt herself walking towards him, and when she reached him, he embraced her. A completeness, as if she had found a home and a soft place to rest her head and belong. Tears filled her eyes and she began to cry. Luna cried so hard that she awoke from the dream. Shivering, Luna wiped her eyes and remembered her dream and the feelings of love and acceptance that came with it.

She gathered her blanket and altar pieces and brought them into the house. The Sun would rise in an hour. Luna dropped herself into bed for more sleep. It was Sunday and she could sleep as long as she needed.

As the weeks passed, Luna felt different. At first it was a sense of loss, coupled with fatigue. An empty sadness engulfed her. She often cried for no apparent reason when she was alone. She allowed herself to grieve the disconnection throughout the winter, and often cried to release the emotion.

By spring, the emptiness subsided and a new self emerged. The crocuses in her front yard announced the arrival of spring. A new chapter was about to begin. Soon she would be back with Grandpa.

Montana Reflection

In April, Luna packed her camping essentials and flew to Helena. Luna and Max met at the airport and split the cost of a rental car. They stopped at a market to buy canned food, instant coffee, water, ice, extra batteries for the flashlights and a cooler. Luna and Max chatted as they drove to Red Eagle's cabin.

"Luna, you look good. I'm so glad we could embark on this trip together. It will be good to get back in the lodge and purify with Grandpa," Max confided.

"Yes, it will. I haven't been in lodge for a couple of years. I need the purification," she replied.

"I met a group that purifies regularly in California and I have been welcomed into their community. I try to purify at least once a month. The elder is a fine native man, but he's no Red Eagle," Max winked.

"I know. I don't think that we will ever meet another Red Eagle. He is one of a kind," she added.

Luna stared at Max as he drove. She had never realized how handsome he was and what a great smile he had. Max was eleven years older than Luna. She had always considered him a brotherly type. Now as Luna looked at him, it was as if a veil from her eyes had been lifted. Her eyes were now attracted to a man. She could see the beauty in his masculinity. His red hair was much shorter and neatly trimmed. His face was clean shaven.

"So Max, have you gotten married or anything yet?" Luna giggled.

"No, but I am dating a lady colleague of mine. It's nothing serious though. What about you, little sister?"

"No. I haven't had time. Readings on the weekends, keep me busy," she laughed.

"Well, you'd better not wait too long. You don't want to get to be an old man like me," Max joked.

"Oh you're not old, Max. It's just that your face is tired," she laughed.

"Thanks a lot. Just like the old times, huh Luna?" he smiled.

"We'd better be ready to work. You remember how much work the quests were. Splitting the wood and lugging it with the truck. Preparing and clearing the quester's spot, setting up the altar, cooking all the food for the feast and a week of little sleep. Remember all the fun?" Max asked.

"Yeah, I remember," Luna reflected. *The days were long and the work was physically hard, but the spiritual gains outweighed it all.*

They arrived at the cabin and were put to work immediately. Luna met three new people that were staying with Red Eagle. One was a young teenager named Mary who was helping with the domestic chores. The other two men would be questing. Each would be sequestered for two days. Tommy was eighteen and had met Red Eagle in Utah. He was half Native American Indian and half Mexican. He was a tall young man, about six feet in height. He could split wood with one swing. The second man was a couple of years older. His name was Roger and he was from Texas. He had come to Red Eagle's lecture in Arizona and was now recovering from alcohol abuse. Red Eagle took him in and helped him stay clean for the past two years. Luna was happy to support the two men.

Once the preparation work was done, Luna had a few minutes to visit with Red Eagle before he became immersed with the spirits. Grandpa welcomed her back with a hug.

"Granddaughter, it's good to see you back here. Are you being human?" he chuckled.

"Yes, I am trying," she replied with a giggle.

"Are you getting along with other human beings? What about your mother?" he asked.

"Things are okay. I've moved out and I have my own life. I am using my gift by doing intuitive readings for clients. I am praying regularly with the Sacred Pipe. I have not yet found love or a relationship, but I am now open to it. I have grown, Grandpa. The spirit helpers come in when I need guidance. My Sky friends come to help as well. I am so grateful for all that I have. But I have no one to talk to and share things with like I did with you. It's slow, but I am learning to be me, a human being with a spirit inside," she said.

"Hau, someday you will share your past and your future with a *half-side,* a partner. He will help you to trust and share yourself with the world. Great Spirit gives us the ability to experience our humanness with all beings here on the Grandmother Earth. We must not waste our lives or wait too long. The human shell deteriorates quickly. Time here is so short and limited. Release your fear and surrender to Great Spirit. Everything will be okay, stop struggling. Let the road open to you. Man sometimes blocks his own path. He struggles because his mind resists what is placed before him. Go with the flow from Spirit. Stay in balance, hau."

Grandpa stood and walked to his bedroom.

"Good night, Grandpa," she replied.

Morning came soon. The men were purified and sequestered on their separate altars on the hill. They were placed about a quarter-of-a-mile from each other to ensure complete solitude. It would be two days before they were welcomed back.

Luna began her daily routine of preparing the meals for the small group of supporters. Max continued to split wood to maintain the fire for the supporters' purifications every evening. The people prayed vigilantly for the questers' safety and strong vision. The camp was quiet as the fire was tended. Meals were eaten. When the supporters ate, they remembered both of the questers, Roger and Tommy. The energy of the food would nourish them on the hill.

On the first night of the quest, Grandpa said the supporters needed to make strong prayers. He said that Spirit told him both men were having a hard time. The evening purification was intense and hot. The steam was so dense Luna could barely keep her eyes open in the darkness. Red Eagle's prayers were strong. He had asked Luna to be the singer for that evening. Luna hoped she could remember the purification songs. She drummed and led the songs when Red Eagle called for them.

She was humbled twice when the steam caught her voice in the back of her throat and made her choke. She allowed her voice to rise above the steam. Smooth Clay Face entered the lodge and took over Luna's voice so that she could continue. Luna relaxed and found that her voice was not her own. She heard the song come from within her, but it was not she who was singing. It was powerful and sweet. It crooned and soothed. Smooth Clay Face's voice entered her body as she became one with the wise woman spirit. The experience was overwhelming. She returned to herself after the last prayer song had been completed.

When the purification was over, the supporters commented on Luna's voice, and how it helped them rise above the heat and stay in their prayers.

Luna thanked them but politely said, "It wasn't me."

Red Eagle came to her aid, "A Grandmother spirit came in to help you. You know her. She is the earth element. She has been with you a long time. It is good you let her help you. When you pray for help, you must learn to surrender. You did good," he smiled.

The next day was long. Luna remembered how slowly time passed on the hill. She remembered her three night quest like it was yesterday. It had been unusually hot for late spring. The temperature almost reached one hundred degrees. The Sun had shone each day and the Sky was clear. No clouds. No overcast. Luna's face, arms and legs had burned in the Sun. On each of her quests, Luna had experienced periods of extreme dehydration that were very hard to endure. But each time, through prayer, the hard times passed. The first and second days of her three day quest had been quiet: there were few birds, and little to no movement of any kind. The third day, however, was the day of surprise. A straggly lone coyote had come from the brush and circled outside Luna's altar and blanket. Luna had begun to pray on her knees.

"Brother, I know you bring awareness and are a trickster. Please give me your message, I am listening."

The coyote had sniffed the blanket, and began to howl and play, running around the blanket. It had made Luna laugh. It had reminded her not to be so serious. It was okay to play and have fun. It had lifted its head to the Sky and howled again and again. It was unusual for a coyote to howl during the day. As it howled, Luna had distinguished a repetitive tune. The coyote was gifting a song to her, a song that warned her against being too serious; a call for assistance to help lighten heavy situations. Red Eagle would later interpret the song as one for Luna to use to help heal the heart and bring joy. What a precious gift it would become for her.

Luna returned from the memory and went back to her supporting chores of cooking. In the evening, Luna entered the supporters' final purification lodge. Max was asked to be the singer for this evening. Red Eagle had spent the last two days in seclusion and prayer with Spirit to remain connected to the two men on the hill. He checked in spiritually to see what prayers they needed to complete their quest.

Red Eagle was in a somber trance-like state. Luna had seen this many times before. He started the purification ceremony by inviting his spiritual helpers. He sang his prayer in his native tongue. He prayed for the men on the hill as did the supporters in the lodge. But now, he spoke very seriously and directly in English. Luna knew it was a message from the spirit world.

"She Falls to Earth, Spirit has a message for you. You are too serious. You think only about your mission. Human life is to be lived and shared. Your service to your human brothers and sisters must not be placed before your needs. Love the whole self. Open your heart to find and embrace your whole being. Not just the spirit inside, the human being too. Then you can be your true self and do what you came to do. Only then can you embrace other humans. Stop hiding yourself. When you embrace the whole self, you will learn love. You can be happy here on the Earth. The spirit within is born from the stars into a human body made from the Grandmother Earth. Be still. Stop looking for acceptance outside of yourself. Do not fear what you know is true. Share it. Great Spirit has given you a life. Live by loving fully. Spirit wants you to pour seven lodges, hau," he ended.

Luna listened carefully. She heard every word and reflected.

Yes, I am afraid. I have feared what my mother told me when I was small. That I would be put away in a hospital away from my parents if I talked about knowing, seeing and hearing things. Wait a minute... Pour seven lodges? That would mean I would have to run purification ceremony. What did he mean? I don't understand. How could I do that? I do not know how to pour or run ceremony. I'm not a leader, or anyone of importance. I've been a part of many purifications but that is not the same. I don't want the responsibility.

Luna began to shake and tremble. Goosebumps covered her body. She shivered and closed her eyes. Her heart began to race faster and faster as she lost her breath and choked for air. She panicked and felt a terrible pain in her chest. The ego was being shattered inside. She had never been afraid to die because she knew her spirit would live on and return to the Center of the Great Spirit. But now, in this moment of human weakness, she began to cry. Her body felt like she was dying from fear. All the physical symptoms were there, pain in her chest and difficulty breathing. She realized she was not ready to leave her body and the Earth Star. She *wanted* to be a human being and have relationships. She needed to share what she had learned from the stars and she needed to fully experience humanness.

Luna had to release her fear and surrender. A small spark of light appeared above her head. Luna opened her eyes wide. *Are they coming to take me now?* The light became large and pulled her into the tunnel. Luna felt her physical body surrender, becoming weightless, floating through the spiraling tunnel. All of her earthly memories came to meet her, the spark of entry into mother's womb, her birth; her mother's tear dropping upon her cheek and her soft voice, calling Luna "her beautiful girl." The overnight hospital stays. The fear in her parents eyes when they had to leave, abandoning her at the hospital, Cyrus' visits, meeting Alcor, Chara and Matar and the memories of Merope, Vega, Etamin and Alpha Centauri.

Her childhood memories were flashing by in an instant. Boys in the schoolyard calling her Lunatic, her teachers sending troubling notes home, her mother's disparaging looks, Grandma Anna leaving the Earth, Cyrus leaving, being on the road with Red Eagle, Native American teachings of ceremony and prayer, questing, reading for clients and disconnecting Rastaban. The memories brought her back to the present moment in the purification lodge. Luna's emotions of anger, resentment, fear and grief consumed her spirit being. Her consciousness heard the message within the lighted tunnel.

"Surrender… Surrender your fear of not belonging. Surrender your fear of abandonment. Surrender your grief and sorrow. Surrender your anger and resentment of those who did not understand you. Surrender and let your light shine within your humanness. Let it go. Release it all. Love yourself and your experiences. You are a perfect being. Let life flow within and through you. Just be."

Luna heard the voice in her consciousness. She understood. Be the human. Be the light of spirit. Just be. Let go of everything else. *I am enough and I need nothing else. Just be and live.* Luna was engulfed with a wave of bliss. The tunnel of light released her. Her physical body was now comfortable in the darkness of steam and heat. The shakes and shivers were gone. She could inhale and exhale easily. The pain and panic were released. The fear was released. The anger and abandonment were gone. She wanted to open and share herself with the world. No more hiding. She wanted to be in and of the world and take her place in life and to experience it fully, using and sharing all of her gifts and knowledge. Opening up to new experiences and being in love with her precious human life. Tears flowed from her eyes. The release of struggling on this Earth had to come to an end. It was a new understanding.

"Thank you, Grandpa. Thank you, Spirit," Luna said quietly to herself. Red Eagle's message came in loud and clear for Luna.

It was a powerful purification indeed.

The next morning, the two men came down from the hill separately and were welcomed back to the community. Red Eagle interpreted each of their quests for them with help from Spirit. Luna and the other women had made a delicious feast for the community. A buffalo roast, rice, beans, corn and a berry pudding fed and filled everyone with contentment. The feast ended with Tommy and Roger's giveaway. The questers, in gratitude, had a gift for each person in the community that supported and prayed for them while they were on the hill. The elder Red Eagle was given tobacco, sage, cedar, a braid of sweet grass (the traditional four sacred herbs) and a beautiful wool blanket. Tommy gave Luna a pair of beaded earrings. Roger gifted Luna a lovely sterling silver cuff bracelet engraved with a bear paw.

Luna was tired from the week of supporting, and was looking forward to spending time with Grandpa.

Max left the next morning, leaving the rental car with Luna. He hitched a ride with Willie to the airport.

Luna sat on the porch with Red Eagle.

"You must pour seven lodges, Spirit said. I will teach you. Spirit will do the rest," Red Eagle commanded.

"I heard you in the lodge. Why me, Grandpa? I am scared. Who am I to run ceremony?" she protested.

"Hau, don't question Spirit. I will tell you what to do in the ceremony and Spirit will help you with the rest. Spirit has given you permission. You would not be asked to do something if Spirit was not going to help. Trust and pay attention," he replied.

Grandpa spent the day going over the teachings. That evening Luna poured the first purification ceremony with only Grandpa by her side. Grandpa called for more water. White Running Trail came into the lodge and hovered above the stone pit. He spoke to Luna about working with the four elements of the purification ceremony. It was time for her to learn how to help other people bridge the Earth and Sky. It was her lineage, and it was time to accept this honor to help people. She had much to learn. She had a choice as to whether or not her lineage would die out. White Running Trail left before the final round of prayers. Grandpa sang the songs for Luna. For the next week, Luna poured the evening lodge.

Everyday, Grandpa gave teachings about the purification ceremony, while Luna accompanied him on day trips to local people needing his healing care. Luna helped mix his herbal tinctures and even accompanied him into the hills at sunrise when it was time to look for a particular plant that he needed. It was always at a moment's notice. No schedule or plan, just the heed of Spirit's call.

Luna was driving the new rental car back to Red Eagle's cabin. Red Eagle was impressed but he felt it was too small. He was used to the old van.

"This pony's too small," he laughed.

"Yeah, but it gets thirty-five miles to the gallon when it gallops," Luna replied.

"Spirit had much to teach you in the quest purification. Guess you decided to stay, huh?" he chuckled.

"What do you mean, Grandpa?" Luna asked.

"You had a chance to leave the lodge during quest, to go back with Spirit. You decided to stay here among us humans," he smiled.

"I was told to surrender the fear, grief and anger. I was shown my life here from the time of my entry. I was shown the stars and the Sky Beings who live there. I was shown my sorrows and fears of being myself, Grandpa. I did not think I could leave. I didn't know I could choose to leave in that moment. I guess I was afraid to leave. I have never felt that before," Luna said.

"If you knew, would you have left?" he asked.

"No, I don't think so. I want to be here. I guess I still want to live in my human body. I was not ready. I never even thought about leaving in that moment. It is interesting," she wondered. "All this time I longed to go Home to the Center. And when it came down to being able to do just that, I was in fear of leaving. I guess I like it here more than I thought," she laughed.

"It is because you have accepted you're a human being, an earth walker, and now maybe you can finally love yourself in this body, uniting your whole self, spirit and body. You are loved because you have the love inside you. No conditions. We are made from Spirit itself. We are all enough. We are connected to the same and we are all the same. As humans, we are responsible to remember our spirit being inside, and as spirit beings we are responsible to take care of and use our human form. There should be no fear. The *robe* or body only transforms when it is time to cross, but the spirit within us lives on forever. You have seen this and know this to be true with all the spirits you have seen. Enjoy and learn from this human experience and help others to know this. Spirit has also given you something else, a right to live your heritage. One needs to know their heritage. You have found yours. You are given the honor of pouring for the next generation. Will you keep it alive? Will you choose to live it? It is up to you. The Great Spirit knows your heart and knows you are a vessel to help humans. This is the way to help people release all the emotional and mental messes that they make. This is a good day for me; to hand the teachings to you. Hau," he said.

"But I have only little Indian blood in me. I am more white-skinned. People won't believe me. What right do I have to pour?" she asked.

"Spirit gives you the right. I will give you the teachings. Spirit has chosen you to continue this way of life, to purify and to pray with the Sacred Pipe. It will help you stay grounded to the Earth and its people, your relatives and relations. Someday you will write about your journeys and tell them all about the spirit and human connection. It will help many who wish to remember. I have seen many things change over the years. I would not have chosen a woman to sing in purification for me, but Spirit chose you. I would not have gifted a Sacred Pipe to you, but Spirit chose you. I would not have chosen to teach you to run purification, but Spirit once again has chosen you. I have always followed Great Spirit and my spirit helpers. I have great trust in them. Granddaughter, *this* is a good day," he said with a smile.

"And writing a book?" Luna asked.

"You will know when it's time. Just shine your spirit. Folks will find you when they need to. Don't worry about the book. Spirit will guide you. Stay in the present and pray. Build your lodge in the future to purify. Live, love and pray. Stay close to Grandmother Earth. The Sky is always within you," he said.

"Thank you, Grandpa. Thank you for all your teachings. I love you," Luna said with misty eyes.

"Hau. Let's get some black medicine," he demanded.

Luna knew he wanted coffee. He took it black with lots of sugar.

The last night of her visit, Grandpa invited a few of his friends to share the seventh and final purification with Luna. Several cars came and ten people were ready to purify. Luna started to panic.

"Grandpa, why are all these people here? I thought we were having the last purification ceremony?" she asked.

"Yup, we are. You're going to purify them," he smiled.

"But…" she stammered. "It has been the two of us all week. I am not ready," she protested.

"Hau, Spirit, says you're ready… sounds like your ego needs a lesson. What are you afraid of? You know what to do and Spirit will take care of the rest. It is not about you. It is about serving Spirit and helping the people. They are your relations. They need help. You can help. You are ready. Open up to Spirit and your helpers. Trust and surrender," he said as walked away.

Luna walked into the wooded area behind the cabin. She fell to her knees and began to cry. Her fear was great.

"Oh Great Spirit, Grandfather, Grandmother, please help me. I am afraid I might burn people with the steam. I don't know what I am doing. Help me."

Luna groveled, hoping an answer would come to her from above.

And then it did. A branch from the tree above her head snapped and fell on her head. It was a good size branch that stung and it awoke her from her hysterical tears.

"Ouch. What the heck?" she asked.

Luna laughed hard and more tears came. What a sight she must have been, carrying on the drama with such frenzy. Spirit had enough. The branch woke her from her ego. She breathed in, relaxed and was ready to pour.

"Thank you, Spirit," she whispered.

The people were ready, standing by the covered lodge. Luna called to the Spirit world and began the ceremony. She trusted her body and mind to her spirit guides. Grandpa sang the prayers and songs for each round. The people made their own prayers, as well. Some released their sadness with tears. Others were grateful. One had asked for healing. When the purification was completed all felt alive and renewed, like infants being born into the world again.

Luna barely remembered what happened inside the lodge during the purification ceremony. She just had a faint recall of one or two things. When one of the men thanked her afterwards for her words, Luna could not remember saying any of it. She asked Grandpa about this.

"This is the way Spirit will work with you. Just be open, like a hollow bone. Don't get in the way. True ceremony is lead by Spirit, not by man," he said.

The next morning, Luna said her goodbyes to Red Eagle. The two weeks were over. She promised to write and visit again.

"I don't know when I'll get to build a lodge for purification. It may be a while," she said.

"Spirit will tell you when. You will remember all that you need when the time is right," he said.

"I'll write to you soon. Maybe I'll come back next spring," she said with hope.

He nodded in gesture.

Grandpa's final words to Luna were, "Remember to live, love and pray. Serve Spirit and help your relations."

She would remind herself of this frequently, when she became unbalanced and old fears tried to creep in. Luna had no idea that this conversation would be the last teaching that she would receive from Grandpa.

A rebirth had taken place for Luna in Montana. A life she would now choose to live.

Love and Acceptance

Upon her arrival back home, Luna returned to her position at the filter plant and, after several weeks, realized she was unhappy. Her heart no longer wished to work at the plant. She only wanted to work with her gift. Many new clients were arranging appointments. Her evenings during the week were now being scheduled with clients.

Luna prayed for guidance as her heart recognized her passion. She remembered Alcor's words.

"Dearest, every human comes to the Earth Star with a special gift and mission. They are given these gifts to use with compassion and love, to help the physical world evolve to goodness and harmony, through the use of writing, art, music, teaching, oratory, invention, technology and healing. Each human has a unique talent. Following one's dreams, visions and aspirations is how one will find their gift and discover their mission. Every mission is similar. To bring love and goodness to the Earth and help each other evolve. But each gift is unique. Some, like you, have more than one. When you are using your gift, it brings great joy within yourself and to the Earth and its beings."

Luna thrived while helping the clients that came to her. This gave her purpose and fulfillment.

Satisfied clients referred her to friends and family. Luna began to take readings by phone. Now she could reach clients from out of state.

One client, a distraught woman from New York, had arranged an appointment. Luna prepared herself for the call through silent meditation and prayer. The phone rang as Luna centered herself.

"Hello."

"Hello. Is this Luna?"

"Yes."

"This is Marianne. I have an appointment with you."

"Good. Let's get started. What questions do you have for me?"

"I would like to know about my dog. He has been missing for over a week now," Marianne replied as she sniffled.

"Okay. Please don't speak anymore. Don't tell me anything else. Let me tune into the energy," Luna said.

Luna saw that the champion, brown Boxer had been retrieved by a white pick up truck. He was taken out of state over the New York border into New Jersey. The dog was a show dog named Champ de Leon. The young man who took him was an acquaintance of Champ's groomer. The groomer was not involved. Luna had seen the dog being treated well and being sold to someone prestigious in the dog competitions. Luna realized the canine would be sent across the country and she could see a sign that said California. When she asked if the dog was already in California, she was given affirmation. The vision offered that the dog would never return to Marianne. When she asked for the name of the new owner, her vision ended. Luna understood. It was not necessary information. Champ was only property to Marianne. Her feelings of loss over the dog came from her ego of financial worth and not from love.

Luna relayed all the information. Marianne was surprised with all the information Luna had seen.

"Okay, so where in California is he? What is the name of the person who bought him?" Marianne demanded.

"I was not given that information. The animal will never be returned to you. Just know that he will be treated well and loved. He will remain a show dog for a few years and then he will be happy and well taken care of after he retires. I am sorry, Marianne. An animal is not property. It is a living thing that should be loved and respected at all times," Luna stated.

"What do you mean he will never be returned to me? Why can't you see who has him and where exactly he is? You aren't very good at this!" Marianne screamed in anger.

"You asked about your dog. I told you what I have seen. I have given you the information and insight as it comes to me. I will also pass on this guidance… if another animal is taken into your home, perhaps you will connect your heart to it and cherish your furry companion next time," Luna said.

"Why tell me all of this if I won't get my dog back? What's the point?" Marianne asked testily.

"Your expectation is what holds you back from truly seeing the big picture. Champ is well and alive. He will be properly taken care of for many years. Isn't that what's most important? You will have a second chance to get another dog and have a better relationship with it than you had with Champ. This is a lesson. That is why we are all here, Marianne; to learn and experience," Luna professed.

The phone was silent. Marianne was probably fuming on the other end of the line. Several minutes went by in silence.

"Marianne, are you still there? Please be happy that Champ is happy. Did you not care about him at all? Of course you did. The loss of Champ has opened the door for you to embrace another dog in a better way, one that will bring you much more joy," Luna soothed.

Luna heard sniffles through the silence. Finally Marianne spoke.

"Maybe you are right. I am glad that you saw that he is alright. I guess I'm more upset that he was stolen. I feel violated and cheated. He was worth a lot of money. Yes, I will get another dog, one that I could have a better relationship with, but not a show dog" she agreed.

"Good," Luna replied.

"Thank you," Marianne replied and ended the session.

Prior to taking the phone reading, Luna wondered whether it might be more difficult to read the energy of a client who was not present in the room with her. But after the call with Marianne, Luna realized there was no difference. Luna allowed her energy to travel to the person wherever they were and the information was channeled easily. She was able to connect no matter how far away the client was.

Luna had the right words to help clients. Luna attributed this to the spiritual help she was given from outside of herself. It was not Luna's own wise and comforting words, but those that were passed through her. She was grateful everyday that this was able to happen.

Luna went to bed early that evening. She needed sleep to replenish her energy. Morning would come soon enough and she had to work at the filter plant.

Months later, Luna had read in the newspaper that there would be an intertribal Indian gathering on the coming Sunday in a nearby town. Luna decided to attend. She called for more information about protocol since she understood that each tribe had its own customs and ways. After asking what she could offer to bring for the feast, Luna decided on a vegetable green bean casserole.

On Sunday, the Penobscot woman whom she had spoken to on the phone welcomed her at the door.

"Welcome. I am Jean. Put your food on that far table with the others. It will be smudged with sage and blessed. Here, let us smudge you, too."

Luna was familiar with the fanning of sage smoke around her to clear her energy and center her being. An elder chief gathered the people in a circle around the tables. He first said a prayer in his language and then repeated it in English. He prayed with a long ceremonial pipe and offered the smoke to the directions. He completed the ritual with reverence and then the whole group sat down to feast. Luna introduced herself to several people.

A group of men sat around a large drum and started to sing in a connected rhythm. The sound echoed against the walls inside. A group of women with rattles stood behind them and began to add their high, shrill voices. The balanced melody created a magnified energy in the room. A circle was created and a chain of people dancing heel to toe emerged. They bent their knees and stepped in one-two timing.

"Come, Luna. Let's dance," Jean said as she draped an embroidered shawl over Luna's shoulders.

The men led the chain of dancers and the woman followed behind. The drum beat vibrated through Luna's entire being. She had only wished she could have been dancing outside on the Grandmother Earth. But it was December and the snow had already frozen the Earth in a blanket for renewal gestation.

Luna met people of many different tribal affiliations; Micmacs, Penobscots and Wampanoags. Many of the New England tribes were lighter skinned like herself; mixed blood, not dark skinned like Red Eagle and others she had met out West. It did not matter to this group how much Native American Indian blood a person had in their veins.

As Red Eagle often said, "We all bleed the same red. We are all earth keepers of the human race. We are all related."

Luna remembered this when she felt unworthy of learning the distant lineage ways.

She noticed an elder man with long white hair. He was dressed in a traditional tanned hide skin shirt. He had a circle of people gathered around him. Wondering if he was a leader, Luna asked Jean who the gentleman was.

"His name is *White Goose*. He is a storyteller. The children just love to hear him talk of the old ways and tell his stories of tribal tricksters like the rabbit and coyote, who teach the people valuable lessons," Jean replied.

Luna joined the group and stood in the background.

"Isn't he entertaining?" the voice behind her whispered.

Luna turned around to see the face of the whisper. Her gaze caught his eyes, and Luna felt a surge of energy within her. Her knees grew weak and became unbalanced. Her breath stopped for a brief moment. His wide smile revealed pearly white teeth. His eyes were green, like shiny emeralds. His dark hair was tied neatly in a small ponytail and framed his face with grace. Luna was quite taken by him. What was this surge of electricity she was feeling through her body from just his gaze? Luna composed herself quickly and lowered her eyes.

"Yes, he is," was all she could say.

"Hi, I'm Sonny. Sam Stafford, actually, but people call me Sonny."

Luna thought Sonny was a great name for him. His presence was bright like the Sun.

"Oh," she paused. "I'm Luna. Luna Belliveau."

"You mean like the Moon?" he chuckled. "I took Latin in high school."

"Yes," she nodded.

"What a coincidence. You're the Moon and I'm the Sun. What a chance meeting this is," he said with a smile.

Luna was overwhelmed. Her pulse was racing. She didn't think this was by chance. She was exactly where she needed to be at this moment in time. She was full of excitement and anxiety all at the same time. They listened to a few of White Goose's stories and then Sonny gently took Luna's hand and led her to a table to sit and talk.

"I haven't seen you here before. Is this your first time at this gathering?" he asked.

"Yes. I saw an advertisement in the newspaper and decided to attend. How about you?" she asked.

"Oh, I have been to many of these over the years. I have no Indian lineage to my name, but I have followed this way of life for several years. I am forty-five years old, have been divorced for ten years and have two sons in college. They are eighteen and nineteen. One is a freshman at the University of Maine. He looks just like his mother. The other is a sophomore at the University of Connecticut. So what's your story? You look young. Are you married?" he asked.

"Boy, you don't waste any time do you? No, I'm not married and have never been married. I have distant lineage that I was told about in my childhood. I've spent a few years learning from an elder in Montana. It was a wonderful experience. In fact, I just went back to visit him this past spring. He is a wonderful man and I'm so grateful to have met him," she said.

As Luna spoke about him she became very emotional. Her eyes filled with tears. Her mind began to float away from the room. She saw Red Eagle sitting in his old rocking chair. The chair was not creaking as usual. As she looked closer, she noticed his eyes were closed and he wasn't breathing. He was slumped in the chair with a smile on his face. Was he sleeping? Or had he crossed from the Earth plane? Was this real? Was it her own fear of abandonment or was it Grandpa's way of telling her of his transition?

"Luna, Luna?" Sonny shook her. "Hey, where did you go? Am I that boring?" he laughed.

"No. I'm sorry. I was just thinking about the elder," she said.

Luna enjoyed Sonny's company. He asked for her phone number and if they could get together for a coffee sometime.

"You mean like a date?" Luna asked with fright in her voice.

"Well, would that be so terrible? Do you think I'm too old? We could just go as friends and talk. I find you very interesting, Miss Luna. I would like to be your friend," he assured.

But the truth was he wanted to be *more* than friends. Since his divorce he had not been interested in dating anyone. But he was intrigued by this young woman, as if he had waited for her all his life. Of course he was not going to tell *her* that. He might scare her and never see her again. He needed to play it cool. But his heart was ready to burst. She had a glow around her that beckoned him to her.

"Well, okay," as she wrote her number down on a napkin, and sheepishly handed it to him.

"Here is my number," she replied.

What's wrong with me? What am I feeling? I'm so nervous. This man's presence had quickened her breathing and made her palms sweaty and her stomach flutter. *Calm down,* she told herself. *He's too old anyways. Or is he?*

Sonny gave Luna a small hug and said he would call her soon. Luna pretended to be nonchalant about the whole thing. Secretly she hoped he would call tomorrow.

When Luna returned home, she had a message on her answering machine. It was Max asking her to call him back. He sounded lifeless and sad. Luna realized what she had seen earlier today had been real. She returned his call and they wept together.

"They found him smiling in his rocking chair. He was eighty. He had no health problems that we knew of. He did purification that morning, and then dressed in his best clothes and sat in his old rocker on the porch of his cabin. Willie said he heard him singing and chanting for a while. When Willie returned from chopping wood, Mary was kneeling and crying at his feet. I suppose it was his heart. He took his last breath with a smile," Max said.

"You know Max, I saw it. This afternoon I had a vision and was transported to him. I believe he was ready for his transition. I guess he completed what he was supposed to do. What a peaceful way to leave the body. We were lucky to have met him," she added. "I will try to go to the memorial. But I don't know if the filter plant will let me take the time off. I have no more vacation time left for this year. Let me know the arrangements."

Luna prayed with the Sacred Pipe to honor her teacher, Red Eagle and offered prayers of gratitude and for his journey home. She sobbed and grieved. When she was finished, she went to the bathroom and began to sing an honoring song. Then she cut off her long waist length hair bluntly, straight across above her shoulders. Red Eagle had told her that Indian women would cut their hair to grieve a loved one who had passed. She decided to honor him and show her grief. Her hair would grow back in time. She cut twelve inches of her dark locks.

Luna returned to work the next day, explained the situation and asked her supervisor for unpaid leave.

"I am sorry Luna, but I can't do that. Then everyone would want to take time off and production would stop. I can't do it for one person and not another. You're asking for four days. That's almost a week of work. I am sorry," he said.

Luna was disappointed. She needed to be there for the memorial. It was important to her. But what should she do? Luna prayed for guidance.

After being told the details for the memorial, she decided to call in sick to work and let the chips fall where they may. If she got fired, she was sure that something else would come.

She wasn't happy at the job anyway. Maybe this was the break she needed. She threw caution to the wind and booked a flight to Montana and put herself in the hands of Spirit. She left on Tuesday morning and called in sick. Her supervisor said she would be fired if she missed any more than one day. Luna thanked him for the opportunity and said, "Sometimes, you have to choose what is right in your heart."

Luna felt free as she flew to Montana. She would meet Max once again at the airport and share a car rental. Luna had rearranged her scheduled clients for the next few days.

She briefly thought about Sonny. She wondered if he would call while she was away. She worried that he would not call again if she did not return his call. *Let it go,* she told herself, *turn it over to Spirit.*

The memorial was a beautiful scene. This man was loved. Hundreds of people came to honor him. It was held in the local high school gymnasium. The group of drummers and singers sang the honoring song. A fire was built outside and the sacred foods were offered to feed his spirit and light the way for his journey home.

Many people shared their stories of happy times and their healings with Red Eagle. The four days came to an end and in his honor; there was a give-away of his possessions to his former students and close family members. Max and Luna were invited. Luna told Max she was uncomfortable with this. She didn't want anything to be given to her. Max said to refuse would be disrespectful.

Red Eagle's daughter, Sharon, (Little Doe) had met Luna several times throughout the years when Luna traveled with Grandpa. Sharon called Luna to come forth and spoke lovingly.

"My father told me of your gifts. He told me last week, to pass these sacred things on to you. He said you would need them one day."

She handed Luna a bundle of herbs, salves and tinctures. The bundle contained a rattle, tail feather and an instrument to call upon her spirit guides.

"I honor you for taking care of my father on the road for seven years and learning your ancestors' ways. Please honor these sacred things in the way he taught you. You will honor his memory each time you do."

"Thank you. I will honor his teachings," she choked.

Luna received the bundle. She had seen him use the sacred things many times over the years. He used the tail feather to fan the smoke, to bless and clear, and also to extract sickness in a specific way. She would keep the bundle in a safe place.

Max received one of Grandpa's favorite belt buckles and Grandpa's sacred hand drum. The buckle was made of silver buffalo nickels. The drum was made by Grandpa many years ago. Max was honored to receive it.

The feast of berries, corn, beans and game meat concluded the give-away. She had no regrets leaving the job at the filter plant. Luna remembered the Sky Being's prophecy, that one day she would use her ability to mend the bands inside people. She wondered when she would begin. Luna surrendered to Spirit, the ancestral guides and the Sky Beings to guide her.

Luna's Heart

Luna returned home. There were no messages from Sonny. Her heart sank in disappointment. There were however, several messages from new clients, ten new appointments to schedule. She trusted she would have enough to pay her rent.

Two weeks went by. During one of her readings the answering machine recorded the call from Sonny.

"Hi, Luna. It's Sonny, from the Intertribal gathering. Sorry I haven't called you sooner. I lost your number. I know that sounds like a load of bull but it's true. I had it in my wallet and somehow misplaced it. Anyway, I found it today. I sure would like that cup of coffee. How about joining me? I could come out your way to meet you. Hope you are well. Please give me a call."

Sonny left his number for Luna to call him back.

Luna had five clients that day and only checked her messages at the end of the day. When she heard Sonny's voice she began to sing and dance around the room.

"He called me, he called me, he finally called me," she chanted like a child.

What do I say when I call him back? I'm not going to ask him out. Wait a minute, he did ask me out first, right? That's what he said on the phone, to get a cup of coffee.

Luna was frantic. She was a nervous wreck. What was it about this man that made her so crazy and childish? Luna never experienced this before. She couldn't think straight.

He would have to drive an hour to meet Luna. He lived at the border in New Hampshire and Luna was in Massachusetts. Maybe she

"While we're talking so openly, I have something to ask you. Do you believe in life on other planets? I mean celestial life out there?" Luna asked, pointing to the Sky.

"Of course, I do. Although, I haven't seen life from other planets, it's hard to believe that Earth is the only place where life exists."

"I have seen life from the stars," Luna gulped hard waiting for the disbelief.

"You mean like aliens?" he asked.

"They don't like to be called aliens. *Sky Beings*, are what they prefer. They have shown and taught me many things. They are real and they are helpful. They keep me aware of my mission on the Earth," she said firmly.

Luna proceeded to explain her mission, sharing pieces of herself that she had withheld from everyone but Grandpa. Luna told Sonny of Spirit's request to write a book when the time was right. Luna tearfully unloaded years of bottled up secrets and emotions. It was as if the dam of emotions was gushing forth to be released. Why was she sharing this with a man she barely knew? Why was she so trusting of him? In this moment, it did not matter if he ran away and she never saw him again. It was time to trust and embrace herself. Sonny just held Luna's hand and soothed her, telling her it was okay and gently wiping the tears from her face.

Luna released more feelings than Sonny really needed or would have wanted to know on a first date. She unloaded a lifetime of emotions that had never been expressed, grieving for the child that felt alone and abandoned and who feared not being loved or accepted if she shared what she had seen and heard. Luna cried and Sonny held her. Luna was always so strong and independent, withholding anger and sadness from the outside world, the anger for not wanting to be here with critical humans who did not understand. But that was precisely why she was here; to show humans what was possible. Luna could not prove that the Sky Beings existed. She could only share her story and maybe help others to remember their own connection to the stars and to the spirit within.

Luna knew all humans were the same. Luna just happened to remember the truth and was guided through her life. Her mission was to share this understanding. Luna felt relieved after talking with Sonny. Her eyes were bloodshot and her nose was red and stuffy.

She looked up into Sonny's eyes to gauge his reactions. She was afraid that he would bolt and she'd never see him again. Luna knew there was a reason for this release. It was a healing and freeing experience that needed to happen, even if he did run away from her. If she trusted one person, in time she could trust many. Sonny's eyes were caring and empathetic. He had no fear or judgment in his eyes, just tenderness and sincerity.

"Luna, I can't imagine what you've held to yourself all these years. You are special. I can't pretend that I understand all you've shared. But I believe everything that you have said. I knew there was something special about you beside your good looks," he joked.

Luna laughed. It felt good to laugh. Sonny was good for Luna. Laughter was not an expression Luna had much experience with. Red Eagle frequently told Luna she was too serious.

"Life is to be enjoyed, Luna. Be happy and be grateful for everything. Happiness is an attitude," the memory made her smile.

"Okay. No more crying," Sonny said. "Let's go and have some fun. It's starting to get dark. Where can we go?"

"It depends on what you would like to do," she replied.

"How about we go to a movie, maybe a comedy?"

"There's a movie theatre twenty miles away. We could go and see what's playing," she added.

"Great. Let's go," he agreed.

When they arrived at the theatre, there was a romantic comedy that was about to start in fifteen minutes. The timing was perfect. Sonny held Luna's hand throughout the movie. Their belly's roared with laughter, while enjoying each other's company. They went for a burger after the movie and talked until the restaurant's closing time. It was nearing midnight when Sonny brought Luna home. Luna was nervous. She didn't want him to leave but she wasn't ready to be sexually intimate. It was too soon. Sonny didn't want to leave either, but did not want to be forward and rush things.

"This has been a fantastic day, Luna."

"It *has* been great. You're a really nice guy. Thanks for listening," she replied.

"Thanks for sharing. Well, I better get going. It's late and I have an hour drive. I'd love to see you again soon. Maybe, we can see each other next weekend? Do you have any plans? Maybe Sunday again?" he asked with anticipation.

"Sure. Next Sunday is good. Maybe I could meet you half-way or come to your place? We could take turns back and forth."

Luna realized she sounded as if she was making long term arrangements.

Oh my God, she thought, *I can't believe I just said that.*

"Maybe... anyway, I'll call you one night this week. When's a good time?" he asked.

"Call anytime after eight," she said.

"Great," he smiled.

Sonny leaned over and cupped Luna's chin in his hand.

"Luna, you're an amazing lady and I look forward to getting to know you better."

Sonny gently kissed Luna's lips. Luna responded tenderly. Within seconds the kiss became passionate. Luna wrapped her arms around his neck and he embraced her around her waist. His tongue was fluttering inside her mouth as hers fluttered inside his. Both of them were becoming aroused. An electrical charge was permeating through each of there bodies and uniting them at the heart.

The kissing lasted for minutes without either of them coming up for air. As they parted lips they both began to chuckle sheepishly.

"Wow, I didn't expect that," he gasped.

"Nor I," she said.

"Well, I better get going before I never leave," he said.

Luna stepped out of the truck. Sonny waited for her to enter safely inside the house.

What a gentleman, she thought.

She waved her final goodbye as he drove off, hoping he would call her. After a kiss like that, she was almost certain that he would.

Human Nature

Luna dated Sonny for a few weeks. They talked twice a week by phone and things were going quite well. Her client base was increasing and she was supporting herself using her gift.

Sonny and Luna were becoming inseparable in their thoughts. They would finish each other's sentences all the time. They had not yet been physically intimate. For Luna, it was becoming apparent she no longer wished to wait. She felt secure in her being but didn't want to be aggressive. She did not know that Sonny felt the same way. He wanted to be closer to Luna. He wanted to fully connect with her. His physical attraction to her was just as strong as his spiritual attraction.

Luna visited her parents every Sunday morning. Claire noticed that Luna's visits had become shorter.

"Luna, you barely visit with us. Are you too busy to visit with your parents? Are you now doing readings on Sundays, too?" she remarked with sarcasm.

Since Luna had told her parents that she quit her job at the plant and was only reading for income, they made their comments and concerns known.

"I think it's foolish. You can't make a living at it. How will you pay your rent if you don't make enough?" Claire said.

"Mom, I will make it. It makes me happy. I like doing it. I am helping people," Luna replied.

Luna and Claire agreed not to talk about it. Luna had not completely mended the relationship with her mother as Grandpa had suggested. Her mother was still critical, and Luna would regress to feeling like the little girl that was unloved and unaccepted. Luna wanted to be able to talk about their Indian heritage, seeing dead spirits and yes, even the Sky Beings. Luna knew that was too much for her mother to handle. Luna was tired of the arguing, criticism and judgment. She longed to be open with her mother and father. Especially her mother, since she was supposed to be the nurturer, the one that Luna needed. Even with her teachings and understandings about unconditional love, she still carried the human ego and need for acceptance from outside of herself.

Luna wondered if she should tell them about dating Sonny. Luna had already met Sonny's sons and it had gone well. They were both very nice young men. Sonny wanted to meet Luna's family as well. Luna decided it was time. She took a deep breath, gathered her courage and spoke.

"Mom, Dad, I have been dating someone lately and have been seeing him on Sunday afternoons. That's why my visits have been short. It's been going quite well. He is a very nice guy."

Luna was smiling but holding back her excitement.

"Really, where did you meet him?" Tom questioned.

"We met at an Indian gathering two months ago," she replied.

"Why haven't you brought him to meet us?" Claire demanded.

"Mom, I don't *have* to bring him here," she answered.

"Well, tell us about him?" Tom asked.

"He's forty-five..."

"He's forty-five?" Tom snapped. "Why he's almost as old as I am," he said with surprise.

"Dad, you're fifty-two. He has two sons from a previous marriage and they're in college."

"Oh my God, he's a divorced man? Does he have a job?" Claire probed.

"Mom," Luna rolled her eyes. "Yes, he has a job. He is in construction. He has a little house in New Hampshire. He is a wonderful man. He is sweet and caring. He makes me laugh."

"Oh, well as long as he makes you laugh," Claire snapped.

"Luna, what else do you know about him? He could be a criminal or murderer," she worried.

"Mom, if he was a murderer, he would have killed me already," Luna retorted in disgust.

"Sonny is a good man and I am going to date him. If you ever want to meet him, then you both had better just stop giving me the third degree about him!" Luna yelled.

Luna had never raised her voice to her father. She was taking a stand. Sonny was important to her; important enough for her to not care about what anyone had thought.

"Okay, Luna, you don't have to yell," Claire snapped. "We just want what's best for you."

"I know, Mom. But I really like this guy. There is something very special here. I want you to give him a chance. Can't you be happy for me?" she pleaded.

"Invite him to visit next Sunday and he can stay for dinner," said Claire.

"Okay. I'll invite him," Luna replied.

Luna met Sonny for lunch at his small cottage in New Hampshire. An inch of fresh snow had lightly covered the pine trees. He was on the wooden porch waiting for her arrival.

"Hi, sweetie," he said as he kissed her gently.

"Hi, honey. I went to visit my parents this morning and I told them about you. They would like to meet you. You're invited for dinner next Sunday. It's okay if you'd prefer to wait to meet them. No rush," hoping he would decline.

"Of course, I would love to meet them," Sonny said with excitement.

"Well, I wouldn't be too enthused. They're worried about your age and that you've been married before."

"It's okay, sweetie. They'll love me when they get to know me," he said with confidence.

Sonny had a gentle confidence about him. He was self-assured and positive. Luna admired this quality the most in him. He was so supportive of her.

"Come on, let's go inside. I have a special lunch planned for us," he said.

The small cottage was rustic. The downstairs had an open floor plan, with a kitchen and living room in a seven hundred square foot space. There were four small wooden chairs and a table in the kitchen. The kitchen had an old gas stove, an ice box freezer and a small white ceramic sink and counter. Two panels of upper and lower cupboards were uniquely carved and added to the coziness. The living room had a futon couch and two old wooden rocking chairs. Native designed blankets neatly covered the backs of the chairs and couch. Hurricane lamps sat on the two antique end tables. The small stone fireplace looked similar to the one in Red Eagle's cabin in Montana. The cottage was homey and comfortable. The kitchen table was neatly set with heavy stoneware plates and mugs. In the middle of the table was a large white vanilla scented candle that Sonny had lit for ambiance.

"I know you like fish. I have prepared baked smoked salmon and wild rice. For dessert, I have chocolate covered strawberries," he said with a wink.

"It sounds divine. Why so special? We could just have had sandwiches," Luna said.

"Well, *today* is special," he replied.

"Why is it so special?" she asked.

"You really don't know?" he looked disappointed.

"No," Luna replied.

"Luna, it is Valentines Day. You know, February fourteenth?"

"Oh no, I'm sorry Sonny. I guess since I've never had a date on Valentine's Day, it's never been special to me," she replied foolishly.

Luna felt awful about being unaware of the date. Sonny was trying to make it a romantic and special day for her. Luna reached over, kissed him on his lips and shyly asked, "Sonny, will you be my Valentine?"

"Forever," he said.

His lips were tender as he returned her kiss. His tongue ran circles inside her mouth. Luna's body became tingly and warm. Her breath was hot and panting. Her mind raced with an overwhelming desire to cry with delight.

"We better sit down and eat before it gets cold," she stammered as she broke away from his lips.

The meal was delicious. They chatted, kissed and held hands. The day rolled into the evening. Time seemed to fly when they were together. Each time it became increasingly difficult to part.

"Sweetheart, you don't have to leave. You could stay overnight. I have to work in the morning on a house I am remodeling, but I don't have to be there until nine."

Luna hesitated as she lowered her eyes to the floor.

"You could sleep in my bed upstairs in the loft," he begged.

The entire second floor was his bedroom. He had a wooden queen-sized bedroom set that he had made himself. Sonny was quite the carpenter.

"I can sleep on the futon downstairs in the living room if that makes you more comfortable."

"Sonny, I really want to stay. But my first client is at ten o'clock. tomorrow. I would need to get back early enough to prepare. I just had not planned for this. I'm not sure that I am ready for this step," she said as she bit her lip.

"Okay. No pressure. But before you go, I have a Valentine's gift for you."

Sonny pulled out a small velvet box with a red bow. Luna was uncomfortable as she did not have a gift for him in return.

"Sonny, I'm sorry but I don't have a present for you."

Her eyes looked away in embarrassment.

"Sweetheart, you're my present. Don't you know that? I have been so happy being with you. You are a gift to me every time we meet," he smiled.

Luna opened the box and her eyes filled with tears, it was a beautiful white gold locket in the shape of a half Moon. Inscribed on the backside of the locket was "To *My* Luna."

"Oh, it's beautiful. Thank you. I love it. Help me put it on," she whispered.

He placed it around her neck and embraced her from behind. He nestled his nose gently into her neck kissing it softly. Luna felt a shiver run down her spine and felt the blood igniting between her thighs. She tingled and could hardly catch her breath. As she turned to face him and looked deeply into his eyes she felt a glow of energy surrounding them.

Sonny lightly brushed her cheek with his lips, allowing his tongue to tantalize her. Luna's body was succumbing to a surge of heat and chills within her body. Her face flushed with a wanton desire and need for him. She desired the full immersion of the energy between them to be fulfilled.

She kissed him with passion and fever. Her tongue wildly roamed inside his mouth. Sonny was breathless. He grabbed her waist and ran his hands over her hips and breasts. The fire ignited between them. It was perfect and natural to allow the life force within and between them to grow. This was the moment, the only moment that existed. Luna was fully present in her body and everything was perfect with the world. She was a woman, a fully embodied human goddess. The Moon was within her ebbing and flowing, beckoning to overflow. Sonny lifted her and began his ascension to the bedroom. Luna's eyes had not left his gaze. She was ready to be with him.

Sonny carefully laid her down on the bed and they started to fervently undress each other. They caressed each other while entwining their bodies. Luna felt her body and spirit merging with him, as he entered her. Luna's moans of delight released all the desires to go Home.

The spiral of energy enveloped them as the pleasure of the immersion grew physically, emotionally, mentally and most importantly, spiritually. Their energies merged together for the first time and created a bonded cord. His tenderness brought waves of physical delight to her body. The lovemaking was slow with building anticipation. Until at last, they exploded together like a celestial nova with primal screams. Luna saw the explosion of energy burst and morph together as one in alignment. For a brief moment they reached high into the cosmos back to the Oneness of spirit.

Luna burst into tears as Sonny held her in his arms. Her humanity and her spirit had now completely joined together on this third dimensional plane. It was emotional and spiritual to fully experience her body this way. Her heart and body did not feel dense and heavy anymore.

They were bonded together human to human and spirit to spirit. They relaxed into each other's arms in exhaustion.

Sonny choked to find the words, "Luna, I know this is soon, but I love you. I really love *you*. I know you are the one I am meant to be with."

Luna looked at him and could no longer see his face. All she could see was his light shining brightly within. Smiling she rolled snuggly into the crook of his arm.

"I love you more," she giggled. "I finally feel connected to my humanness... I belong on the Earth," she replied.

Luna realized she was fully a human being in a loving human relationship on the Earth Star, no longer an observer. She was a participant in humanness, embracing the human with the spirit within and would someday write of her childhood experiences. It was all coming together now. She smiled and drifted off into peaceful bliss.

Healing the Bands

Luna returned home the next morning and started the day with meditation and prayer. She was in a joyous mood. She had five clients scheduled for readings. The day went by quickly. As she was ready to turn in for the night, the phone rang. It was 10:00 p.m.

"Hello?"

"Luna, this is Leana. Mom and Dad are at the hospital. Mom was having terrible pains in her stomach and side. She couldn't stand. We had to have the ambulance take her. Dad wants you to meet him at the hospital. She had thought it was just gas. The pain kept getting worse, until she finally buckled over."

"Okay. I'll meet you at the hospital," Luna replied.

"How is she?" Luna asked on her arrival to the hospital.

"They took her in for tests. They think it is her appendix. The doctor said her gums were black, a sign of poison in her system."

Tom began to well up with tears. Luna had never seen her Dad so emotional.

"Luna, I can't lose her. I would be lost without her."

"It's okay, Dad. I'm sure they're taking good care of her," she replied.

A couple of hours went by as they waited anxiously. Finally a doctor came for Tom.

"Mr. Belliveau? I am Doctor Todd. We removed her appendix, but it burst and filled her system with poison. We're giving her heavy doses of antibiotics. Her breathing collapsed, so she's on a ventilator and she is still unconscious. Her lungs and kidneys have been infected. We had to give her a blood transfusion, too. She's in tough shape. The next forty-eight hours are crucial. She is a young woman and has no other health issues. If we can get rid of the poison, and if her organs cooperate, she will recover. Time will tell. I'll keep you posted."

"Can we see her?" Tom asked.

"Sure, but only for a few minutes. She is on intravenous and hooked up to a dialysis machine and a ventilator. Only a few minutes at a time," he answered.

"Dad, you and Leana go in first," Luna directed.

Luna sat in silence. She closed her eyes and began a long prayer of affirmation, holding and envisioning her mother being well. Twenty minutes passed. Tom and Leana came from her mother's room in tears.

"Oh Luna, she looks bad. I can't see her like this. What am I going to do?" her Dad cried.

"Dad, you need to go home and get some rest. Take Leana and come back in the morning. I'll stay. I'll call you if anything changes."

Luna knew her father was not good at things like this. He had never been apart from Claire. Leana was a mess as well. Luna needed to hold a space of healing for her mother. Luna hugged her Dad and Leana as they left and then entered her mother's room. The noise of the air going in and out of the ventilator was dreadful and the beeping of the heart monitor were the only sounds in the dimly light room. Luna sat beside her mother's bed. She gently and carefully held her hand.

Luna bent over her mother and whispered.

"Mom, I love you and I am here for you. You are going to be well," Luna choked on the last words, trying to hold back her tears and be strong.

"You need to fight, Mom. You have a strong will. You are going to be well. Fight to come back to us."

Luna closed her eyes and placed her hands on her mother's forehead and abdomen. Luna relaxed her breath and opened herself up to a vision. She saw inside her mother's body. The orange, yellow and green bands were weakened. Luna offered a silent prayer and asked for help. She allowed the energy to pass through her hands to her mother's head, lungs and abdomen. She focused her attention on the energy running back and forth to lift her mother's vibration. She alternated from band to band for twenty minutes every hour. The bands were being woven back into place and becoming stronger. Luna repeated this process for four cycles of energy transfer. Luna held a silent vigil with trust that her mother would recover completely. At 7:00 a.m., Luna left the hospital to rest.

Tom and Leana arrived, passing Luna in the hallway.

"I will be back later. I need to rest a while. Call me when things change," she said with certainty.

Tom and Leana waited two hours for the doctor's report.

"Mr. Belliveau, we may be able to take her off the dialysis soon. Her kidneys are recovering. She's responding to the antibiotics and the blood transfusion. She has improved greatly overnight. She is still unconscious, but has improved."

Upon returning home, Luna removed the Sacred Pipe from the bundle and began to pray.

"Great Spirit, I ask for your help here for this woman, my mother. I ask for you to do what is best for her. I ask for her highest healing. I offer this sacred way of prayer from my ancestors. I ask my ancestors to help on her behalf. Help her find her way back to us if that is what is best for her, so that she may fulfill her life here. Spirit, I forgive and release all resentment towards her. I release my attachment to this. I lovingly accept my mother for the wonderful woman she is. Let her feel my deep love for her and find the strength in that for her healing," Luna broke into tears. "I love her. Have pity on her, Spirit. It would be good to have more time with her," she cried.

Luna had become unattached or so she thought, as she got older and withdrew from her mother. But in this moment, she realized she was still attached. A human child and its mother had a cord of energy and a bond that was deeper than anything on this Earth. A mother carried her and ate for her and supported her inside her womb. She hoped for her and dreamed for her and wanted good things for her child. The bond was deep and strong. She did not understand that bond, but it was there. She could no longer deny it. She was bonded to Claire. She felt it deeply. The love bond between them would not be severed. That is why Luna continually desired acceptance from her mother. Luna could now see the silvery cord between them, navel to navel, as she prayed. The silver fluid flowed through the cord from mother to child and child to mother. Her mother did and said things only because of her love for her daughter. She tried to do her best. In this space of prayer for her mother, Luna pleaded for her mother's life because of the bond of love. Luna could now see and feel the bond that had always been there. The cord tugged at her. She could feel every emotion her mother ever had from when she was a child to the present, her fears and anxiety, her sadness and grief, as well as her physical pain around the tissues and muscles of her body where the appendix had been. Luna felt the pain in the kidneys as they desperately tried to release the toxins and the pain in the lungs as they were forced to breathe through the ventilator. Luna became her mother's body. She realized Claire wanted Luna's love as much as Luna wanted her love. Luna understood this now. Their connection was born from love.

It was *Luna* who needed to love and accept herself as human, and to accept life here on the Earth. She needed to love the human being in herself. She realized no other human being could truly give that to her, not even her mother. Self love. Spirit was love. Love was within. That was enough. She was enough. No one needed to give that to her. *She* was love. Love was eternal, one with the spirit; just as Grandpa and the Sky Beings had taught her.

"Now you see," a voice spoke.

Luna opened her eyes and before her was Red Eagle in spirit form.

"Grandpa," Luna cried. "You're here."

"Hau, your mother will be well. Healing the bands is a gift Spirit has given you. You will begin to use the energy from Spirit. Your spirit relations will come to help you. Make ceremony and pray. Spirit will hear you. You will know when and who to help. It's almost time to share your story of the Sky and our connection to the whole. It should be a good one," Red Eagle laughed.

Luna was faint and losing her physical balance. The room became a blur of brightness. Light exploded around her until she became one within it, no longer seeing her hands, legs or arms. There was no longer a physical form of self.

"What is it you seek?" a gentle voice spoke. "What is it you seek?" the voice asked again.

There was no form or figure that she could see, just a shroud of light. Luna's consciousness spoke.

"I seek the balance of human and spirit. I ask for my mother's human form to be filled with light and health," she responded.

"Then it must be accepted, honored and used wisely. One has the human form for only a short time. One must love and honor one's life because the light of spirit loves you. Love and help others to realize this," the light spoke. "The spirit must evolve through the human. The human must evolve through the spirit. Love the human. Love the spirit. Your mother is you and you are your mother. You are one and are connected. You are never separate. All life is connected. The spirit within connects you to the whole in the Sky and all its beings and forms of life."

"Be the light of spirit in human form. Shine for others. Share all that you have been shown. Others too, will remember and evolve," spoke the being.

Luna awoke on her living room floor. The Sacred Pipe, now empty, was still tightly grasped in her hands. Red Eagle's spirit had come and the light spoke. Luna cleaned and placed the Sacred Pipe back into the bundle. She napped peacefully knowing her prayers would be answered.

Luna had slept four hours when the phone rang. She jumped from the bed to answer it.

"Luna, Mom's awake. She's conscious and off dialysis. She still has the ventilator. I just wanted to let you know," Leana said.

"That's great. I'll take a shower and then I'll be there," she replied.

"Thank you, Great Spirit, for helping her to become well," she whispered.

Luna lit the sage and cleansed herself. She took three deep breaths and relaxed. She found herself inside her mother's hospital room. She saw the band around her mother's lungs. It was better, but not yet healed. Luna focused the energy into her mother's lungs. Allowing the energy to flow, she saw the light start to mend and fill the lungs. She envisioned the ventilator being removed and Claire breathing on her own. Luna ended the energy transfer and again offered a prayer of gratitude.

Luna showered. The water cleansed and energized her. As she stepped out of the shower the phone rang again. She went to answer, but the answering machine had already begun to tape the message.

"Luna, this is Leana. I don't know if you've left for the hospital yet, but they are taking Mom off the ventilator. She's breathing on her own. Luna, it's a miracle!"

Yes, it is a miracle, Luna reflected. *Life itself is a miracle. Life goes on with or without the human body. It is wonderful to live in a human body. We are all connected to each other with the Divine Spirit Light within.*

Luna was glad to be human and was happy her mother would remain in the human form longer. She rushed with anticipation to see her mother.

Realizing time was so short; she now fully embraced the spirit and the human. It did not matter what others thought. She accepted her life and mission with great peace.

Luna arrived at the hospital and entered her mother's room. Claire still looked weak and was sleeping. Leana was holding one hand and Tom was holding the other.

Luna placed a large bouquet of roses on the tray table and bent down to kiss her mother's cheek.

"Dad, Leana, can I be with Mom alone?" she asked.

Tom and Leana nodded. They quickly kissed Claire and left the room. Luna held Claire's hand for the next hour sending love from her heart to Claire's.

The next day Luna returned to the hospital. Her mother was awake and was now able to hold a conversation.

"How are you doing, Mom?" Luna asked.

"I am still weak. Everything hurts. The doctor says I'll have to be on antibiotics for a couple of weeks. But they believe there is no permanent damage," she responded.

"That's good," Luna said, as she caressed her mother's hand and forehead.

"Mom, I know I have been a difficult child to understand, maybe something of a disappointment. But I have to be me. I have to be the woman who sees dead people and helps them cross Home. I have to be the person who has seen and been taught by Sky Beings. I am not mentally unstable. I never realized how hard this might have been on you, fearing for me. I love Sonny and he accepts all of me, my abilities and weaknesses. This is the man I am supposed to be with."

She continued, "I love you, Mom. I have seen the cord that ties a mother to her child. It is beautiful. It is one that has to release its tension as the child grows older and allows it space to grow. Mom, I don't want you to worry anymore. I will be fine. Thank you for my life and bringing me into this world. I realize that I resented you for bringing me into a world that did not understand me. I did not want to be here. It was too hard. I felt unloved when you didn't understand or believe me. But I'm not different. Humans are all the same. We all come from the same place and we all return to the same place. We are all connected by the spirit light inside of us. I know you did the best you could for me. But I have to live my life the way I came here to live it, accepting and loving all parts of myself. I want you Mom, to live your life fully as well. It was almost taken from you. I'm glad you're still here with me," Luna choked back the tears.

Claire was speechless, listening to every word her daughter poured from her heart. She, too, choked back the tears.

"Luna, yes, I worried for you. Yes, I did not understand you. But, I have always loved you, my beautiful girl. You were such a strong-headed child. You are so much like your grandmother, Anna. I see that now. Maybe you do have a mission. You used to say that over and over when you were a child. Maybe *my* mission was to bring you into the world. I want to share something with you...," she paused. "When I was unconscious, I could hear your voice. I swear I could feel heat moving inside of me. I felt you were here with me all the time. It was strange. It was as if you were giving me some part of yourself. If I hadn't experienced it myself, I wouldn't have believed it. When I was unconscious, I heard your voice telling me that I would be well. I felt your hands on my body. They were warm. Although I couldn't move, I felt something moving inside of me. There were colors all around me. I also saw Grandma Anna and she explained that you were helping me, the same way she helped other people. She told me how much you loved me. She said that you had so much love and help to give others and that this was my chance to see and feel it. Luna, I believe that you helped me. I don't understand it, but I believe it. You *are* gifted. I understand this now," she said. "Thank you Luna, for helping me."

"I asked the energy to flow to you and heal the bands or places inside your body that were sick," Luna said.

"Does it work all the time?" she asked.

"I don't know. I have only done it twice; once when Leana was a baby and now for you. I suppose it depends on the person receiving it and his or her free will, and whether or not they choose to accept it. I'm just glad that you're on the mend," she smiled.

"Luna, I'm sorry that I have been hard on you. I thought and hoped you would outgrow it. Now, I see I've made a mistake. I was trying to protect you from a hard life. I guess I did the very thing that I did not want to do. I drove you to withdraw from me, just as I did with my mother. A parent makes mistakes. I did it with the best intentions. I did out of love, Luna," she said as she filled with tears.

Luna remembered back to when she was an infant, and her mother's tear fell on her face while speaking the words, "I love you, beautiful girl."

"Mom, I realize now, that I had to love myself first," she said with contentment.

Forgiveness and love will always heal human beings, she thought. *It was that simple.*

Luna and Claire hugged, a long full embrace, one that would start the healing of past wounds that they both carried in this life. They held each other and cried tears of release until at last Claire spoke wiping her eyes.

"Now, let's talk about this Sonny."

Luna began to share her thoughts and heart. She held nothing back. She spoke of her nervousness and sweaty hands. The excitement she felt when she was with him and yes, even her first night with him.

"Don't worry Mom, it was safe sex," they both laughed.

Luna noticed her mother's energy was fading and that she needed to rest.

"I'll come back later, Mom. Just rest now." Luna kissed her cheek.

This was a day she would remember forever. Grandpa would have been proud. A healing had shifted her mother to see Luna as an adult with a mission. When Luna finally embraced her whole self, her mother was able to shift and embrace Luna.

Claire smiled. Her heart was lighter. It was the beginning of a relationship with her daughter that she had always hoped for. Happy, she drifted off to sleep.

A New Chapter

Luna visited often the next month and helped with the household chores while Claire was recuperating. Claire enjoyed the time with Luna. She was getting to know her adult daughter. Luna shared her life and stories from the road and native teachings. It took Claire weeks to fully recover and return to work.

Once fully recovered, Luna brought Sonny to Sunday dinner. Claire made a pot roast and one of her famous chocolate cakes for the occasion. As Luna and Sonny arrived on time, Claire, Tom and Leana excitedly greeted them at the door. Claire gave Sonny a warm hug. Tom grinned and shook his hand.

"Well, come on in," Tom said.

"Please sit down," Claire said, as she led him towards the living room.

"Sonny, thank you for sending me flowers while I was in the hospital. That was very thoughtful. Dinner will be ready shortly."

Sonny felt at ease and accepted. The conversation was light. Luna and Sonny barely took a break from holding hands. Claire noticed his affection towards Luna.

I think Luna is right. This one is going to work out. He's a keeper.

Claire's heart was happy because Luna's heart was happy. Life was good.

Before he left, Sonny motioned to Tom to speak to him privately.

"Mr. Belliveau," Sonny said.

"Please call me Tom."

"Tom, I know I'm a bit older and have been married before, but I love your daughter and only have good intentions. I hope in time to make her my wife. That is, if she'll have me," he laughed.

"That's great. But take your time. Get to know each other well. We welcome you to the family," Tom smiled.

Luna's life was going well. Her mission was shaping into a life. The readings increased with many new clients. She was happy with Sonny. After a year of dating, Sonny proposed to Luna. She excitedly accepted.

Sonny sold his cabin and moved into the rental house with Luna. They planned to join together in union in a traditional Native American Indian ceremony that would make them half-sides to each other. For the next year, they saved for a down payment on a house with land. Life was going well. Luna was evolving and learning to balance the Earth and Sky within herself.

With a realtor's help, Sonny found a home nestled in the woods with twenty acres of land.

"Luna, I found a house that we should look at. It's in our price range," he said.

"Honey, are we ready?" she cautioned.

"It's time. Then maybe we could have the wedding ceremony on the land," he smiled.

Luna agreed to see the house and land on the following Sunday afternoon. They drove down a secluded country road lined with oak and pine trees. When they reached the property, they parked at the bottom of the long steep driveway. The quaint, three bedroom cape rested on a small hill, surrounded by raspberry bushes. Luna began to cry. The Earth beneath her feet vibrated. Her sense of knowing was felt throughout her entire being. A butterfly flew over her shoulder and danced up the driveway. It was guiding her and confirming what she already knew. She reached for the tobacco pouch that she carried in her purse and offered a pinch to the four directions, the Sky and the Earth.

"Great Spirit, I offer gratitude to you for leading us here. If this is where we belong, I ask that the spirits of this land, the trees and animals and all life that dwell here to allow us to join them as we take care of and live in union with this land, to all my relations," she said releasing the tobacco.

"This is it, Sonny. This is our place," she said tearfully.

"But you haven't seen the inside of the house yet," he said with surprise.

"This is it. I feel it in my bones, with my feet and in my heart," Luna rejoiced.

"I get it, I get it. It's the right place," he chuckled.

The inside was small and cozy. There were three rooms downstairs and three bedrooms upstairs. A beautiful farmer's porch in the front of the house made it perfect. The sale went easily and within three months they moved in to what would be their long time home.

Months later, in a wonderful and private wedding ceremony under the afternoon Sky on the land on which they lived, an elder Native American Indian Holy Man united them as half-sides, joining them with the smoking of the Sacred Pipe. Luna wore an off-white deer skin dress with long fringe around the arms and at the hem. A beautifully beaded feather was gifted to her by an elder Native American Indian Grandmother named, *Generous Woman*. The feather was tied in her long dark hair.

Sonny wore a brown buckskin shirt and leggings and matching moccasins on his feet. He, too, was gifted a beaded feather from Generous Woman to wear in his hair. Generous Woman and her sister, *She Who Heals*, both elder Grandmothers stood within the Sacred Circle to support and witness this sacred union.

When the ceremony ended, the elder grandmothers placed a Pendleton blanket over the couple's shoulders to solidify their union. Luna remembered the exact vision of the wedding before they had even had their first date. It was a déjà vu moment. It was a day they both would treasure for the rest of their lives.

During the blissful first year of marriage, they built a small lodge from saplings to purify themselves and pray in the old way. The ceremonial purification lodge was hidden amongst the acres of oak trees.

Luna was living as Grandpa taught her. Purification helped Luna to remain in balance and in gratitude.

Sonny continued to build environmentally friendly houses. Luna continued with client readings.

Now, as Luna looked into the night Sky from the bedroom window, she no longer yearned for Home. Much had changed for her since she met Sonny. She had found a partner with whom she would share her life's mission.

Luna completely accepted her mission, to live here and balance human and spirit. She would willingly remain as long as it took. Chara, Matar and Alcor continued their visits when she needed them. Her ancestral spirit guides also guided her in ceremony.

Although Sonny could not see her Sky Being friends, he could tell when they came for her during the night for Luna's breathing would change. He accepted it all as part of being with the woman he loved.

As Luna remembered the Sky Beings, she looked up into the night Sky and three stars began to twinkle brightly. Their points elongated and glowed. It was a reminder they would always be there for her.

"Thank you, Sky Beings, for all of your teachings. Thank you, Red Eagle for teaching me the Red Road of the ancestors and how to be a human being. I will help people to remember the spirit light within all beings and the teachings of the Sky Nation. I will return someday when my mission is complete and when I do, it will be forever," she whispered.

Luna smiled and walked away from the window with contentment. Sonny was fast asleep, snoring to beat the band.

My beloved, she thought as she giggled.

Luna felt drawn to the kitchen to retrieve a pen and some paper. Words were being channeled to her brain and she needed to write them down. She sat at the kitchen table, as if she was in a guided trance scribbling down her memories as a child and her travels to the distant stars. When she awoke on the couch in the morning, she read the channeled thoughts, barely remembering the actions of the night before. As she read the pages, she was overwhelmed, realizing that her writings contained the first chapter of the book.

Luna remembered Mr. Anderson, the English teacher from high school and his words of encouragement, *"One day I hope to see your name on a book. You have great imagination and spirit in your writings."*

Luna smiled. She wondered where he is now, and if he is still teaching and encouraging students.

Thank you, Mr. Anderson. I hope to make you proud, she thought.

This was the beginning. It would be *the* book. Luna would be helped and guided. Through her writing, another level of courage would be tested as she revealed her experiences to the world. The Sky Beings helped her to remember and write. It was now time for the story to be told.

As Luna read the opening line of the chapter, she knew the next part of her journey was upon her. This was the start of completing the purpose of her life on Earth. Reading her words out loud for the first time brought a smile to her lips and goose bumps to her skin.

"Beyond the blue and dark up high,
the story of remembrance,
There's a *Whole* in the Sky."

Acknowledgements

To the Great Spirit, that creates and moves through all life, whose insight and direction led to the creation of this novel.

To my Celestial and Spirit teachers who have guided me throughout all of my life and for whom this story is told.

To my beloved half-side, husband, lover, partner and friend, Paul Samuels, who has filled my life with the joy and love I had only hoped to find on this Earth. Love you, baby.

To my parents, Raymond and Theresa Dubeau, who through their love for each other, created a loving space and home for which my life could begin and grow. I love you big, big.

To the memory of my beloved friend, elder Grandmother and Sundancer, Joyce Doyle, whose teachings of kindness and generosity have forever changed my life.

To the memory of Native American elders, Wallace Black Elk, Vincent "Sun Bear" La Duke and Marcellus "Bear Heart" Williams, I offer my gratitude.

To my beloved teacher, spiritual mentor and elder, Grandfather C.W. Duncan Sings-Alone, whose love, teachings and belief in my calling from Spirit gave me the opportunity to be of service to the People.

To elder Grandmother, Mary Dobson, whose unconditional love and teachings for healing have helped me to become a better human being.

To elder Grandmother, Alloday Gatoga, for her love, teachings and initiations to the Good Medicine Society.

To my best friend, Lorraine Tetreault, for her many years of treasured friendship and valuable feedback to the story's first draft.

To my friend and award-winning author, Pricilla Cogan, who has mentored and inspired the storyteller within me.

To my soul sister, Sandra Corcoran, for sharing the teachings from her respected elders.

To my friend, author and earth keeper, Lesley Shore, who provided the tranquil and sacred place at Harmony Center for workshops.

To my friend, Del Bachard, for providing a warm, welcoming space at Generations Herbal Apothecary and Gift Shop, for my consultations and classes.

To my editorial eye, Justin Clifford and the publishing team at Balboa Press for their hard work and expertise.

To author, Rita Schiano, who provided valuable advice on manuscript development.

To my sister, Denise Wongkam, who shared her graphic art expertise and provided valuable feedback to the story's first draft.

To Dr. Peter Pingalore, whose chiropractic hands, provided healing relief from long hours of writing.

To Emily Maiella ND, who guides me along the natural path to health.

To Bernice Bernhagen, whose spirit, encouragement, and love of the Arts, had a hand in making it possible for this book to be published.

To my high school English teacher, John Palermo, whose words of encouragement over thirty years ago, found their way into this novel.

And finally to my beloved pet and ceremony companion, Sammy, whose unconditional love has brought an incredible peace to my life.

About the Author

Loralee Dubeau is an educator, consultant, spiritual advisor, Reiki Master, Teacher of the Good Medicine Society and a Universal Life Minister. She has a private consulting practice for Intuitive Readings, Dream Analysis, and Flower Essences. She provides both lectures and workshops for mind/body/spirit.

"There's A Whole in the Sky" is her first fictional novel and was inspired by her own spiritual and professional experiences. She resides in Massachusetts with her husband, Paul Samuels and her beloved cat, Sammy.

Contact www.dream-flowerconsultant.com for more information.

CPSIA information can be obtained at www.ICGtesting.com
Printed in the USA
BVOW041618010812

296805BV00001B/4/P